LGBTQ Social Movements

LGBTQ Social Movements

Lisa M. Stulberg

polity

First published in 2018 by Polity Press

Polity Press
65 Bridge Street
Cambridge CB2 1UR, UK

Polity Press
101 Station Landing
Suite 300
Medord, MA 02155, USA

ISBN-13: 978-0-7456-5607-6
ISBN-13: 978-0-7456-5608-3(pb)

A catalogue record for this book is available from the British Library.

Library of Congress Cataloging-in-Publication Data

Names: Stulberg, Lisa M., author.
Title: LGBTQ social movements / Lisa M. Stulberg.
Description: Malden, MA : Polity Press, [2017] | Series: Social movements |
   Includes bibliographical references and index.
Identifiers: LCCN 2017023462 (print) | LCCN 2017031945 (ebook) | ISBN
   9781509527397 (Mobi) | ISBN 9781509527403 (Epub) | ISBN 9780745656076
   (hardback) | ISBN 9780745656083 (pbk.)
Subjects: LCSH: Gay liberation movement--United States | Sexual
   minorities--United States.
Classification: LCC HQ76.8.U5 (ebook) | LCC HQ76.8.U5 S78 2017 (print) | DDC
   306.760973--dc23
LC record available at https://lccn.loc.gov/2017023462

Typeset in 11 on 13 pt Sabon by
Servis Filmsetting Ltd, Stockport, Cheshire

For further information on Polity, visit our website: politybooks.com

Contents

Acknowledgments

I love that feeling just before I start to read a new book. I take it all in before I even read a word: the cover design, the feel of the paper, the typeface, the Table of Contents. No matter where I am or how quickly I have to digest a book, whether I'm reading fiction or nonfiction, for pleasure or for work, I am immediately calmed when I read. Put a book in my hand on a crowded subway and I'm good. Everything just melts away, and it's just me and the pages. And starting a new book is especially exciting. I just know I'm about to start feeling something, or learning something, falling in love with some quirky and flawed character, writing furiously in the margins, staying up way too late reading by the light of my phone.

And it all starts with the Acknowledgments for me. Acknowledgments are the first thing I read when I start any book. I said this once in a class, and I got a much more surprised reaction from my students than I would have expected. It doesn't seem that weird to me, but I guess it is. For me, Acknowledgments are a window into the personality and the relationships of the author. They are usually written in a different voice from the text itself, and I love hearing how the author's voice sounds when they're not working so hard to be artful or articulate. I feel like I'm learning something about the way they rely on people, who they have in their lives, their sense of humor and humility and gratitude.

Anyway, all that is to say that these Acknowledgments sections are very important to me, and I want to make sure I don't forget anyone. I apologize in advance to those I have inevitably left out here.

First, thank you to the amazing staff at Polity. Emma Longstaff initially expressed interest in this book and was my first editor at the press. Her enthusiasm and support were incredibly motivating and appreciated, and I will always be grateful to her. Jonathan Skerrett has been a wonderful editor of the project – always so accessible and insightful. My copyeditor, Sarah Dancy, had great attention to detail *and* the amazing ability to put up with me and all of my anxious notes. Thanks too to Geraldine Beare for compiling the index. The team at Polity – including Amy Williams, Adrienn Jelinek, Neil de Cort, and Rachel Moore – has been a pleasure to work with. I have to say, I got the most helpful and thorough reviews of the initial manuscript of any I've ever received on any project. Thanks so much to these three anonymous reviewers for their feedback - the book is immeasurably stronger because of it – and to the Polity team for soliciting these wonderful reviews.

Claudia Castañeda, editor extraordinaire, read the entire manuscript draft *twice* and was exceedingly patient and responsive to all of my questions and concerns. I can't imagine having written this without her feedback and input. Of course, all of the book's shortcomings are my own.

This project began because I wanted to write the kind of book that I could use in the kinds of classes I teach at New York University. At NYU, I have had incredible friends, colleagues, and students who have supported me and the book in so many ways over the years. The Department of Applied Statistics, Social Science, and Humanities has been by home at NYU for 15 years, and I am so grateful for it. The NYU Steinhardt PhD students who have been especially supportive of this project include Bryan Rosenberg, Nina Mauceri, Hilary Lustick, Maggie Fay, and Sarah Klevan. Undergrads in my spring 2016 and spring 2017 Social Movements classes read and engaged with earlier drafts of the book in ways that were incredibly helpful to me along the way. Thanks, especially, to Besjana Hoxha, Marcha Johnson, Samantha Padavick, and Jordan Reynolds, for being willing to read and give feedback on draft chapters. The NYU LGBTQ working group - an amazing group of faculty, students, and staff – gave me a close read, valuable time, a supportive community, and incisive feedback along the way. Sebastian Cherng provided a crucial cover suggestion at a critical moment. Joe Salvatore has taught me so much over the years and has always been a willing, supportive, and caring listener, colleague, and friend – and also great with cover design feedback!

Then there are those friends who just always ask, in exactly the right way, how my writing is going, and they are always there to celebrate accomplishments, to weigh in on small decisions, and to lend encouragement and fun diversion when exhaustion sets in. For this project, those friends and family members especially include Ian Stulberg and Bob Berman, Lauri Hornik, Tony Chen, John and Melissa King, Cori Flam Meltzer and Brad Meltzer, and members of "the fam" text group who always have grammar advice and cute Bitmojis to share at any time of the day or night. And, while I cannot thank him directly, the late Eric Rofes has frequent conversations with me about this book, even if he doesn't know it. I am regularly inspired by the example he set of how to live life, do politics, write, and teach.

Thanks go, too, to my local coffee shop – you know who you are – for allowing me to sit there for hours with my wall of books, nursing my extra large decaf iced coffee with extra ice. Thanks, too, to our miniature poodle, Gryffindor (Griffy) for keeping my feet warm while I wrote and for never minding when I needed to take walks or runs with her while my head was in this book. And to the late George Michael, thanks for getting me through a last, intense week of writing the first draft of this book, especially the song "Freedom," which I played basically incessantly. I like to think that the lyrics "sometimes the clothes do not make the man" are not just a commentary about fame but are also, in the context of this project, a comment on the complexities of gender.

Finally, to my amazing, incredible family – the East Coast and Midwest contingents – I love who you are and I love who you allow me to be. Any sentence that I've started and deleted over and over here does not do justice to just how much you mean to me and how much purpose you give my life. To all of the young people in my immediate and extended family and the young people whom our kids have brought into our lives: I am in awe of how brave, generous, social justice-minded, and loving you are, and I can't wait for you to write the next chapter of this ongoing story of social change.

1

Introduction

"I was going to die, if not sooner then later, whether or not I had ever spoken myself. My silences had not protected me. Your silence will not protect you." I have carried these words with me since the moment I read them in college. They belong to Audre Lorde, an incredible African American lesbian activist and writer, and she wrote them after she had been diagnosed with cancer, when she was facing her own mortality. She continued:

> We can learn to work and speak when we are afraid in the same way we have learned to work and speak when we are tired. For we have been socialized to respect fear more than our own needs for language and definition, and while we wait in silence for that final luxury of fearlessness, the weight of that silence will choke us . . . [I]t is not difference which immobilizes us, but silence. And there are so many silences to be broken. (1984, pp. 41, 44)

I read this on the last day of my undergraduate social movements class each spring. Silence is debilitating. Silence is dangerous. "And there are so many silences to be broken." This is the same sentiment that moved AIDS activists in the 1980s. They proclaimed that "Silence = Death," and they mobilized around being as loud as possible for their cause and their survival.

This is a book about people who have broken past their silences. The book is meant for students and others who are new to lesbian, gay, bisexual, transgender, and queer (LGBTQ) social movement history and politics. I have taught an American social movements class to undergraduates at New York University a number of times since the early 2000s. I have found that students had learned almost nothing about LGBTQ history and activism in high school or in their other college courses and that they are eager for and incredibly receptive to this material. They have a strong and quite visceral reaction to the history and present-day injustices faced by LGBTQ Americans and the ways in which they and their allies have fought back. In the few years in which these young students have been politically conscious or active, they have experienced the national debate on same-sex marriage, and they want to grasp why marriage is such a hot-button issue. They have watched as states have debated so-called "bathrooms bills," and they want to know why providing equal access to transgender people is so controversial. They debate LGBTQ politics with their families, and they are excited to use their new knowledge at the holiday dinner table. They are LGBTQ themselves or have queer friends and family members and want to understand their rights and the challenges they face and are likely to face as they plan to enter the workforce or start families. They want to mobilize for LGBTQ justice, and they want to learn from previous generations of activists.

I attempt to tell a story of more than 70 years in a short, accessible way, and that has felt nearly impossible. LGBTQ social movements in the United States, like any other movement, contain so many different approaches to social change within them and are characterized by both diversity and inevitable internal conflict (Ghaziani, 2008). I cannot possibly do justice to this varied, complicated, and dynamic set of movements and movement actors in a short, introductory book. But the story I tell here is one about the mainstream LGBTQ movements since World War II in the US.[1] I have chosen to include here those events, organizations, and people that help raise key themes that I believe are central to understanding the politics of gender and sexuality of the past few generations.

This book is a starting point for those who want to know just a little bit, so they can contextualize the current politics of gender and sexuality in the US, or who want to know much more but need a foundation and a set of resources to explore further. I hope this is a good first stop. I hope this book will prompt you to learn more, to flip through the bibliography to find those resources that resonate with you, and to pay attention to the current politics of LGBTQ social change (maybe having picked up here a bit more knowledge to guide your understanding). Pairing this book with a look at the primary historical and political documents of these movements (some of which are cited here) is another wonderful way to further explore the themes and events that are introduced here.

This is a story about marginalized people and communities using a wide range of political and cultural tools at their disposal to make demands on the state – their government – to fight for full citizenship and to realize their full humanity in a country that often thinks of them as less than fully human, less than fully deserving of basic rights and freedoms. The unifying idea of this book is that LGBTQ social movements, like most others by oppressed peoples in the US, have always been about marginalized groups' relationships to their country and its institutions. They interact with history in dynamic, complex ways on multiple fronts. Ultimately, they raise central questions about the mechanisms of change and the limits and possibilities of democracy.

We see this in a few key ideas that I highlight in my discussion in these chapters: in the way that marginalized communities and their activists work to either assimilate into existing cultures and institutions or lose faith in these cultures and institutions and remove themselves from them, building alternatives instead; the way they view the law as both a vehicle for and a constraint on social change; and the way they use many tools at their disposal to not just change law but to change hearts and minds. The themes that structure this book's discussion of LGBTQ social movements in the US are: (1) assimilationism and liberationism as complex sets of strategies for equality and social justice; (2) the limits and possibilities of law and policy; (3) the role of art and popular culture in social change; (4) the interconnectedness of social movements; and (5) the role of privilege in movement organizing.

Introduction

In LGBTQ movements, participants and analysts have often understood the ways in which activists orient themselves toward the state to be either *assimilationist* or *liberationist*. Sociologist Steven Seidman argues of this distinction: "At the heart of this political division are contrasting images of America" and its potential (2002, p. 183). The distinction is both strategic and philosophical. As political scientist Craig A. Rimmerman writes, liberationists embrace "more radical cultural change, change that is transformational in nature and often arises outside the formal structures of the U.S. political system." On the other hand, "[t]he assimilationist approach typically embraces a rights-based perspective, works within the broader framework of pluralist democracy . . . and fights for a seat at the table" and tends to be more gradualist and "patient with creeping toward long-term movement goals" (2008, pp. 5, 133). Writer Michael Bronski adds, on the cultural politics of assimilation versus liberation: "The assimilationist position is predicated on a deeply held belief in the worth of such basic social structures as traditional sexual morality, monogamous marriage, accepted gender roles, and the nuclear family" (1998, p. 3), and this has characterized the mainstream movement since its inception after World War II (Rimmerman, 2002).

LGBTQ people and activists have had the same debates and tensions as other marginalized Americans about whether it is best to assimilate to mainstream norms and institutions or whether these American institutions are fundamentally broken and in need of rejection in favor of community-controlled alternatives. These movements have also, since the beginning of social action, targeted the law for change, used the law to advance civil equality, and, conversely, recognized the limits of the law in changing culture and everyday private behavior. Social movements are not and have never been just about mass, collective action. Art, media, culture, and popular culture have always been sites and vehicles for social change, for bringing in new voices, for resistance and community-building, and for telling stories that can build sympathy and empathy. So, too, we will see, social movements develop in relationship to each other, whether that is building on movements with the same general political orientation from the

4

Introduction

Left or responding to movements that are directly opposed from the Right. Finally, people who come together in communities and social movements may share something of their biographies and experiences, but they also differ in important ways, by race, gender, gender identity, class, sexual orientation, religion, ability or immigration status. These differences matter a lot in the way that movements are shaped. The way that I tell this story of diversity and difference here is to focus on *privilege* and the role it has played in LGBTQ movements over time.

It was only in the second half of the nineteenth century that homosexuality began to be named and mobilized around as an *identity*; the mid-twentieth before gender identity would become politicized.[2] In the US, gay and lesbian people began to develop their own cultures and communities in the early part of the twentieth century. But it was not until World War II, when both gay and lesbian visibility and repression rose significantly, that the seeds of the modern movements were sown in the US and around the world. The first lesbian and gay political organizations in the US were founded in the 1950s, as small, mostly secretive groups known as the *homophile* movement. Through the 1960s, when gay men and lesbians now had other contemporaneous examples of social movements from which to draw inspiration and practical lessons, they began to organize for change. The Stonewall rebellion, when New York City bar-goers and their supporters fought back against the kind of police repression that had become routine for them, changed the future of LGBTQ politics.

After Stonewall, the gay liberation movement blossomed and produced more than a thousand organizations dedicated to a wide range of lesbian, gay, bisexual, and transgender efforts for social change. The liberation movement, at the height of the radical late 1960s and early 1970s, shifted within a couple of years into a kind of gay pride and gay rights movement – a *gay identity movement* (Armstrong, 2002) – that has continued to this day. When AIDS blindsided the community with such force in the early 1980s, AIDS activism became another – separate but related – part of the broader sexual identity movement. Out of AIDS activism, too, came a challenge from the Left to broaden the movement, making space for bisexual and transgender activists to both join the pan-identity movement and to continue to articulate their own interests and politics. Since then, over the past few decades, we have seen efforts for social change on scores of different fronts: from explicitly political fights to change civil rights laws, to efforts to change school culture and sports culture, to media campaigns to increase visibility, to the renewal of longstanding fights to recognize and fully honor intersectional identities.

One of the primary arguments of this book is that movements for social change take many forms. When you think about social movements, you might envision large groups of people holding hands in solidarity or marching in a mass with signs and bullhorns: those iconic images on posters, stamps, and in the pages of history texts. Or, you might recall a sketch from a children's picture book or grainy documentary of a small, brave group of people – maybe even one person at first – sitting, standing, fighting back, riding a bus or not riding a bus in a public act of defiance. These are collective, public actions for change. This kind of activism often focuses on the state, on changing laws and policy. But, these are just some of the kinds of activism that are part of LGBTQ – and many other – movements.

From the social movement literature that specifically takes up LGBTQ organizing,[3] I draw specifically on that which understands the *cultural* to be an important part of the *political*.[4] Some of this kind of activism focuses on the state – on making demands on the government for social welfare or for civil rights protections.[5] Other forms of LGBTQ activism that are central to my discussion are not primarily state-centered and may be, instead, about raising visibility, building alternative communities and identities, and changing hearts and minds both for and beyond the purpose of changing laws. Some may be a combination of both – using cultural and symbolic tactics for the purposes of effecting law and policy change.

Sociologist Joshua Gamson, for instance, identifies an "orientation towards identity and expression" in the direct action AIDS activism of the late 1980s, which, while "cultural" and "theatrical" in nature – as we will see in chapter 3 – was nevertheless aimed at changing science, industry, and public policy (1989, p. 355). Sociologist Verta Taylor and colleagues write of the 2004 mass wedding protest in San Francisco – featured in chapter 4 – that those who participated in this kind of cultural protest, a wedding that had the mayor's blessing but was not certified by the state, was a form of laying claim to a state-given civil right (marriage) and had the effect of spurring its participants into "more traditional forms of political action" (2009, p. 886). They argue that "social movements often adapt, create, and use culture – ritual, music, street theatre, art, the Internet, and practices of everyday life – to make collective claims" (2009, p. 866). Similarly, as sociologist Amin Ghaziani writes, even cultural forms of mobilization – like making a residential choice to live in the "space of freedom" of gay neighborhoods – have the political impact of providing an incubator for political engagement and action from a position of strength (2014, p. 3). So, too, do drag shows, as Leila J. Rupp and Taylor argue, which are both cultural performances of and commentary on the complexity of gender and sexuality and protest-oriented "political events" (2003, p. 3).

Focusing on this understanding of social movements that combines the cultural and the political – and that understands the cultural *to be* political – in the chapters that follow I look at a number of efforts within US LGBTQ social movements that I feel are particularly instructive and central to the way that social change around gender and sexuality has occurred since World War II. The first three chapters are roughly chronological and illustrate the main themes of the book, introducing us to some of the primary fights of recent generations that focus both on state-directed and cultural change. Chapter 2 examines the early days of gay and lesbian organizing, the period before Stonewall, and the years through the 1970s that were so impacted by the Stonewall rebellion. This chapter, too, focuses on the rise of the Religious Right and the way that this new conservative movement gained strength and numbers from its anti-gay activism. Chapter 3 focuses on AIDS activism from the early 1980s to the mid-1990s, with attention, as well, given to the role of the Right in LGBTQ experience and organizing. Chapter 4 looks closely at marriage politics: this issue that has been so central to mainstream LGBTQ organizing since the early 2000s.

For the next two chapters, I have chosen examples of LGBTQ organizing that show both the range and the nuance of the movement as well as cultural change at work. These are two sites of change that I believe are going to be at the forefront of the movement in the years to come: youth activism – through schooling and media – and activism around the complexity and diversity of sexuality and gender. Chapter 5 focuses on young LGBTQ people: their experiences in and around schools, the ways they have responded to the homophobia and transphobia they have experienced in schools, and social change efforts that have developed around young people to support them and help them build communities in school and through popular culture. Chapter 6 looks specifically at bisexual and transgender experience, exclusion, and politics and the ways in which the "B" and the "T" prompt us to recognize and understand many forms of diversity, privilege, and division within LGBTQ communities and movements and orient us toward the future of the movement and its reaction on the Right.

As with almost any other book on LGBTQ issues, it is important to say a little bit about terminology and scope. I have chosen to use the term "LGBTQ" to generally apply to the communities and the set of movements that I have included in this book. I have worked to be historically and politically accurate in my writing, in that I attempt to use the self- and community-given language of the time and try not to be *more* inclusive in my language than activists were in their time (by, for instance, using "LGBTQ" when an organization did not, in fact, have anything to do with trans people or issues). This might seem inconsistent in the way this is written. For instance, activists in the 1950s and 1960s often used "gay" to be inclusive of gay men and lesbians. By the 1970s, "and lesbian" was added as lesbian feminists asserted their own identities and interests and called out the sexism in the gay movement. These lesbian and gay movements through the 1960s and 1970s did not have a politics or theory of bisexuality. While there was a lot of talk of gender fluidity and performance, and people who were gender nonconforming were absolutely leaders of and participants in these earlier movements, there was no explicit "transgender" inclusion or politics until the 1990s at least, when "LGBT" came to be the label that activists used to define their work and their communities. For the current time, and just within the past few years, the "Q" in LGBTQ is increasingly, though not universally, used. Some people still prefer "LGBT," particularly in describing the mainstream civil rights movement. As we will see in chapter 3, the reappropriation of the word "queer" in the early 1990s was and remains controversial. Throughout the book, I will say more about the meanings of each of these terms in their historical context.

Of course, it is important to remember that gay, lesbian, bisexual, and transgender identities and labels have not always existed in the same way they do now. All identities are socially constructed and historically contingent. This does not make them any less *real*. It simply means that we need to understand labels, terms, and identities as having particular histories, as *coming from some place* rather than being naturally given, and as necessarily and constantly changing over time. For example, Rupp (2009) writes of gender fluidity and about same-sex desire and love between women around the world and since prehistorical times, well before any labels defined or circumscribed these individuals and their relationships. And historians Rupp (2009), Carroll Smith-Rosenberg (1975), and Lillian Faderman (1991) all write of a time in late eighteenth- to early nineteenth-century Europe and the US, a time of supposed repressive sexuality and restrictive sexual and gender norms, when some women were allowed – even celebrated for – a level of physical and emotional intimacy with each other that would come to be pathologized in the twentieth century. *Lesbians*, as a social and political category of people, did not exist yet, even though same-sex love and sex between women did. Faderman argues that the lesbian category came into being through the development of an increased faith in science and through a series of economic, demographic, and social changes, such as the possibility of women's financial independence and the development of women's educational, military, and social institutions.

Similarly, it is important to remember that terminology shifts in its use and connotation substantially over time. In the late nineteenth and early twentieth centuries in the US, men who had sex with men were distinguished – as *fairy*, *queer*, and *trade*, for example – by their gender expression and sometimes by the gender expression of their lovers, rather than by their orientation toward men as romantic and sexual partners (Chauncey, 1994). It was only in the 1930s and 1940s that these distinctions consolidated around the term *gay*, and then this term may have also referred to lesbians, bisexuals, and even transgender people (Faderman & Timmons, 2009).

Even in using LGBTQ for the way in which the modern movement frames itself, I have made some specific choices here about which groups I am including and which I am leaving out. I do not, for example, talk at all about *intersex* politics, which have developed since the 1990s (Chase, 1998; Stryker, 2008; Morland, 2014), nor do I examine the politics and identity of *asexuality* that have gained visibility in recent years (Decker, 2014; Gremore, 2016). There are so many variations on the pan-identity acronym these days. One capacious label is "LGBTQ+." Some use "queer" as a broad, inclusive term for gender and sexual minorities, others find this term to be alienating. I have made the choice, however, that "LGBTQ," while admittedly limited, best represents the history and politics as I tell it here of movements for gender/sexual social change in the US in the past few generations.

In this book, we will encounter just some of the many activists over the generations who marched and demonstrated and argued cases before the Supreme Court. We will also meet activists who built movements around alternative cultural institutions, or around their music and art, their science, their bars, and their music festivals. We will see that LGBTQ Americans have broken their silences in so many ways over the generations. It is to those ways that we now turn.

2

Before and After Stonewall

One hot summer night in June of 1969, at the seedy Stonewall Inn bar in the heart of New York City's West Village, a diverse group of gender and sexual minorities stood up to the police brutality and repression that had become so familiar to them. The Stonewall Inn was not the first or only place that LGBTQ people had fought back. But it was the one that stuck, the one that sparked an organizational revolution that led to the modern LGBTQ movement. It is probably the one you know about, if you are familiar at all with LGBTQ history in the US. It is where most popular accounts of the mass movement for LGBTQ social justice tends to start. Yet to understand the ways in which LGBTQ people have defined and understood themselves in the US, built communities, and developed a complex and wide-ranging set of politics, we need to reach back further in history, to the early twentieth century. Stonewall *was* a beginning, but it was also a culmination.

By learning a bit about this history, we can find the roots of some of the key themes of the modern LGBTQ movements. First, we see that social organizing and resistance take many forms. We see that early gay liberationists organized mass demonstrations and marches, as well as smaller direct actions. We also see that people have used culture, language, and alternative institution-building to create collective identities and safe spaces for themselves that were in themselves a form of resistance. Second, we see how movements develop in relation to one another, gaining language, strategies, and confidence from other social movements of the time.

11

Post-Stonewall movements took what they learned both directly and indirectly from civil rights, Black Power, the New Left, and second wave feminism as they built LGBTQ-focused organizations. Third, we see that some of the key ideological divisions in LGBTQ movements have their roots in the homophile movements of the post-World War II era. Perhaps the most significant of these is the division between assimilationists and liberationists (Rimmerman, 2008). This division dates at least as far back as the early 1950s. Faderman writes of a "bitter clash" in 1953 between "radicals who'd regarded homosexuals as a different species from heterosexuals" and "assimilationists who'd insisted homosexuals and heterosexuals were almost exactly the same," which "would divide lesbian and gay communities even into the twenty-first century" (2015, p. 73). Finally, we see, in the anti-gay backlash – which developed first in an organized way during and after World War II and then with unprecedented vitality in the late 1970s with the rise of the Religious Right[1] – that social action often produces a response, which then impacts and shapes subsequent social action, such that repression and revolution often occur together.

Culture, Community, and Organizing Before Stonewall

There were thriving gay and lesbian cultures, communities, and even organizations in the decades before Stonewall.[2] Here, I focus on three pre-Stonewall institutions: cities, the military, and medical and psychological sciences. These were three of the most important sites for lesbian and gay visibility and community-building in the first half of the twentieth century in the US. They presented opportunities for lesbian and gay people to come together, develop distinctive cultures, and build a sense of shared experience and common language. They also, conversely, presented opportunities for state and cultural subjugation of gender and sexual minorities. This combination of increased visibility and community with heightened institutional repression created the political opening into which Stonewall emerged at the end of the 1960s.

Gay men and lesbians were creating their own vibrant and visible communities in large US cities by the beginning of the twentieth century. In *Gay New York*, historian George Chauncey "challenges three widespread myths" of pre-Stonewall gay life: "isolation, invisibility, and internalization" (1994, pp. 1–2). Gay men in New York City built successful institutions and neighborhoods throughout the city, developing an "immense gay world" around their city's streets, bars, bathhouses, restaurants, and hugely popular drag balls (1994, p. 2). Rather than separating themselves, they were integrated into the social lives of their straight neighbors and neighborhoods, while inventing "a highly sophisticated system of subcultural codes – codes of dress, speech, and style – that enabled them to recognize one another on the streets, at work, and at parties and bars" (1994, p. 4). Finally, gay New Yorkers in this pre-World War II era generally did not internalize a view of themselves as "sick, criminal, and unworthy," but instead "celebrated their difference" and pushed back against homophobia (1994, pp. 4–5).

Chauncey argues that gay culture- and community-building was itself a kind of innovative and collective "everyday resistance" that pre-dated the explicitly political organizing of the 1960s and 1970s (1994, p. 5). This included individual ways of asserting visibility and presence through, for example, fashion (like red ties) and language. Other acts of resistance were communal. Gay men in New York City made communities out of their city's institutions: the YMCA (popularized as a gay institution, but not first discovered, by the Village People!); bathhouses that they made their own; drag balls that drew crowds of hundreds, even thousands; and local cafeterias and lunch counters. Well before Stonewall, gay New Yorkers – and people in other cities around the world – built lives and communities for themselves, fashioned out of their cities.[3]

While Chauncey focuses on men in New York City, Faderman (1991), Faderman and Stuart Timmons (2009), and Rupp (2009) write about the vibrant and visible lesbian urban communities that flourished during this same time in a number of other cities, in the US, Canada, and Western Europe.[4] Women had more economic and cultural constraints, and some of their public communities developed a bit later than those of men; but lesbians did create thriving community institutions – like, for example, working-class lesbian bars that catered to butch-femme couples (D'Emilio, 1998; Rupp, 2009).

With increased visibility and vibrancy for urban gay men and lesbians – and in the context of 1920s and 1930s politics and economics – came increased repression. Chauncey argues that the closet did not always exist and was not inevitable, nor has the history of the past century been a story of linear progress *out* of the closet. Rather, the closet was a product of the mid-twentieth century, starting in the 1920s. It was a deliberate construction by the state. He contends that the apparatus of police control, surveillance, and repression that developed in a broad way during the Prohibition era was applied to gay nightlight and public socializing. So, too, the Great Depression at the end of the 1920s put many men out of work, which meant that they could not fulfill their traditional gender roles as economic providers for wives and children. "Lesbians and gay men," Chauncey writes, "began to seem more dangerous in this context – as figures whose defiant perversity threatened to undermine the reproduction of normative gender and sexual arrangements already threatened by the upheavals of the thirties" (1994, p. 354).

Just as cities like New York and Los Angeles provided opportunities for lesbian and gay visibility and community in the early part of the twentieth century, so the World War II-era military offered a much broader opportunity for community-building across the country. This military also proved to be a site for a new level of persecution and marginalization. The war created an institutional space that allowed people who may have been otherwise isolated from each other, who may have "grown up in rural areas or small towns and . . . regarded themselves as singular freaks" (Duberman 1993, p. 76), to find each other. The war also created a demand for women workers, and, with it, a new dominant narrative about femininity that allowed a broad range of women to come out of their homes and into new all-women's communities (Faderman, 1991).

Allan Bérubé (2010) writes that the US military had not historically excluded gay service members as *people*. Rather, it had criminalized sodomy between men as an *act* – and generally had no policy at all about sex between women. As it mobilized for a massive draft for World War II, however, the Selective Service initially set a number of explicit restrictions on draftees. It excluded women, *homosexuals* as a category of people, and, in some branches, African Americans, on the assumption that "their integration would turn the military into a testing ground for radical social experimentation rather than a strong fighting force" (2010, p. 2). However, after the bombing of Pearl Harbor in December 1941, the military could not afford to exclude people so categorically. And, once enlisted, gay and lesbian service members found one another, developed collective identities and a new sense of shared experience, came out, and built communities.

These new GI communities endured beyond the war years. An expanded gay and especially lesbian bar scene developed out of the war, as did the growth of enclave cities like San Francisco and Los Angeles, as new veterans chose to maintain the ties they had formed in the service.[5] Their experience through the war had changed gay and lesbian GIs, giving them a lasting sense of collective identity and strength and a pride in their contribution to the war effort. Their experience also gave them a sense that they constituted a *group*: a persecuted minority – both in and outside the military – that shared a common experience and that could and should fight for its own rights and receive the entitlements due to other GIs (Bérubé, 2010). It also brought a new experience of public community. Ghaziani argues that new urban institutions, like bars, "cemented dense social networks and inspired gays and lesbians to assert a right to gather in public places" (2014, p. 15).

World War II also brought new repression for gay and lesbian GIs. First, the military moved from a criminal justice model to a reliance on psychiatrists and a psychiatric model for defining, sussing out, and punishing homosexuality. This move was meant as a *liberal* and decriminalizing reform effort, but it had the effect of shifting the focus from the *act* of sodomy as *criminal* to the *person* of the homosexual as *sick*. At the time, as Bérubé argues, in the service of "pursuing their agenda of showing how psychiatry could contribute to the war effort," psychiatrists introduced broad-reaching mental health screens for new recruits (2010, p. 9). This involved developing and administering elaborate screening tests to detect and root out any possible male homosexuals in their midst (women were less actively targeted initially).[6] Repression and anti-gay panic grew all the more emphatic in the military by the late 1940s, as it no longer needed the millions of recruits it had relied on during the war. An October 1949 memo from the Department of Defense declared plainly: "Homosexual personnel, irrespective of sex, should not be permitted to serve in any branch of the Armed Forces in any capacity, and prompt separation of known homosexuals from the Armed Forces is mandatory" (Faderman, 2015, p. 32).

In the Cold War era, when Senator Joseph McCarthy stirred up anti-Communist hysteria and a concern for national security, gay men, especially, became ready scapegoats, and military discharges increased significantly (Adam, 1995; D'Emilio, 1998). In December 1950, a Senate report urged that any "sexual pervert" should also be refused all federal jobs. Their "lack [of] emotional stability" and weak "moral fiber" were so great that they "[tend] to have a corrosive influence upon . . . fellow employees" (D'Emilio, 1998, p. 42). Officials further argued that (closeted) gay government workers were national security risks as they would be easy targets of blackmail. In April 1953, soon after taking office, President Dwight D. Eisenhower codified this exclusion by signing Executive Order 10450.

This unprecedented state-sponsored framing of gay and lesbian veterans and government workers as national threats played out against a postwar return to restrictive gender roles that pathologized independent and working women. Lesbians might have been allowed to be the "hero" during World War II, but they were the "sicko" of the 1950s (Faderman, 1991, p. 119). As Bérubé (2010) argues, the psychiatric framing of homosexuality as a mental illness, which had originated with military practice, became part of public culture. Gay men and lesbians were subject to police intimidation, random raids, and entrapment in bars and public spaces, even in private spaces like their homes. "Lewd and lascivious conduct" was a common charge against gay men, while women were most commonly picked up and harassed by police for the charge of "masquerading" in clothes that authorities considered masculine or for men only (Faderman & Timmons, 2009, pp. 81, 93). Amid anti-Communist fervor, gay men and lesbians during this period became "invisible enemies who could live next door and who threatened the security and safety of children, women, the family, and the nation" (Bérubé, 2010, p. 258). This framing was new (Chauncey, 1994), and – as we will see – powerfully enduring.

Along with American cities and the military, science was a third pre-Stonewall site of both early gay and lesbian visibility and community and a repressive backlash against it. First, there was the science at work in the military, as we saw it in operation during and after World War II. Service members were prodded and interrogated, all for the goal of categorizing and rooting out homosexuality. On the other hand, after the war, sex researcher Alfred Kinsey published two bestselling and widely reviewed reports on male and female sexuality (in 1948 and 1953 respectively) that indicated that there was much more same-sex desire and sexual activity among Americans than anyone had previously imagined. The reports, based on interviews with more than 10,000 white women and men, were broad looks at sexual desires, practices, and identities. They both spent months on the *New York Times* bestseller list, selling close to 250,000 copies each, and Kinsey was featured on the cover of *Time* magazine (D'Emilio, 1998).

Kinsey's work revealed that 37 percent of men in the study reported having at least one adult same-sex experience, while 13 percent of women reported the same. In addition, 50 percent of men and 28 percent of women reported that they responded sexually to people of the same sex, regardless of their sexual behavior, and 10 percent of men reported that they were "more or less exclusively homosexual" for three years or more (Faderman, 2015, p. 5; also see D'Emilio, 1998, p. 35). These numbers, which Kinsey and his colleagues found to be surprisingly high, were headline news for the American public.

Out of this increased visibility and a McCarthy-era national and local atmosphere of fear, intimidation, and state-sponsored repression grew the first modern gay and lesbian rights organizations and activists. These new organizations were part of the burgeoning *homophile* movement (*homo* meaning same and *phila* meaning love; see Faderman & Timmons, 2009, p. 111). Although they operated in secret initially, they represented the first sizeable political groups organized around shared sexual identity in the US. They were also the first organizations to grow out of a new self-understanding of gay men and lesbians as *minorities* with a defined identity and with claims to rights and to civil equality (Bérubé, 2010; Armstrong, 2002). This mirrored the ways in which other movements – like the civil rights movement for African American equality – framed identity and social change at the time.

The Mattachine Society, founded in Los Angeles in 1950, was the first of the newly formed groups. Harry Hay, a member of the Communist Party living as a struggling actor and writer in Hollywood, had been moved by Kinsey's report and by the federal postwar program of anti-gay suppression and exclusion. Hay and a very small group of men founded the organization, with its radical roots and its progressive understanding of homosexuals in American society as a marginalized minority. The group's name came from the Italian *Matachinos*, masked court jesters who could speak truth to power behind their masks. The group met secretly in Los Angeles homes, in basements or with shades drawn, and with someone always on the lookout for police raids. By 1953, political splits within the group had pushed Hay and his radical allies out of Mattachine as "accommodation replaced militancy ... [T]he Mattachine Society pursued respectability and abandoned the quest for self-respect" (D'Emilio, 1992, p. 46). As we will see, the debate over assimilation versus radicalism that led to Hay being ousted would continue to mark the politics of LGBTQ social change.[7]

Over the course of the early 1950s, small Mattachine chapters were founded throughout California and in other cities across the country. Mattachine had not really attracted women, however, and there was as yet no substantial lesbian organization in the US. The Daughters of Bilitis (DOB), a lesbian group founded in San

Francisco in 1955, became another primary organizational player in the homophile movement of that era. It took its name from "Songs of Bilitis," a collection of late nineteenth-century French lesbian erotic poetry. The DOB was small, with just a few hundred members across all of its chapters nationwide. But its monthly magazine, *The Ladder*, reached a broader audience, notably women in areas with little lesbian visibility or community. Although the founders of DOB did not know about the Mattachine Society at first, they did eventually work with the group, but they were aware of the sexism in these gay male spaces. "Lesbians are not satisfied," said one of DOB's founders at a Mattachine meeting in 1959, "to be auxiliary members or second-class homosexuals" (D'Emilio, 1998, p. 105; for this paragraph, also see Faderman, 2015).

The founders of DOB, couple Del Martin and Phyllis Lyon, together with a small group of others, initially were not especially interested in politics. They were looking for ways for lesbians to meet and find each other in venues other than bars. In time, however, splits developed in DOB, such that Martin, Lyon, and other middle-class members eventually took the group in a more outward-facing direction, while the working-class members left to start their own solely social group (D'Emilio, 1998; Armstrong, 2002).

Both the Mattachine Society and the Daughters of Bilitis ascribed to the goal of gay men and lesbians "fitting in" to their broader communities, which included conforming to normative gender presentation and expression. "To be invited to Mattachine," one man recalled, "you had to be wearing a Brooks Brothers three-piece suit. Those who were unusual dressers or had unusual hairstyles were not invited. If you made the mistake of bringing someone who was too flamboyant, you could be asked to leave" (Faderman & Timmons, 2009, pp. 113–114). Rejecting alternative gender presentation, the DOB warned in an issue of *The Ladder*: "The kids in fly front pants and with butch haircuts and mannish manner are the worst publicity that we can get" (Rupp, 1999, p. 163). In explanation of this political strategy, sociologist Barry D. Adam wrote: "After the McCarthy terror, accommodation seemed the only realistic choice" (1995, p. 70).

By the mid-1960s, the burgeoning gay and lesbian movements

were growing in the context of, and in many ways directly out of, other 1960s movements for social change, thereby becoming more explicitly political and less accommodationist (D'Emilio, 1992). Frank Kameny, a Washington, DC astronomer who worked for the Department of Defense's Army Map Service, and who was fired for being gay as he was starting his career, embodied this new political approach. He went on to found the Mattachine Society of Washington (no connection to the national Mattachine) in the fall of 1961 and then a coalition group called the East Coast Homophile Organizations (ECHO) at the end of 1962 (Long, 2014; Faderman, 2015). Kameny described himself, and even his early work, as "activist militant" (Marcus, 2002, p. 83) and as directly in contrast to the work of the preceding homophile movement. He took direct lessons in strategy and approach from the African American civil rights and Black Power movements, particularly in being unapologetic and stridently proud of his marginalized identity: "I take the stand that not only is homosexuality . . . not immoral, but that homosexual acts engaged in by consenting adults are moral, in a positive and real sense, and are right, good, and desirable, both for the individual participants and for the society in which they live" (D'Emilio, 1998, p. 153).[8]

As the gay and lesbian movement grew increasingly visible and active, no longer hiding behind drawn curtains and in basements, it drew on the language and symbolism of movements for racial justice in particular. In 1967, the new national gay magazine, *The Advocate*, used the slogan "Gay Power" for the first recorded time. It also drew on the tactics of these movements: from nonviolent sit-ins to more aggressive pushing back against state repression and police brutality. A general radicalization of social movements in 1968 and 1969 – with the assassination of Dr. Martin Luther King, Jr. in April of 1968, the anti-Vietnam War movement, the student movement and the New Left, and the radicalized racial justice movements and feminist movements – all inspired and set the tone for the emerging gay and lesbian liberation movement. Many LGBTQ people already had taken part in other movements at the time and, by the late 1960s, began to move to apply what they had learned as activists to their gay and lesbian activism.[9]

The first use of gay *pride* in this context was probably in the name given to the organization Personal Rights in Defense and Education (PRIDE), which was founded in Los Angeles in 1966. It described itself as an "activist militant" group that encouraged pride and openness and protested against police brutality and other forms of repression (Faderman & Timmons, 2009, pp. 155–156). By 1968, the North American Conference of Homophile Organizations (NACHO) had embraced the slogan "Gay is Good," which Kameny developed in line with the African American freedom movement's "Black is Beautiful" campaign (Faderman, 1991; Carter, 2004; Chauncey, 2005). This was also the beginning of the time when activists began to use the word *gay* explicitly. The label was a move away from *homosexual*, which had come from a psychiatric, pathologized view of same-sex love, desire, and connection (Armstrong, 2002; Stein, 2012).

These years before Stonewall also saw many forms of gay and lesbian collective protest, often led by the most disaffected and marginalized of the broader community in terms of age, race, income and professional status, and gender identity. As we know, the most marginalized people tend not to be the subject of American historical narratives, textbooks, or celebrations. So, even these few (pre-Stonewall) events that I mention here are evidence of a much greater absence in the telling of American history. Cooper Do-nuts in downtown Los Angeles was the site of "perhaps the first homosexual uprising in the world," according to Faderman and Timmons (2009, p. 2). But it did not get much press at the time and has been largely ignored by historians. The coffee and doughnut shop, whose customers were mostly Black and Latino hustlers, drag queens, and their friends, was a regular focus of the local police department. One night, in the spring of 1959, two officers came into the shop and insisted on collecting identification from some customers, before commanding them to get into their waiting squad car. Some customers fought back, throwing doughnuts, cups, sugar cubes, and coffee stirrers (also see Faderman, 2015).

In San Francisco, Gene Compton's Cafeteria was a Northern California version of Cooper Do-nuts, a spot for cheap coffee, food, and community. As at Cooper's, the largely Black and Latino clientele was used to police harassment and intimidation. But, one night in the summer of 1966, as Faderman describes: "As a policeman approached a queen to demand identification, she threw hot coffee in his face. It sparked California's second homosexual brush fire – fifty young homosexuals hurling dishes, breaking windows, vandalizing a police car parked outside the cafeteria, setting a nearby newsstand on fire" and fighting back against police intimidation (2015, p. 119; also see *Screaming queens*, 2005).

In sum, by June 1969, just before Stonewall, there was a small but active and complex gay and lesbian movement. The movement was centered primarily on the US coasts. D'Emilio (1992) estimates that there were likely about 50 groups with a few thousand members in total. Through this early organizing, gender and sexual minorities began to develop collective identities and to mobilize these as they built the beginnings of an organizational infrastructure. There were also already ongoing disagreements within the movement over the kind and pace of change. Some held onto the older, homophile strategy of accommodation, and they stressed *sameness* between gay and lesbian and straight people and communities. Some, on the other hand, emphasized that "gay is good" and *different* and worthy of pride and of legal protection (Rupp, 1999; Faderman & Timmons, 2009; Ghaziani et al., 2016). It was out of this movement and all of its complexity that the Stonewall moment took hold.

Stonewall

Located at 53 Christopher Street in the West Village, New York City, The Stonewall Inn was a seedy club that had been bought by a small group of Mafia men and reopened as a gay bar in the spring of 1967. It was officially a private "bottle club" rather than a public bar, to get around the fact that it lacked a liquor license. It was dark, dingy, and did not even have running water to wash glasses. It served diluted drinks, had filthy bathrooms, and played music through a jukebox and a shabby sound system. But the bar and its two dance floors were popular, crowded, and profitable. Martin Duberman writes that the bar mostly appealed to a younger crowd: teenagers to people in their early-30s. It did not attract many lesbians or "full-time transvestites," but it did serve a wide "melting pot" (1993, pp. 188–190). David Carter (2004) writes that the bar attracted a racially mixed but segregated clientele. White customers tended to hang out in the front room, while the back room was sometimes called "the 'black' or 'Puerto Rican room'" and was mostly for the younger crowd. Some of those who frequented the Stonewall were homeless. In the words of gay writer and activist Vito Russo, the Stonewall "was a bar for the people who were too young, too poor or just too much to get in anywhere else" (Carter 2004, pp. 73–74).

For many decades in many US states, it was illegal for gay men and lesbians to congregate in public and to be served alcohol. These laws were changing through the 1960s, but for years they provided a perfectly legal rationale for police raids on gay bars and the use of vice squads and undercover agents to arrest patrons for their behavior and to close down bars that served gay and lesbian customers (D'Emilio, 1998; Faderman, 2015). One of the reasons why these police raids set high stakes for bar patrons is that many felt they would have a lot to lose both personally and professionally if they were outed as gay or lesbian in the course of a raid and arrest (Armstrong & Crage, 2006; Stewart-Winter, 2016).

In New York City, as Carter (2004) notes, gay bars were raided routinely (every month or so), but there was often close coordination between the police and the bar staff, facilitated by the bars' regular police pay-offs. The Stonewall's mob owners – who also were dealing drugs from the bar – paid off corrupt Sixth Precinct cops on a weekly basis, and this kept the bar–police relationship relatively low-key. For instance, officers in the Sixth Precinct often warned Stonewall employees before taking action and would time their raids to occur earlier in the night, when there were fewer patrons in the bars. Stonewall management also kept close watch on the door, with a bouncer who collected cover charges and carefully monitored entrance. When bright lights suddenly illuminated the dark bar, this was the bar staff's warning to patrons of a raid.

On this particular summer weekend in 1969, police were ending an active couple of weeks of raiding gay bars in the area and already had been to the Stonewall earlier in the week. This raid was different, though. It came later at night, without warning, when the bar was already packed with about 200 patrons. At about 1:20 a.m., on what was technically Saturday, June 28, six members of Manhattan's First Division Public Morals Squad entered the Stonewall and joined two undercover women officers from inside the club. They locked the doors, collected and seized alcohol stock, and began checking IDs of bar patrons, looking for underage and "masquerading" customers. The police released most patrons but placed some under arrest.

This raid then took an unexpected and very unusual turn when bar patrons began to fight back. Deputy Inspector Seymour Pine, who had organized the action, remembers the growing resistance and the role that transgender women took, as police urged them into the bathrooms to be "examined" on "masquerading" charges: "We separated the few transvestites that we had, and they were very noisy that night. Usually they would just sit there and not say a word, but now they're acting up: 'Get your hands off me!' 'Don't touch me!' They wouldn't go in, so it was a question of pushing them in, fighting them" (Carter, 2004, pp. 140–141). As patrons were released into the street, or were roughly arrested outside the bar and shoved into a waiting police wagon or squad cars, they quickly gained the support of others who had been called on payphones to join in this unusual response to the raid and of passersby who were out at a prime time on this first hot, humid weekend night of the summer.

The growing crowd outside the Stonewall began to resist, throwing pennies, glass bottles, cans, bricks, and Molotov cocktails, and yelling at the police. At least one man yelled "Gay power!" A few others started a round of "We Shall Overcome." Police retaliated, brutalizing Stonewall customers and others who had gathered to join the protest on the street. Eventually, the officers took cover inside the bar as they called for backup, and the crowd outside battered the building with anything they could get their hands on, including trash cans and a parking meter that had been ripped from the sidewalk. The backup was the Tactical

Patrol Force (TPF), whose members arrived in riot gear, marching in formation and carrying billy clubs and tear gas. They worked to break up the crowd, which kept re-forming. They were met with what Duberman describes as "their worst nightmare: a chorus line of mocking queens, their arms clasped around each other, kicking their heels in the air Rockettes-style and singing at the tops of their sardonic voices: '*We are the Stonewall girls / We wear our hair in curls / We wear no underwear / We show our pubic hair . . . / We wear our dungarees / Above our nelly knees!*'" (1993, pp. 200–201). The clash continued until about 3:30 a.m., when the 1,000 or so protesters and hundreds of police officers finally dispersed.

The next night (technically later that day, on Saturday night), protesters returned to the streets outside the Stonewall as word had spread through press and by word-of-mouth. A couple of thousand people gathered, singing the "Stonewall Girls" song again, shouting "Gay power," "Equality for homosexuals," and "Liberate Christopher Street." They again clashed with police, including the TPF, who came in droves, again in riot gear, and brutalized protesters. The demonstrations lasted until the early hours of the next morning. On Sunday afternoon, Mattachine New York posted a sign on the wreckage of the Stonewall Inn urging peace rather than protest: "We homosexuals plead with our people to please help maintain peaceful and quiet conduct on the streets of the Village – Mattachine," it read (Carter, 2004, p. 196). The end of the weekend and the increased early police presence likely discouraged large numbers of protesters on that third, Sunday, night. There was only a small number of incidents on the subsequent rainy Monday and Tuesday nights. A larger, 1,000-person protest – and clash with TPF, again – took place on Wednesday, the last of six nights of Stonewall actions.[10]

Although press coverage of the Stonewall uprisings was limited and derisive, especially in the mainstream press and outside New York City (Rupp, 1999; Faderman, 2015), the uprising was immediately significant and generative for the movement. "[T]o many homosexuals, male and female alike," Faderman wrote, "the Stonewall Rebellion was the shot heard round the world" (1991, p. 195).

By all accounts, this action had been started and led by people who were marginalized within LGBTQ communities. Some of the best-known activists to come out of the Stonewall moment were young, gender nonconforming people of color. Latina drag queen (her self-identity) Sylvia Rivera and African American drag queen Marsha P. Johnson, who had known each other since they were very young hustlers in Times Square, were both central to the Stonewall uprising. Rivera was not yet 18 years old, and Johnson was just a few years older (Duberman, 1993).

Sociologists Elizabeth A. Armstrong and Suzanna M. Crage (2006) argue that Stonewall and its significance in the LGBTQ campaign reveal the complexity of power within the movement and the telling of its history. Marginalized gay and gender nonconforming people, especially young queens and hustlers, had stood up to police a number of times before, most notably, perhaps, at Compton's, three years before Stonewall. But "[w]hat Stonewall had, and Compton's did not, were activists able and willing to capitalize on such rioting: high-resource, radical gay men" (2006, p. 744). In other words, Stonewall came at a time and place when the actions of marginalized members of the community – by race, class, age, and gender presentation – were celebrated and built upon by privileged members of the mainstream of the movement, often white, gay, middle-class, gender conforming men. Also, coming in the late 1960s, in the midst of countercultural shifts and the rise of racial justice movements, feminism, and the New Left, this moment resonated in new ways. This had the impact of turning the Stonewall uprisings into a symbol for the growing movement and a catalyst for broad organizational development.

Gay Liberation and the Organizational Revolution after Stonewall

Even before the Stonewall weekend, there was already a fight under way about how to move forward in the gay and lesbian movement. This divided approach mirrored similar discussions in other social and political movements at the time, particularly the

African American movement, which had seen the birth of Black Power out of the civil rights movement. While the civil rights movement focused on using existing American institutions, such as the law, to bring about social change, Black Power refused this assimilationist approach in favor of claiming pride and power for African Americans, building internally controlled institutions that would better serve their Black communities (see, e.g., Van Deburg, 1992).

Stonewall was politically and culturally controversial, another example of a response to oppression that divided those who were hanging on to a politics of respectability that still characterized the homophile movement from those who were on their way to becoming proud and militant gay liberationists. The Stonewall-era gay and lesbian activists saw themselves as the young vanguards of a new revolution and they saw their older homophile siblings as dated and submissive. The older, more experienced homophile activists and community members saw these newcomers as immature, inexperienced, and probably a bit ungrateful and short-sighted (Duberman, 1993; Rupp, 1999; Armstrong, 2002; Marcus, 2002).

The gay liberation movement took off mere days after Stonewall. Carter (2004) describes in detail how Mattachine New York leaders worked to corral the energy into peaceful protests and reform. Yet, over the course of a few meetings in July 1969, they were met with frustration, impatience, and anger by activists who wanted to take a more radical approach. By the end of July, the Gay Liberation Front (GLF) had emerged out of this divide, rejecting assimilation and championing a more liberationist stance. The GLF took its name from the Communist Vietnamese National Liberation Front, signaling its connection to other parts of the New Left and linking its view of gay and lesbian oppression to the capitalist oppression of others in the US and around the world.

The GLF framed its mission in radical terms from the beginning: "We are a revolutionary homosexual group of men and women formed with the realization that complete sexual liberation for all people cannot come about unless existing social institutions are abolished. . . . Babylon has forced us to commit ourselves to one thing . . . revolution" (Carter, 2004, p. 219). In its mission, it displayed a critique of capitalism that was consistent with the Marxism of other Leftist groups at the time, and it urged an alliance with these groups. In answer to the question: "What makes you revolutionaries?" The group articulated:

> We formed after the recent pig bust of the Stonewall, a well-known gay bar in Greenwich Village. We've come to realize that all our frustrations and feelings of oppression are real. The society has fucked with us . . . within our families, on our jobs, in our education, in the streets, in our bedrooms; in short, in has shit all over us. We, like everyone else, are treated as commodities. We're told what to feel, what to think [. . . .] We identify ourselves with all the oppressed: the Vietnamese struggle, the third world, the blacks, the workers . . . all those oppressed by this rotten, dirty, vile, fucked-up capitalist conspiracy. (Carter, 2004, p. 220)

Carter writes that the GLF laid the blame for the construction of the closet at the feet of capitalism, theorizing that capitalism was particularly oppressive to gay and lesbian people in that it constructed and reproduced a "system of taboos and institutionalized repressions." As a result, GLF's politics focused on visibility as a goal: on coming and being "out of the closet" (2004, p. 220). For the first time in history, coming out was not simply a personal and private act, but a highly important *political* one (D'Emilio, 1998; Armstrong, 2002). From the beginning, the GLF also emphasized the importance of community and culture, distributing its own publication, called *Come Out!*, and organizing community-building events, like its popular dances. Soon there were GLF groups in cities and college towns across the country as well as in a few European countries (Rupp, 1999; Faderman, 2015).

Many other radical gay and lesbian groups arose alongside the GLF. "Gay liberation," Armstrong wrote, "burst onto the scene. It accomplished more in two years than the homophile movement had in the previous twenty, as measured by organizational growth, visibility, and political action" (2002, pp. 56–57). While 50 or 60 groups already existed before the summer of 1969, by just a few years after the Stonewall uprising this number had grown to more than 1,000, maybe more than 2,000 (D'Emilio, 1992; Rupp, 1999; Carter, 2004).

Not surprisingly, divisions and disagreements within and between groups existed from the beginning of this radical phase of the movement. One of the most divisive issues was the extent to which gay liberation efforts should remain "single-issue" – focused on gay issues – or should ally with other Left movements of the time (Armstrong, 2002, p. 75). In November 1969, just months after GLF New York was founded, the group bitterly debated (and ultimately rejected) a motion to donate $500 to the Black Panthers. Those who argued strongly for supporting the Panthers saw the GLF work as connected to racial justice efforts. Those who argued vehemently against it believed that the GLF should prioritize gay issues. They also worried about the homophobia they had seen displayed by the Panthers and some other Black nationalists at the time (Duberman, 1993; Carter, 2004).[11]

Like many movements and organizations of the time, the GLF began to fall apart as its members failed to resolve volatile internal disagreements. The organization had been unstable from the start, rife with ideological divisions and no clear organizational or leadership structure (D'Emilio, 1992; Faderman, 2015). After the Panther debate in GLF New York, the more liberal members, who wanted to focus on gay causes exclusively and who had a more rights-focused approach to change, broke away and founded the Gay Activists Alliance (GAA) in December 1969. Armstrong (2002) argues that the brief *gay power* phase of the movement gave way, with the founding of the GAA and then the organizational proliferation that followed, to a *gay rights* and *gay pride* movement. For some, this signaled that those with privilege and a single-issue commitment had succeeded in defining the movement's focus. Because the GAA formed initially out of the split with the GLF over the support of the Black Panthers, Armstrong argues, "the conflict between gay pride and gay power" had "a distinctively racial cast. Some GLF activists viewed the abandonment of gay power and the formation of GAA as an expression of the class, race, and gender privilege of middle-class white gay men" (2002, p. 94).[12]

The GAA had a clear organizational structure, an explicit attention only to gay and lesbian issues, and founding documents that were modeled on US founding documents, like the Constitution (Hirshman, 2013; Faderman, 2015). This new group was focused on civil rights and was therefore more assimilationist. As Duberman notes, it wanted to "win acceptance for gays within the country's institutional structure – not to topple or transform that structure, as was GLF's intent" (1993, p. 232). But, the GAA also had a direct action focus that was quite different from the Mattachine-like accommodationist style. The GAA articulated its mission this way:

> We as liberated homosexual activists demand the freedom for expression of our dignity and value as human beings through confrontation with and disarmament of all mechanisms which unjustly inhibit us: economic, social, and political. Before the public conscience, we demand an immediate end to all oppression of homosexuals and the immediate unconditional recognition of these basic rights. (Carter, 2004, p. 235)

To this end, GAA activists began to engage in high-profile, disruptive, theatrical direct actions that they called "zaps." For example:

> When *Harper's* magazine published an article by intellectual heavy hitter Joseph Epstein, expressing his wish to "wipe homosexuality off the face of the earth," GAA activists brought cakes and a big coffee urn to the offices of the magazine, interrupting publication to demand equal time to reply. As each of *Harper's* employees walked into work that morning, he or she was greeted by a GAA demonstrator: "*I'm a homosexual*," the activists said. "Have a doughnut." (Hirshman, 2013, pp. 122–123)

In keeping with its more assimilationist approach with regard to its faith in existing American institutions, the GAA also focused its zaps efforts on fighting for policy change, like its effort to add sexual orientation to a New York City nondiscrimination law and to call attention to a New York City clerk's denial of wedding licenses to same-sex couples (Rimmerman, 2002; Faderman, 2015).

The GAA signaled the beginning of the end of the short-lived radical gay liberationist phase of the movement that had developed out of Stonewall. This phase was essentially over by early 1972. Then, throughout the 1970s, the gay liberation phase gave way to a prolific period of culture and political organizing within a more rights- and pride-focused movement. LGBTQ groups formed to fight on a number of different political fronts, and a wide range of LGBTQ communities built and controlled their own cultural institutions (Armstrong, 2002).

One enduring contribution to the movement of the post-Stonewall era was the pride march and parade, which began in 1970 as a way to memorialize the Stonewall uprising. The first New York celebration on June 28, 1970 was a 51-block march of thousands of people up Sixth Avenue from near Christopher Street to the Sheep Meadow in Central Park, throughout which participants carried "Gay Pride" placards and yelled "Gay Power" and "Say it clear! Say it loud! Gay is good! Gay is proud!" At the same time, Los Angeles held Christopher Street West, a march down Hollywood Boulevard, and Chicago, for its part, hosted a "Gay Pride Week." Armstrong notes that, from the beginning, these events were framed less as political "demonstrations" and more as "celebrations" of "pride" (2002, p. 108). The parades grew quickly in the years that followed, and spread to a wide range of US cities throughout the country and in Western Europe. From the beginning, these pride events relied on and built upon the existing organizational infrastructure and institutions (like community media) in local gay communities (Armstrong & Crage, 2006).[13]

A lesbian feminist movement also grew out of the post-Stonewall moment of gay liberation. It articulated a distinctly gendered analysis of the experience of sexuality and an intersectional understanding of gender and sexuality. Lesbians had experienced sexism within the homophile and gay liberation movements *and* homophobia within the feminist movements of the time.[14] Within the mainstream second wave feminist movement, which developed in the 1960s, the most infamous example of homophobia came from Betty Friedan. In 1963, Friedan had published *The Feminine Mystique*, which helped to inspire a mainstream feminist civil rights movement.[15] In 1966, she also had co-founded the National Organization for Women (NOW), which became one of the primary players in mainstream feminism, a civil rights organization focused on legal and policy change for women's equality. Calling lesbians the "lavender menace of the women's movement," Friedan worried that they would scare away from feminism those women who "wanted equality but also wanted to keep on loving their husbands and children" (quoted in Faderman & Timmons, 2009, p. 184; Faderman, 2015, p. 235). She worked explicitly to exclude lesbians and lesbian organizations – like Daughters of Bilitis – from the women's movement.[16] Later in the decade, radical feminists, who were critical of the assimilationist, civil rights agenda of Friedan and other liberals, were nevertheless not particularly inclusive of lesbians either. As historian Alice Echols writes of many radical feminists: "Most commonly, they dismissed lesbianism as sexual rather than political"; the women's liberation movement of the early 1970s was "convulsed by the gay–straight split" within it (1989, pp. 211, 220).

Even as they faced homophobia within both mainstream and radical feminism, lesbians within the gay movement often felt marginalized by gay male activists. Both the GLF and the GAA were primarily founded, led, and joined by men (Carter, 2004; Faderman, 2015), and women within these organizations experienced male activists as sometimes aggressive, dismissive, and stuck in their own traditional notions of gender roles. These women activists also felt that lesbians and gay men had different experiences of their sexuality, and that even the most radical parts of the gay movement had been organized primarily around gay male experiences and priorities (Faderman, 1991; Duberman, 1993; *Pride Divide*, 1997; Faderman & Timmons, 2009).

By 1970 and 1971, lesbian activists began to organize a "parallel revolution" (Faderman, 2015, p. 227) for themselves and to claim the label of *lesbian feminist* explicitly. Taylor and Rupp define lesbian feminism as "a variety of beliefs and practices based on the core assumption that a connection exists between an erotic and/ or emotional commitment to women and political resistance to patriarchal domination" (1993, p. 33). Lesbian feminists worked in an explicitly politicized way to build and sustain community-controlled cultural, artistic, athletic, and health institutions and spaces. Just as it demonstrated a division between men's and women's cultures and organizing (*Pride Divide*, 1997), so this kind of lesbian organizing was another example of the political split in the broader gay and lesbian movement, between assimilationists whose interest was in integrating into existing American institutions and separatists who believed that the path to equality and justice was through the creation of their own institutions.[17]

In this short period in the early 1970s, radical lesbian feminist groups proliferated across the country (Stein, 2012). On the explicitly political front, for instance, a short-lived group, the Radicalesbians, developed out of the frustration of women in the GLF, including charismatic writer and activist Rita Mae Brown (Hirshman, 2013). She had briefly joined the Student Homophile League at Columbia and the New York chapter of NOW, before exploring a radical feminist group called Redstockings. Having found the Columbia group to be sexist and the NOW group to be elitist, she concluded that Redstockings lacked any attention to lesbian needs and politics (Echols, 1989; Faderman, 2015). Brown turned to the GLF hoping for something more inclusive of lesbians, but did not find it there. With a small group of women, she ultimately produced the influential and heavily circulated manifesto "The Woman Identified Woman." This 1970 document defined "lesbian" broadly and, primarily, *politically*: "A lesbian is the rage of all women condensed to the point of explosion. She is a woman who . . . acts in accordance with her inner compulsion to be a more complete and free human being than her society . . . cares to allow her" (Faderman, 1991, p. 206). Challenging the mainstream feminist movement of the time, Brown organized a protest of NOW's Second Congress to Unite Women in New York City in the spring of 1970. As the lights went out in the meeting space, a group of women wearing Lavender Menace shirts took over the stage as Brown took to the microphone, over conference organizers' strong objections. "This conference," Brown said, "won't proceed until we talk about lesbians in the women's movement" (Faderman, 2015, p. 236). Brown was also at the center of another short-lived early 1970s radical lesbian political group in Washington, DC, The Furies. The group took a separatist stance and viewed lesbianism as a form of radical gender politics. As one founder noted: "Lesbianism is a threat to the ideological, political, personal and economic base of male supremacy" (quoted in Echols, 1989, p. 232).

During this time of organizational proliferation in the lesbian and gay movement, racialized and gendered exclusion inside the movement also spurred activism by lesbian, gay, and bisexual people of color (Cohen, 1999) and transgender activism. For example, Sylvia Rivera had been active in both the GLF and the GAA for a while, even though many in those organizations exhibited transphobia. Rivera and her longtime friend Marsha P. Johnson, co-founded STAR, the Street Transvestite Action Revolutionaries, in New York City in 1970 (later renamed the Street Transgender Action Revolutionaries). STAR provided housing and services, especially for young homeless LGBTQ people. It was, Rivera said, "for the street gay people, the street homeless people, and anybody that needed help at that time" (Feinberg, 1998, p. 107) and it had chapters in New York, Chicago, California, and England. Rivera felt that STAR and trans people were often marginalized in the broader movement after Stonewall. "Gay liberation but transgender nothing!" she reflected in a speech in 2001 (n.p.).[18]

By the early 1970s, gay and lesbian activists were putting their efforts into other areas of politics and culture, demonstrating a broad range of approaches to social change. Some turned to public policy and traditional, assimilationist civil rights pursuits through organizations like the National Gay Task Force (NGTF) and the Lambda Legal Defense and Education Fund, both founded in 1973 (Marcus, 2002; Chauncey, 2005). These were part of a new "professionalized" gay and lesbian rights movement, which, as Bronski notes, "sought change through legislative and electoral channels and worked within the system to make gay people full American citizens" (1998, pp. 73, 70). There were gendered aspects of the shape this movement took. As law and society scholar Kimberly D. Richman (2009) notes, it was only when women began to take on leadership roles that family law issues – like lesbian mothers' child custody cases – began to be a priority for this civil rights focus of the movement in the 1970s, and new national organizations developed around new legal goals of the movement – for example, Lesbian Mothers National Defense Fund in 1974 and the Lesbian Rights Project, which later became the National Center for Lesbian Rights (NCLR), in 1977.

Other activists turned "inward," toward building community institutions of various kinds (Faderman & Timmons, 2009, p. 192). Some organizations provided health and social service supports – like the Los Angeles Gay Community Services Center, founded in the early 1970s, and the Gay VD Clinic in Chicago. Others provided religious support – for example, the Metropolitan Community Church (MCC), which had been founded in Los Angeles by gay Pentecostal minister Troy Perry in 1968 and expanded tremendously through the early 1970s; and other religious organizations, like the first gay and lesbian Jewish congregation, Beth Chayim Chadashim, founded in Los Angeles in 1972–73. Other groups focused on race/ethnicity, gender, and sexuality – for example, Gay American Indians and the Combahee River Collective. In fact, as historian Marc Stein notes, it "was a period of transformational mobilization" for lesbian and gay activists of color (2012, p. 123). Finally, others provided a range of artistic and cultural outlets, like discos and bars, bathhouses, bookstores, record labels, choruses, and coffee shops.[19]

Stonewall-era revolutionaries might have celebrated the size and public nature of the broad, diffuse, and visible gay and lesbian movement, but they would have lamented the direction it had taken – like the other social justice movements of its time – toward civil rights and assimilationism rather than alternative community-building and liberationism. Longtime LGBTQ progressive activist Urvashi Vaid noted of the movement by the late 1970s: "From that period on, the gay and lesbian political movement pursued social, legal, cultural, and political legitimation – what I call mainstreaming – rather than social change" (1995, p. 36).

The Emboldened Right Responds

The proliferation of these visible and varied lesbian and gay mobilizations coincided with the beginnings of the flourishing of the American Right in the mid- to late 1970s. Historian Dagmar Herzog (2008) details the rise of the politically active Religious Right and its dependence on a very narrow view of legitimate, moral sexuality. The Religious Right moved away from the church, inserting itself boldly into politics by targeting two issues: abortion and gay rights (also see Diamond, 1995; Vaid, 1995). Sociologist Tina Fetner argues that the Right had a rich and effective internal network and set of community-controlled institutions – like media, churches, and schools – on which to draw for its anti-gay activism, which "marked the entry of evangelical Christians into secular politics" (2008, p. 10). During this time, three moments stand out as historically and politically significant to the development of both LGBTQ movements and movements on the Right: Anita Bryant's Save Our Children Campaign; the Briggs Initiative in California; and the assassination of Harvey Milk, the first openly gay person elected to the San Francisco board of supervisors.

Anita Bryant's anti-gay campaign in 1977 was the moment of the birth of a highly visible and organized anti-gay Religious Right (Fetner, 2008). Bryant was an Oklahoman evangelical Southern Baptist and a well-known celebrity who had been a long-time Miami (Dade County) resident. She had been a singer, a beauty queen, a professional Christian with book contracts and speaking tours under her belt, and a Florida orange juice spokesperson with a national platform for her views. Prompted by members of her church, she launched a frenzied and theatrical effort to overturn a Dade County nondiscrimination law that had been newly revised to include civil rights protections for "affectional or sexual preference." This was the first sexual orientation nondiscrimination law – of approximately 40 laws like it at the time in other regions – to be adopted by any southern city (Shilts, 1982).

Bryant's Save Our Children campaign collected nearly 65,000

signatures to put a repeal of the law on the June 1977 ballot. Bryant drew on all the Cold War-era depictions of gay men as dangerous, untrustworthy pedophiles who were obsessed with molesting and converting America's children. As she famously wrote at the time in her autobiography: "[H]omosexuals cannot reproduce – so they must recruit. And to freshen their ranks, they must recruit the youth of America" (Fetner, 2008, p. xiii). The campaign ran a full-page ad in the *Miami Herald* that read: "There is no 'Human Right' to Corrupt Our Children" (Faderman, 2015, p. 337).

Just as the rise and success of the Religious Right was a response to progressive gender and sexual politics of the time, so the gay and lesbian movement emerged in new ways in the late 1970s to respond to the growing public activism of the Right. These two contemporaneous movements arose, were reinforced, and were energized by each other (Fetner, 2008). Gay and lesbian activists fought back against Bryant – including urging a national boycott of Florida orange juice. To ask a majority to vote to protect or extend the rights of a minority is always a tall order, though. Bryant's campaign had broad appeal and visibility across the country (Faderman, 2015) and in June of 1977 Dade County voters handily revoked the rights that had just been bestowed on lesbian, gay, and bisexual residents.

At her victory celebration in a Miami Holiday Inn, Bryant spoke as if this were just the beginning for the anti-gay Religious Right. She pronounced: "Tonight the laws of God and the cultural values of man have been vindicated! . . . The people of Dade County – the normal majority – have said 'Enough! Enough! Enough!'" (Faderman, 2015, p. 353). She vowed to extend her campaign and, on the heels of the Miami vote, St. Paul (Minnesota), Wichita (Kansas), and Eugene (Oregon) all repealed their nondiscrimination protections (Stone, 2012). Bryant also inspired Republican Senator John Briggs of Orange County, California (Fetner, 2008). An evangelical Christian with gubernatorial ambitions, Briggs bet on homophobia to raise his profile, calling gay politics "the hottest social issue since Reconstruction." He organized to place an initiative before California voters in November 1978. Proposition

6 proposed that teachers or anyone working with children in schools would be fired for "advocating, soliciting, imposing, encouraging, or promoting private or public sexual acts defined in the penal code between persons of the same sex in a manner likely to come to the attention of other employees or students, or publicly and indiscreetly engaging in such actions." The initiative, which placed in voters' hands the power of the state to fire teachers for being gay or "promoting" homosexuality in any way, drew on the same tropes of gay perversion and child endangerment as Bryant's campaign had done. One Proposition 6 flyer, for instance, read: "Preserve Parents' Rights to Protect Their Children from Teachers Who Are Immoral and Who Promote a Perverted Lifestyle. Vote 'Yes' on 6!" (see Faderman, 2015, pp. 368–369).

The Briggs Initiative became another national lightning rod in gay rights politics, mobilizing high-profile support as well as opposition. It was the first time that California voters statewide weighed in on gay and lesbian civil rights (Shilts, 1982). The measure had been leading in the polls in California. In a turning point, conservative former California governor Ronald Reagan *opposed* the initiative. He was a small-government conservative, and he believed that this law would bring government to the classroom in intrusive, potentially messy ways. Reagan's involvement went a long way toward sinking the Briggs Initiative. Ultimately, it failed at the polls on November 7, 1978, when Californians voted against it, 58.4 to 41.6 percent. This handed the anti-gay Religious Right a high-profile defeat, but it still had the effect of "consolidat[ing] an activist network opposed to gay rights" (Diamond, 1995, p. 171; also see Faderman, 2015).

A new result of the high-profile anti-gay rightwing bigotry of Bryant and Briggs was that straight allies began to participate in the lesbian and gay movement in an unprecedented way. Faderman argues that young, progressive straights had not previously viewed gay rights as *their* issue. "But," she writes, "Anita Bryant's Bible-thumping took away their neutrality. The sexual sanctimoniousness of Bryant and her ilk were a threat to heterosexual freedoms, too, and straight hip culture began reflecting antipathy" (2015, p. 363). The rise of the Right energized the gay and lesbian movement, helped it develop organizationally, and brought in more allies and more national visibility (Armstrong, 2002; Fetner, 2008).

At the end of the 1970s, the assassination of Harvey Milk became another site and symbol of the clash between the Right and the gay and lesbian movement. Milk's death and the unjust, inadequate criminal sentence of his murderer further fueled gay and lesbian activism and helped to build a movement that was increasingly national in scope. Milk, a San Francisco Supervisor (equivalent to a city council member), was one of the first openly gay elected officials in the country and had fought hard against the Briggs Initiative. A transplant from New York, a former banker and political conservative-turned-hippy, gay rights activist, and the co-owner of a small camera shop in San Francisco's heavily gay Castro neighborhood, Milk had run unsuccessfully for the San Francisco Board of Supervisors in 1973 and 1975. He finally won in 1977. With humor and a huge amount of charisma and energy, Milk became a national gay rights superstar. He spoke frequently about the importance of visibility, of coming out, and of gay leadership.[20] He was an energizing force for the local and the national movement, making a strong case for gay rights and linking this fight to other movements and causes.[21]

A few days after the failure of the Briggs Initiative, conservative Supervisor Dan White, who had sparred with Milk on a number of local issues, including gay rights, resigned from the Board of Supervisors. Just 10 days later, he asked the liberal San Francisco mayor, George Moscone, for his job back. On November 27, 1978, while awaiting final confirmation from the mayor that his reappointment would not be accepted, White walked into City Hall and fatally shot both Mayor Moscone and Harvey Milk, five times each. His guilt was not in question: he confessed to the murders. But, when a jury handed down a verdict, in May 1979, it was an incredibly light one: voluntary manslaughter in both cases. For this charge, White was sentenced to the maximum possible total of seven years and eight months in prison.

The jury's failure to charge White with murder spurred an immediate response in San Francisco. With calls of "Out of the bars and into the streets" and "Dan White, Dan White / Hit man for the New Right," a gathering crowd of eventually thousands made their way from the Castro to San Francisco's City Hall, where they smashed windows and eventually clashed violently with police (Shilts, 1982; also see Shepard, 1997, ch. 3). Harry Britt, the gay man who was appointed to Milk's place on the Board of Supervisors after the assassination, said, the day after the confrontation at City Hall: "Now the society is going to have to deal with us not as nice little fairies who have their hair dressing salons, but as people capable of violence. This was gay anger you saw" (Faderman, 2015, p. 409).

It was in the wake of Milk's assassination – following on the heels of the anti-gay work of Bryant and Briggs – that the first national gay and lesbian march in Washington, DC, was organized. Armstrong writes that there had been "little enthusiasm" for a national march prior to this time, though Milk advocated it. "Sentiment about a national march on Washington," however, "changed dramatically" after Milk's assassination (2002, p. 130). Ghaziani argues that one impact of the local organized responses to Bryant and Briggs and to Milk's assassination was the development of a gay and lesbian "national consciousness" and the awareness of a need to build a movement with a broad reach (2008, p. 36). The October 1979 march, which drew between 75,000 and 125,000 participants from across the country, "gave birth to a national movement" (2008, p. 43). It was, according to the *San Francisco Chronicle*, the "coming out of the movement on the national political agenda" (quoted in Armstrong, 2002, p. 130).

Beyond Stonewall

Once lesbian and gay people found each other in large numbers and developed a sense of identity as a collective and as a minority group, they began to resist state oppression – like police raids – and to make demands of their country. The Stonewall uprising crystallized and accelerated a movement that had been building for almost two decades already. Out of it came organizational proliferation and a national movement – and a vehement backlash from a Religious Right that was in the midst of its own moment of growth and accomplishment.

Historians and analysts often understand the divide between assimilationists and liberationists to characterize the LGBTQ movement, dating back to the split within Mattachine in the early 1950s. We see this at play here in many ways throughout these first few decades of the organized movement, between the homophile movement and gay liberation, then between the groups that formed after Stonewall. As Bronski nicely summarizes: "While the homophile movement promoted the idea of private, responsible citizenship, the gay liberation movement called for public displays of identity but did not actively promote a civil rights platform that demanded full participation in the state. This was because, on a deeply political level, the movement deplored the state and its power" (1998, p. 68).

It is important to recognize, though, as you continue to read, that this assimilationist/liberationist distinction is not an easy or an absolute one. Frank Kameny, for instance, understood himself as a militant and urged self-acceptance and pride. Yet he had his own conservative guidelines during protests, urging participants to be "lawful, orderly, dignified," noting: "If we want to be employed by the Federal Government . . . we have to look employable to the Federal Government" (Duberman, 1993, pp. 210, 111). When he saw two women holding hands, he broke them apart, scolding "None of that! None of that!" (Carter, 2004, p. 217). He had both a radical and a cultural accommodationist side. So, too, organizations that demanded rights from the state (as assimilationists tend to), like the GAA, adopted direct action tactics, in the form of their protests, that some might describe as quite militant. Later in the 1970s, lesbian women and gay men developed their own community organizations – a strategy that might be called liberationist. But, many of these were cultural in nature (like religious organizations) or social service-oriented and did not necessarily make policy demands. As you read, keep the liberationist/assimilationist distinction in mind, as it is a central lens through which to understand the complexity of LGBTQ politics. But also keep in mind that the distinction can be complex and messy.

Finally, if a national LGBTQ movement was born from the moment at Stonewall when young, marginalized by race and class, gender nonconforming members of the community spontaneously stood up to police repression, so, too, we can understand the Stonewall moment as solidifying the reality that the mainstream movement would center around white, middle-class, gay men. We will see this in the remaining chapters, that this group has always held a lot of privilege in the mainstream LGBTQ movement. Armstrong argues that the development of this national movement was predicated on this privilege: "Race, gender, and class exclusions were built into the gay identity movement" (2002, p. 153). She argues that the mainstream, national movement *did* develop in a way that celebrated diversity and that saw itself as representing the broad interests of a diverse group of gender and sexual minorities. In reality, though, the movement was largely led, and its agendas primarily set, by privileged white, gay men who believed that their interests and issues were shared by people who were economically less-advantaged, women of all backgrounds, and people of color of all genders in the movement. In other words, they *universalized* their interests, believing they spoke for a diverse movement. "The movement," Armstrong argues, "understood itself as in the general interest of all people engaged in nonnormative sexuality, while concretely embodying the evolving interests of middle-class, white gay men" (2002, p. 135). This, too, is a legacy of Stonewall that we see play out in the generations to come.

3

Activism in the Early Days of AIDS

Before AIDS, the mainstream gay and lesbian movement had settled into a civil rights focus and had moved away from the short-lived liberationist phase of the early 1970s. Movement leaders and activists aimed primarily to gain rights, recognition, and civil equality from the state. There was, of course, a long way to go, but there had been victories and there was strength and momentum. Then came the tragically destructive Acquired Immune Deficiency Syndrome (AIDS). Longtime San Francisco gay leader, Bill Kraus, worried: "Anita Bryant couldn't destroy our community. The FBI could never destroy our community; the police couldn't; Dan White couldn't; the government couldn't do it . . . But AIDS might. We've made all this progress only to be undone by some virus" (Shilts, 2007, p. 319). AIDS changed everything for the LGBTQ movements that came after it, but it did not destroy activism.

The ways in which conservative Republican President Ronald Reagan ignored AIDS for years provided one more historical example of government hostility toward and neglect of marginalized and maligned minorities. Reagan's colleagues on the Religious Right flamboyantly put an exclamation point on the president's homophobia, publicly framing AIDS as the price of admission to – in their view – a dangerous, immoral, perverse lifestyle. The private response to AIDS – from medical providers, the mainstream media, and the broader American public – underscored the extent to which LGBTQ people were still largely a dehumanized other. This response uncovered longstanding homophobia and brought a new means through which anti-gay discrimination could thrive. And when the state failed people with AIDS – not just LGBTQ people of all backgrounds and experiences, but also straight people of color and poor people and intravenous drug users and sex workers – it drew limits around citizenship (Patton, 1996). As Bronski observed, AIDS brought back the "image of the diseased outsider as a threat to a healthy America" (1998, p. 76).

AIDS ravaged gay communities, killing young, vibrant, politically and artistically active people. It threatened and called into question the sexual liberation that was part of the prize of the post-Stonewall movements. But, this decimation did not mean the demise of gay and lesbian organizing. On a very basic level, AIDS brought new visibility to gay people and communities because visibly sick, unambiguously dying people came out of their closets, both voluntarily and involuntarily, both practically and as a political act. As Vaid notes: "In a sense, AIDS outed our entire community. Perversely put, we won visibility for gay and lesbian lives because we died in record numbers" (1995, p. 81; also see Sontag, 1988; Bronski, 1998; Chauncey, 2005). This new exposure also led to institutional homophobia, individual prejudice, and heartbreaking rejection by loved ones. At the same time, however, it created opportunities for the *opposite*: for acceptance, care, and merciful humanity (Padug & Oppenheimer, 1992; Vaid, 1995; Faderman & Timmons, 2009).

The social movement that developed to respond to the AIDS crisis centered both around building community-controlled service provision in the absence of government support and care *and* around pushing the state to fulfill its role and responsibilities to its citizens. This was liberationist in its alternative institution-building tactic and its strong critique of the state. It was also assimilationist in that – especially in the later years, after 1987 – it worked in direct relationship to the state and relied on it, ultimately, to live up to its promises to protect its citizens. While AIDS activism grew out of the organization- and community-building of the 1960s and 1970s and the previous generation of gay and lesbian activists, it was its *own* movement, not identical to the gay and lesbian movement of the time (Armstrong, 2002). As we will see in the discussion below, this AIDS movement did, however, impact the shape of LGBTQ movements in the decades to follow. It also prompted both a new queer liberationist politics and a mainstream, assimilationist gay and lesbian politics of the 1990s.[1]

In the politics of AIDS, we see again the ways in which social movements are interconnected and responsive to each other. We also see the many ways in which art and popular culture were mobilized for social change and social action, to express anger, fear, and frustration and to spur action. Finally, we see a number of ways in which privilege – particularly the politics of race, class, and gender – played out in AIDS activism. The discussion that follows focuses on the first 15 years of the AIDS epidemic, when it was in its deadliest phase in the US and when the US-based AIDS movement was most active. However, there is, as of yet, no vaccination against the virus that causes AIDS and no cure, and effective treatment is incredibly expensive and inaccessible to many people throughout the world. Every day, thousands of people around the world are newly infected with the virus that causes AIDS. The politics of AIDS therefore continues in the US and across the globe.

Science, Media, and the Beginning of AIDS

Young gay American men began getting mysteriously sick toward the end of the 1970s, and we know now that, by the end of the year 1980, the virus had presented itself in Europe and Africa as well.[2] In late 1980, an immunologist at the University of California at Los Angeles, Michael Gottlieb, began to see young, gay, otherwise-healthy men in his practice who were presenting with a rare form of pneumonia, *pneumocystis carinii* (PCP), which was known to strike people with severely compromised immune systems. At around the same time, in early 1981, doctors in San Francisco and New York City were beginning to report that young gay men were presenting with Kaposi's sarcoma (KS), a virus-induced, very rare form of cancer that presented as purple skin legions and was typically found in older men with compromised immune systems. Meanwhile, a staffer at the federal agency, the Centers for Disease Control (CDC), began to note an uptick in doctors' requests for the drug that commonly treated the rare PCP. On June 5, 1981, the CDC published the first widely circulated piece on what would come to be known as AIDS, in its *Morbidity and Mortality Weekly Report (MMWR)*.[3] Dr. Gottlieb's report noted that his five young patients in Los Angeles were "all active homosexuals," and two had already died from PCP (Epstein, 1996, p. 45). Less than a month later, the *MMWR* reported on 26 cases of young gay men in New York City and California, eight of whom had already died, who presented with Kaposi's sarcoma (Shilts, 2007; Faderman, 2015).

The *MMWR* reports began to attract a little – but just a little – press attention, within both the mainstream and the gay press.[4] From the beginning, both the medical community and the press linked these new, mysterious cases of what came to be dubbed "gay cancer" to gay men and raised questions about what in their "lifestyles" might be related and relevant to this new illness. The first CDC report noted that the five Los Angeles cases of pneumocystis pneumonia might be connected to "some aspect of a homosexual lifestyle" or might be a "disease acquired through sexual contact" (Epstein, 1996, p. 46). On July 3, 1981, the *New York Times* ran its first article,[5] one column long and buried on page A20. The short piece indicated that little was yet known about the cause of these cases in young gay men: "The reporting doctors said that most cases had involved homosexual men who have had multiple and frequent sexual encounters with different partners, as many as ten sexual encounters each night up to four times a week" (quoted in Epstein, 1996, p. 46). Later that month, the *New York Native*, a gay newspaper in New York City with a wide, national audience, published an article called "Cancer in the Gay Community," which also raised the question of the link between sexual behavior and the new cases: "At this time, many feel that sexual frequency with a multiplicity of partners – what some would call promiscuity – is the single overriding risk factor." It also cited a medical hypothesis that two inhalant drugs popular in some urban gay male communities, known as poppers, might suppress the immune system and be related to the KS outbreak (Epstein, 1996, pp. 46–47; also see Kinsella, 1989).

Gay men were not the only people presenting with and dying from pneumocystis pneumonia or Kaposi's sarcoma. Intravenous drug users (of all sexual orientations) were also among the early cases. Yet, as sociologist Steven Epstein (1996) argues, the relative race and class privilege of some gay men meant that they generally had better access to doctors and to care at teaching hospitals, where reports of their cases could find their way to the public via medical and academic journals. These earliest cases were being noted in San Francisco, Los Angeles, and New York City. This privilege and access contributed to the connection between the new disease and gay men. By early 1982, some were using the acronym GRID – Gay-Related Immune Deficiency – to identify the new illness.

Because the mainstream media tended to understand the phenomenon as primarily impacting gay men and other marginalized people, they saw it as being not generally interesting to their audiences, so press coverage in the first two years of the epidemic was extremely sparse (Altman, 1986; Kinsella, 1989; Streitmatter, 2009). Analysts point to other medical stories of the time that garnered much broader media attention. In October 1982, for instance, by the time that 260 people had died from AIDS-related complications (Shilts, 2007), seven deaths occurred as a result of a tampering incident involving the pain reliever Tylenol. The *New York Times* published six stories on AIDS in 1981 and 1982, but fifty-four stories about the cyanide-laced Tylenol – it was front page news for months (Vaid, 1995). By the middle of 1983, however, there was a significant increase in general public recognition of AIDS. As more cases appeared among non-gay Americans and non-drug users (for example, babies and people who had received blood transfusions), fear spread that AIDS could have a wider reach (Altman, 1986; Kinsella, 1989).

As more young gay men succumbed to AIDS, gay communities themselves reacted with fear, anger, and denial. Gay men were wary of press reports that seemed to pathologize their sexual identity and to prescribe a change in sexual practice. The gay press downplayed the severity of the new epidemic, even refusing to run stories with basic medical information (Armstrong, 2002). Randy Shilts, a well-known gay reporter, was on the staff at the *San Francisco Chronicle* in the early 1980s. He would go on, in 1987, to publish one of the defining books on the politics and medicine of the early AIDS epidemic, the bestselling *And the Band Played On*. But his reporting on the early days of the epidemic was met with angry claims by other gay men that he was needlessly airing community dirty laundry. When he reported on the surprising reach of the "gay disease" in the *Chronicle* in March 1983, critics dubbed him "gay Uncle Tom," a traitor to his community (Kinsella, 1989, p. 169; also see Marcus, 2002).

Meanwhile, the science marched on. While initially the new epidemic was identified only with young, gay men, this had shifted within a year of the first *MMWR* report, when cases presented among not necessarily gay intravenous drug users, Haitians, and hemophiliacs. Soon after, AIDS was found to be prevalent in central Africa, where there seemed to be no correlation between the illness and same-sex sexual practice (Altman, 1986). By the middle of 1982, scientists settled on a name: Acquired Immune Deficiency Syndrome (AIDS). The name highlights that AIDS works on the body by attacking the immune system, specifically by working to decrease the number of infection- and bacteria-fighting T-cells (a type of white blood cell). It was not until 1983 and 1984 that AIDS was found to be caused by a virus, which came to be named HIV, the human immunodeficiency virus.[6] AIDS, then, is caused by HIV and is a late stage of that virus, which is defined by the low number of T-cells present in the blood (and, therefore, a significantly reduced immune system).[7] HIV can be found in all bodily fluid but is most commonly transmitted through blood exposure and is most readily spread through sexual intercourse (Whiteside, 2008). An HIV antibody blood test, to test for HIV status, was developed and became widely available in the US in early 1985.[8]

The Right Ignores and Responds

At the end of the 1970s, just as AIDS was on the horizon, both the gay and lesbian movement and the Religious Right were at a crossroads (Shilts, 1982; Fetner, 2008). As Vaid notes, AIDS had an enormous impact on both movements: "The impact of AIDS on the right and on gay and lesbian communities cannot be over-stated. AIDS gave the right the ammunition it needed to expand its war against homosexuality, and AIDS more than any other factor helped build a national gay and lesbian movement" (1995, p. 326).

The defeat of California's Briggs Initiative in November 1978 was a huge win for the gay and lesbian movement and a significant setback for the Right. Anita Bryant's influence, too, was fading. She was the target of regular protest and pop cultural derision, as her values were easily portrayed and parodied as being out of touch and old-fashioned (Faderman, 2015). Her divorce – announced in 1980 and seemingly at odds with her embrace of traditional marriage – diminished her credibility with her conservative Christian base (Fetner, 2008). But 1980 brought the election of Ronald Reagan and the beginning of a new, energized, national movement: the birth of the Christian Right.

Fetner (2008) argues that the first phase of this new movement in the early 1980s was characterized by the growth of the Moral Majority, a short-lived organization that started in 1979 and was led by the televangelist Reverend Jerry Falwell. This contributed to the development of the Christian Right and, with it, many new conservative activists. The second phase built on this new grass-roots mobilization by creating "institutional infrastructure" and by inserting the movement into national politics (Fetner, 2008, p. 56; also see Diamond, 1995).

The Christian Right gained mainstream legitimacy by solidify-ing a relationship with the Republican Party and becoming active in electoral politics through the 1980s. This flourishing new movement leveraged the AIDS crisis to fuel its homophobia and to grow its ranks (Vaid, 1995; Polikoff, 2008; Stone, 2012). The movement's leaders characterized AIDS as chickens coming home to roost. Articulating a theme that the Christian Right would echo frequently over the years, media personality and Republican presidential advisor (and eventual presidential candidate) Pat Robertson wrote about AIDS in May 1983: "The poor homosexuals – they have declared war upon nature, and now nature is exacting an awful retribution" (Shilts, 2007, p. 311; also see Hooper, 2015). Following up a few months later, Reverend Falwell said, on TV: "When you violate moral, health, and hygiene laws, you reap the whirlwind. . . . You cannot shake your fist in God's face and get by with it" (Vaid, 1995, p. 327).

This portrayal of gay men as the authors of their own demise allowed Christian Right commentators to propose policy solutions to AIDS that involved framing gay Americans as "dangerous outsiders who threatened the nation: diseased and dangerously hard to detect" (Chauncey, 2005, p. 41). In a column in early 1985, for example, conservative writer William Buckley suggested that people with AIDS should be marked with tattoos: "[E]veryone detected with AIDS should be tattooed in the upper forearm to protect common-needle users, and on the buttocks, to prevent the victimization of other homosexuals" (Epstein, 1996, p. 187).

For his part, President Reagan completely ignored AIDS for the better part of six years. He did not give his first public address on AIDS until the middle of 1987, after more than 36,000 Americans had acquired AIDS and more than 20,000 Americans had died (Shilts, 2007).[9] Reagan's administration displayed, at *best*, a complete lack of empathy for, and even blatant derision of, gay men and this new epidemic that was striking their communities.

In one telling example, in October 1982, more than a year after AIDS had been reported on by the CDC and major mainstream media around the country, a reporter asked Reagan's press secretary, Larry Speakes, if the president could react to the fact that the CDC had documented more than 600 cases of AIDS and was now calling it an epidemic. Speakes responded: "What's AIDS?" The reporter responded: "It's known as 'gay plague'," which got a laugh in the room. The reporter continued: "I mean it's a pretty serious thing that one in every three people that get this have died.

And I wondered if the President is aware of it?" Speakes replied, to more laughter from the room: "I don't have it. Do you?" The reporter replied: "In other words, the White House looks on this as a great joke?" to which Speakes replied: "No, I don't know anything about it" (Cohen, 2001, pp. 3–4; Faderman, 2015, pp. 417–418). When, in December 1984, the same press secretary was again asked for a presidential reaction to the fact that the CDC was then estimating that 300,000 people had been exposed to AIDS, Speakes again responded by joking about the epidemic and indicating that the president had expressed no views on AIDS and that he had never asked him about it (Cohen, 2001, pp. 14–15).

Reagan's official response to AIDS was informed in part by his overall philosophy on the role of government in the welfare of American citizens. In his view, the federal government should be small, and responsibility for social welfare should fall to the private sector and to states. In many areas of governing, Reagan was pulling the feds back from their role in social service provision and was working actively to shrink the size of the federal government. As a result, this provided few federal resources to combat this new epidemic, whether through research funding, treatment development, or social services. This continued in 1983, even when the Reagan administration finally responded to some internal pressure and months of heavy media attention to AIDS by declaring the epidemic to be its "highest priority emergency health problem" (Altman, 1986, p. 47).[10]

Reagan and his staff also influenced his administration's messaging and education on AIDS, constraining public comment until well into the 1980s. Reagan's Surgeon General, Dr. C. Everett Koop, a pediatrician by training, was a social conservative known for his work as an anti-abortion advocate. But, by the middle of the 1980s, he began to take AIDS as a public health crisis seriously and wanted to treat it with a broad, extensive, and direct public education campaign free of morality plays. In early 1986, Reagan asked Koop to prepare a report on AIDS, which was published in October of that year. The report, which drew substantial media attention and criticism from conservatives, urged more federal action, broad condom distribution and use, and a comprehensive approach to AIDS education for young people that "should start at the earliest grade possible" (quoted in Shilts, 2007, p. 587). Koop also distributed an education booklet, *Understanding AIDS*, to 107 million American households and modeled for the public and the press what open, factual conversations about the epidemic could look like. As Shilts noted, the United States was the only major country in the industrialized world that, by early 1987, did not have a broad AIDS education campaign.[11]

Reagan's critics believe that he, presiding over the introduction and spread of this epidemic, had the power to contain it. His neglect was not simply benign: an earlier response could have very possibly led to a more limited epidemic. Analysts and activists believe that Reagan's failure to respond was due to homophobia, classism, racism, and prejudice against those afflicted by addiction. As AIDS activist Russo urged: "If AIDS were happening to the straight, white, middle class, non-drug-using population, there would be global panic" (1987, p. 325). It was "government's murderous neglect" (Chauncey, 2005, p. 41) that allowed the virus to spread so quickly and so deeply. Shilts wrote: "The bitter truth was that AIDS did not just happen to America – it was *allowed* to happen by an array of institutions, all of which failed to perform their appropriate tasks to safeguard the public health" (2007, p. xxii; emphasis added).

The AIDS Movement:
Both Liberationist and Assimilationist

AIDS service organizations

The grassroots mobilization around AIDS in the early days came from community-run and -controlled social services. These AIDS service organizations (ASOs) were a response to the outright hostility and rejection of people with AIDS and the resulting lack of adequate support from outside the community. A number of writers and activists have documented the heartbreaking indignities that people with AIDS faced while they were dying, when they most needed support and compassion. Fearful for their own health, doctors and nurses sometimes left AIDS patients unattended in emergency rooms and hospital beds, even when those patients were completely incapacitated. After their death, some were placed in trash bags, and some funeral homes refused to take anyone who had died of AIDS-related causes (Altman, 1986; Shilts, 2007; Faderman, 2015).

ASOs developed to do what mainstream care providers refused to do respectfully, adequately, or even at all. One of the first such organizations was the Gay Men's Health Crisis (GMHC) in New York City. As more and more people in his social circle were falling ill, well-known white, gay writer Larry Kramer sought to fashion a community response. In the summer of 1981, he invited a group of prominent gay men to his Greenwich Village apartment to learn about the emerging crisis from a New York University doctor who had experience in treating a growing number of young gay patients with the telltale AIDS-related symptoms. Out of this initial meeting came GMHC, which Kramer founded with five other men in early 1982 to provide accurate and straightforward information about AIDS and to deliver daily care and emotional and legal support to people with AIDS and to their loved ones (Tanne, 1987; Marcus, 2002). In its first year, the group raised hundreds of thousands of dollars from the gay and lesbian community. It also eventually raised public city financial support. As it grew, GMHC organized hundreds of volunteers to serve as "buddies" to people with AIDS (not all of whom were gay) on a daily basis; to staff the GMHC hotline; and to help with legal, housing, and psychological support. By the early 1990s, GMHC was "the largest and most recognized AIDS-specific agency and gay organization in the world" (Kayal, 1993, p. 2).

Like GMHC, the AIDS Project/LA (APLA) was founded in 1982, along with Cleve Jones's co-founded San Francisco organization that came to be called the AIDS Foundation. So too, the pre-existing Shanti Project in the Bay Area turned its work primarily to AIDS service provision. Other direct service groups developed across the country outside these major coastal cities, in Atlanta, Dallas, and Kansas City, as well as, outside the US in these early years, in London, Toronto, and Sydney. At a time when the federal government refused to talk about AIDS, and before the Surgeon General had launched his active public education campaign, gay communities took control of educating and supporting themselves and disseminating information about AIDS transmission and prevention.[12]

Communities of color also developed their own community-based responses to AIDS (Patton, 1990; Vaid, 1995; Rofes, 1998). In her book on AIDS and Black politics, political scientist Cathy J. Cohen writes that the *early* response within Black communities to African American people with AIDS was to offer support through individual families and other individual support networks. As GMHC and other predominantly white groups were growing in the early 1980s,[13] for African American people and communities, "the predominant activities during this first stage were increasing recognition and acceptance of AIDS as a disease affecting black communities and obtaining basic services for those in need" (1999, p. 98). The earliest AIDS organizations specifically by and for African Americans and other people of color were generally focused – like GMHC – on education and on social service provision. Founded and led primarily by Black gay men and lesbians, the Minority Task Force on AIDS in New York City, the Kupona Network in Chicago, and Minority AIDS Project in Los Angeles, among others, developed to meet the growing needs of, especially, Black and Latino communities, which were disproportionately impacted by AIDS. By 1990, for instance, African Americans made up 12 percent of the American public and almost 28 percent of all adult AIDS cases; Latinos were 9 percent of the American population and almost 16 percent of adult AIDS cases (1999, p. 21).

A number of commentators have noted that, as a community approach that took the care of Americans out of the hands of the American government, this early social service response to AIDS was well aligned with Reagan's approach to privatizing social welfare (Patton, 1990; Kayal, 1993). Others have noted that this approach worked *within* health service provision rather than working to change it. As Rimmerman writes: "The primary critique is that AIDS service organizations focused too much on accommodating themselves to the existing health care system rather than linking health care service delivery to class, race, and gender concerns." They "pursued a mainstreaming, insider-politics assimilationist strategy" (2008, pp. 47, 48).

An important related critique is that these service organizations failed to provide a political response to AIDS. They were an early and necessary response to a crisis, and they were able to develop quickly to meet the urgent needs of the sick and the dying, because they built on pre-existing organizational and knowledge resources (Altman, 1986; Epstein, 1996; Armstrong, 2002; Chauncey, 2005). These included the principles and practices of the feminist health movement of the 1970s (Taylor & Rupp, 1993), a community-controlled response to the sexism built into mainstream medical practice that insisted on generating knowledge about and attention to women's health from within the community. AIDS service provision also built on a gay and lesbian health movement that had developed in the 1970s to challenge the anti-gay assumptions of medicine and psychiatry. But while these movements were explicitly political, the ASOs that developed out of them were not. The feminist and early gay and lesbian health movements offered broad critiques of the structures and institutions that produced a range of intersectional gender- and sexuality-based inequalities; the ASOs did not. "[W]e went for the AIDS fix," Vaid notes, "and left systemic problems largely unaddressed" (1995, p. 87). Some of these organizations grew into large, well-funded service bureaucracies, earning the generally-used derisive term "AIDS Inc." (see, e.g., Rofes, 1998, p. 265), which signaled the mainstreaming of AIDS activism as institutionalized social service provision essentially devoid of a political project.

In this way, ASOs played into conservatives' view of the role of government, stepping in when government failed to serve its people, and doing so in a way that was not explicitly political. On the other hand, ASOs were community-controlled responses to the homophobia and neglect of the federal government. This early stage of the AIDS movement was not about working within or asking anything of the state. It was about working to fill in, through private money and service, to make up for the state's negligence. It was about survival by whatever means were feasible at a time when people with AIDS could not even count on their president to name what was killing them. This was a kind of liberationist political strategy that looked outside the state for power. As sociologist Benita Roth found, in her interviews with AIDS activists, "each operated in a social movement culture where service was understood as a form of politics" (2017, p. 176).

Early community debates

As the rise in deaths from AIDS continued, despite the work of GMHC and other ASOs, criticisms of this approach grew. Kramer, for one, was increasingly convinced that social services were not the solution to the AIDS epidemic. By 1983 he had founded an explicitly political group called the AIDS Network, working with National Gay Task Force executive director Virginia Apuzzo. Kramer also publicly called on GMHC and the service provision movement to politicize the AIDS crisis rather than simply tend to it. The dispute between service and politics was one of the earliest debates within the gay community about the direction of the AIDS movement: should it focus on providing direct services to the people with AIDS who were being mistreated and ignored, or should it become more involved in public policy and in holding the government accountable for its meager response to AIDS (Shilts, 2007; Gould, 2009; Faderman, 2015)?

In March of 1983, Kramer published a searing essay in the *New York Native* called "1,112 and Counting." It began: "If this article doesn't scare the shit out of you, we're in real trouble. If this article doesn't rouse you to anger, fury, rage, and action, gay men may have no future on this earth. Our continued existence depends on just how angry you can get" (1983, p. 33). The essay was a call to action, to anger, and to a shift in the direction of the young AIDS movement. "Why," Kramer wrote, "isn't every gay man in this city so scared shitless that he is screaming for action? Does every gay man in New York *want* to die?" (1983, p. 35; emphasis in original). He charged that government inaction and lack of support for research and treatment were a result of institutional bias, not just benign neglect: "There is no question that if this epidemic was happening to the straight, white, non-intravenous-drug-using middle class, that money would have been put into use almost two years ago, when the first alarming signs of this epidemic were noticed" (1983, p. 39). He implored: "How many of us must die before *all* of us living fight back?" (1983, p. 49; emphasis in original). The essay circulated widely and represented a watershed in the AIDS movement. As Shilts assessed: "Larry Kramer's piece irrevocably altered the context in which AIDS was discussed in the gay community and, hence, in the nation . . . [it] swiftly crystallized the epidemic into a political movement for the gay community" (2007, p. 245).

Kramer was forced out of GMHC, as his stylistic and philosophical differences with the organization became increasingly evident. "I eventually quit GMHC," he said, "because I knew they wanted me out. I was too difficult and too opinionated" (Marcus, 2002, p. 252). In addition, his article, while widely read, did not have the impact he desired. It did not, as he had hoped, spark a mass direct action movement aimed at changing public policy and government action on AIDS.[14]

Kramer's essay contributed to another central debate in the AIDS movement, one that has continued through the decades: how should *sex* be implicated in the fight against AIDS? This is an extension of a longstanding set of tensions within the gay and lesbian movement about how central sex is or should be to gay and lesbian identity and politics. "Tensions over sex," Michael Warner writes, "have marked the gay movement from the outset" (1999, p. 42). Kramer was a controversial figure in this conversation, even before he became an activist. In 1978, he had published a bestselling novel titled *Faggots*, which was a fictionalized account of the gay scene on Fire Island and New York City. The book was read by many as a sanctimonious indictment of a culture of sex and drugs among a certain set of New York's gay men (Shilts, 2007). Kramer's "1,112 and Counting" essay was also read by many as "sex-negative" (Shilts, 2007, p. 245; also see Gould, 2009); as Kramer wrote: "I am sick of guys who moan that giving up careless sex until this blows over is worse than death. . . . I am sick of guys who think that all being gay means is sex in the first place" (1983, p. 46).

Within ASOs and gay male communities, the question of whether and how to alter sexual behavior as a way of curbing the spread of AIDS was incredibly controversial. Kramer believed, for instance, that GMHC should counsel gay men to significantly scale back on sex and the number of sexual partners (Shilts, 2007). Others felt – and argued bitterly – that modifying and moderating sexual practices when they had just gained sexual freedom was self-hating, misguided, and a dangerous overreaction that smacked of capitulation to homophobic repression.[15]

This debate crystallized in many community discussions over whether to close bathhouses as a way to curb the spread of AIDS. Armstrong writes that the baths were "a cornerstone of gay men's public sexual culture" and had also been found to be a "major site of HIV infection" (2002, p. 160). Gay men disagreed vehemently about whether these community institutions should be closed. In San Francisco, in 1983, some called for the city's Department of Health to intervene by posting safer sex announcements in bathhouses, effectively turning these community institutions into sites of public education. Some called for bathhouses to be closed altogether as a way to discourage the spread of AIDS by taking away opportunities for anonymous and multi-partner sex between men (though many had already closed because gay men were modifying their sexual behavior and staying away on their own). Some felt it was the city's or state's role to intervene in a public health crisis, while others felt that this was a homophobic, anti-sex overreach. Those who opposed this public action were "very vocal, sometimes even hysterical," Armstrong notes: "Governmental intervention recalled the police harassment of gay bars that had been a routine part of homosexual life in the 1950s" (2002, p. 160; also see Altman, 1986).

This bathhouse debate also tapped into a broader split between assimilationists and liberationists in gay and lesbian movements and communities, in the sense that it revealed a split between those who celebrated cultural difference and those who asserted sameness. As Bronski argues, "AIDS made it impossible to pretend that sexuality was not central to gay male lives" (1998, p. 77). Some liberationists celebrated this as an opportunity to come out about that which was different and valuable about gay men's cultures, while others, those in the "more culturally conservative gay rights movement," saw this focus on gay men's sex as a threat to the argument that "[w]e are just like everyone else" and were "still wedded to the idea of privacy as the path to acceptance and assimilation" (1998, p. 77; also see Warner, 1999).

Direct action AIDS activism: ACT UP

By 1986, many years into the AIDS crisis, there still was no real government response or treatment for AIDS. Yet there was so much death and dying. This year marked the beginning of a new phase of the AIDS movement, one that was more explicitly politicized and radical, more focused on direct action mobilization and a confrontation with the state over its neglect. This shift was due to years of built-up anger and frustration. It also was due to other gay politics at play during that year, including responses to the Supreme Court's June 1986 *Bowers v. Hardwick* decision, which upheld states' rights to criminalize oral and anal sex, finding that "[t]he Constitution does not confer a fundamental right upon homosexuals to engage in sodomy" (n.p.). The ruling forged a connection between gay rights and AIDS advocacy, in that, as Linda Hirshman argues, the Court essentially articulated "that gays and lesbians were immoral actors, unworthy of the protections of the United States Constitution. ... In the face of this decision, no one could say that the government's inattention to AIDS was innocuous" (2013, p. 188).

The AIDS Coalition to Unleash Power (ACT UP) is perhaps the most prominent symbol of the AIDS movement's shift to political action (Armstrong, 2002). ACT UP was founded in March 1987 in New York City, after a speech given by Larry Kramer to an audience of about 250 people at the Lesbian and Gay Community Services Center in Greenwich Village that was a version of his "1,112 and Counting" essay. Kramer had been inspired by

Lavender Hill Mob, a direct action group founded in the fall of 1986 by a former member of the 1970s Gay Activists Alliance. The Lavender Hill Mob rejected the GMHC service provision model, calling instead for a visible and aggressive shift in public policy on AIDS science, education, and treatment. ACT UP was officially born within days of Kramer's speech, modeling itself on the Lavender Hill Mob's theatrical direct activism. Ghaziani and colleagues note that ACT UP also had its roots in lesbian feminism and the feminist health movement: "Feminist beliefs about control of one's body, resistance to medical authority, patient inclusion in medical decision making, and discriminatory practices in health care fueled" the founding of ACT UP (2016, p. 170).[16]

The mission of the strident new organization focused on education, treatment, and policy change. According to Gamson, who observed the movement, "ACT UP pushes for greater access to treatments and drugs for AIDS-related diseases; culturally sensitive, widely available and explicit safe-sex education; and well-funded research" (1989, p. 354). ACT UP adopted slogans and symbolism that advertised its bold politics – for example, "Silence = Death" with a pink triangle pointing up, a reappropriation and an inversion of the downward-facing pink triangle that the Nazis had used to brand homosexuals.

In keeping with its GAA and Lavender Hill Mob forebears, ACT UP designed actions that were high-profile, theatrical, and used both anger and humor to gain attention. They were designed to indict and to attract the attention of mainstream institutions like the church, the media, public scientific and health agencies, and the private pharmaceutical industry. They made bold announcements like "The side effect of AIDS is death" (Signorile, 2003, p. 14), and they did not shy away from anger. This made their work quite compelling. As Vaid's insider account observes: "The life and death drama of people with AIDS and HIV being angry and screaming at officials and bureaucrats who opposed them riveted the nation's attention for several years" (1995, p. 101).

ACT UP/New York's first action occurred just a few weeks after Kramer's March 1987 speech. On the morning of March 24, 1987, about 250 demonstrators blocked traffic on Wall Street, protesting the US Food and Drug Administration's (FDA) slow progress on AIDS drug development and targeting the company Burroughs Wellcome for the astronomical cost of its treatment drug, azidothymidine (AZT). Other actions were similarly devised to attract media attention and to put pressure on decision-makers to change policy and practice, particularly around the issues of scientific research on AIDS and the affordability and accessibility of treatment drugs. ACT UP regularly targeted the FDA with its actions, because activists perceived the agency as a roadblock to progress on AIDS treatment. The group organized other high-profile and high-impact actions – for example, a "political funeral" at the White House, where grieving loved ones threw ashes of people who had died from AIDS-related complications on the White House lawn; and an interruption of a live CBS news broadcast while anchor Dan Rather was on the air.[17]

In one of the most controversial actions, hundreds of ACT UP/ New York activists targeted St. Patrick's Cathedral and Catholic Cardinal O'Connor, specifically attacking the Catholic pronouncement that the use of condoms went against church teaching. In the "Stop the Church" action on the Sunday morning of December 10, 1989, ACT UP demonstrators held a "die in" in the aisles of the church. Activist Michael Petrelis, who was very sick at the time, stood up and yelled "O'Connor, you're killing us! Murderer! We will fight O'Connor's bigotry!" Another activist, Tom Keane, visibly spit out his communion wafer, and thousands of protestors – from ACT UP and abortion rights activists from the Women's Health Action and Mobilization (WHAM) – demonstrated outside the church. In the end, 111 people were arrested, and this dramatic action was front-page news around the world (Northrop, 2003, pp. 27–29; Faderman, 2015, pp. 433–435).

ACT UP grew quickly. In New York City, the group's Monday night meetings in those early years regularly drew in hundreds of people. These energized and eroticized sessions were run democratically and effectively and attracted accomplished gay and lesbian activists, like Vito Russo, Urvashi Vaid, and activist journalists Ann Northrop and Michelangelo Signorile.[18] For many, ACT UP provided a community and support, as well as a political outlet: "it gave people a sense of belonging and a creative outlet for despair" (Vaid, 1995, p. 98). Beyond New York, within just a couple of years, there were more than 100 ACT UP chapters in cities and towns across the country and around the world. This growth was partially attributable to the gay and lesbian rights movement at the time. The forceful "militant tone" of the second national gay rights demonstration, the 600,000-person March on Washington for Lesbian and Gay Rights, in October 1987, inspired activists to return home to organize direct action responses to AIDS (Gould, 2009, pp. 131–132; also see Faderman, 2015; Roth, 2017).[19]

As the years went by, some ACT UP activists began to work more and more closely with those government health officials who had the authority and the means to fund research that would advance the science of AIDS treatment and make treatment drugs more accessible. In his book on the politics of science and AIDS activism, Epstein writes that this approach created scientific "lay experts" who produced and disseminated knowledge (1996, p. 17). It was the Treatment and Data Committee of ACT UP that primarily took on the scientists and the scientific research on HIV and AIDS. By 1992, this group had left ACT UP to form its own organization, the Treatment Action Group (TAG).

Both ACT UP's direct action tactics and the strategy of working *with* rather than directly in protest of the government were highly controversial. ACT UP, which had grown so quickly and so visibly in 1987, had just five or six years of prominence. Analysts point to a range of external and internal factors that contributed to the decline of ACT UP by the mid-1990s, including the simple, brutal fact that so many activists were dying. "Despair," sociologist and former ACT UP member Deborah B. Gould writes, "destroyed ACT UP" (2009, p. 395; also see Crimp, 1993; Vaid, 1995).[20]

The internal politics of privilege also caused substantial fractures within ACT UP. Vaid argues that the organization did have wide appeal and drew a diverse group of activists, "from closeted gay professional men who were HIV positive, to veteran lesbian-feminist organizers, to gay activists frustrated by traditional political strategies, to straight celebrities, to young gay and straight activists whose first-ever political involvement was an ACT UP meeting and demonstration" (1995, p. 95). Others, too, noted that, although media representation and recognition tended to focus on white male leaders, the organization *was* a diverse space (Shepard, 2002). Nevertheless, chapters tended to be composed of primarily young, white, gay men who were already highly politicized and disproportionately highly educated (Gamson, 1989; Epstein, 1996). Some activists perceived that differences of race, class, gender, sexuality, and HIV status mapped on to differences in purpose that caused substantial cracks and tensions in the organization. Reflecting back years later, Northrop said that while many activists – particularly many women and others who had been long-time political activists – were attracted to the group as a way to articulate a broad and intersectional critique of American power, many privileged, white, gay, HIV positive men were drawn to their activism as a way to advocate for their own health:

> I think that gay white men thought they had privilege in this country and were shocked to find out they didn't, and that people in power were prepared to let them die. And when they figured that out, they got very angry about it . . . and that's what made ACT UP happen. . . . [T]he gay white men there with HIV were there for their own personal survival, and out of their own anger at not having privilege. And that's why the rifts eventually developed in ACT UP, because there was a group of people who were there only for their own survival, and who did not see that their survival, to a large extent, depended on them seeing the larger issues. (2003, pp. 13–14)

Some participants – including some of these privileged men themselves – understood that white male involvement often was a reflection of the anger, fear, and lack of agency they felt when their needs as HIV positive men were being disregarded. One activist said: "We're middle class white guys and we're not used to being ignored and so what can we do to get what we want?" (quoted in Hirshman, 2013, p. 196).

These privileged men tended to be the treatment activists, and this was controversial within ACT UP. Some viewed the Treatment and Data Committee, then TAG members, as opportunists who were more interested in their own power, access, and health than in truly holding government accountable (for discussion, see Epstein, 1996; Rimmerman, 2008; Gould, 2009; Faderman, 2015). For his part, Kramer wrote: "TAG breaks my heart. . . . I'm angry at them for what I think has been a massive case of selling out" (1994, p. 303).

Ultimately, ACT UP's motivating politics and tactics were a complicated combination of liberationist and assimilationist. ACT UP activists were highly critical of, and had lost faith in, the government for its inability to meet their needs (Kramer, 1994; Shilts, 2007). Yet they knew that the federal government had the authority, resources, and platform to adequately respond to AIDS as a public health crisis. To put their demands into action, they worked in partnership with federal health agencies, like the FDA, because they knew they needed to. In this way, ACT UP was liberationist in its critique and in its direct action tactics, and assimilationist in its targeting of public administration and public policy as a site for change (Rimmerman, 2008). As a lobbyist for another direct action AIDS group noted of this contradiction and shift: "The traditional gay and lesbian agenda is [for government] to stay out of our lives. Now we're saying we need affirmative programs that will save our lives and that we need a much closer relationship with the government" (quoted in Hirshman, 2013, p. 181). Along the same lines, Vaid wrote: "Paradoxically, government was the obstacle . . . and salvation" (1995, p. 389).

From AIDS Activism to Gay, Lesbian, and Queer

It is important to remember that ACT UP and other direct action and service provision responses to the AIDS crisis were *AIDS* activists groups, not *gay* rights or identity groups (Armstrong, 2002). Of course, there was overlap, and many people involved in the AIDS fight identified as gay and lesbian. But many AIDS activists fought to articulate a political and health response to AIDS that was separate from their commitment to the politics of gay identity, equality, or liberation (Marcus, 2002; Faderman

& Timmons, 2009). As the years went on, these AIDS organizations had increasingly close ties to the state, through funding and through their relationships with federal health agencies. They were also much more professionalized, institutionalized, and well funded. Armstrong notes that this led to a sense, by the late 1980s, of tension and "competition between gay and AIDS organizations for resources of all sorts (funds, leadership, volunteers, and members)" (2002, p. 173).

Many activists felt that this focus on AIDS was taking attention away from a broader focus on lesbian and gay social justice. Eric Rofes, who was both an AIDS and a gay activist, wrote that the "growing rift" in the movements "appears to be pushing our community toward civil war" (1990, p. 9). He referred to the "deliberate de-gaying of AIDS" (1990, p. 11), which Vaid defined as "removing the stigma of homosexuality from the stigma of AIDS in order to win the access and attention we needed" (1995, p. 75). Vaid argues that some activists saw a kind of decoupling of AIDS from gay people and identity as a necessary response to homophobia – a calculation that AIDS would receive more attention and response if it did not have to contend with a stigmatizing connection to gay men.

This "de-gaying" of AIDS took many forms. For instance, the October 1987 National March on Washington for Lesbian and Gay Rights was, Ghaziani argues, "in large part a reaction against AIDS and federal negligence" (2008, p. 86). It also marked the debut of the giant NAMES Project AIDS Memorial Quilt, which consisted of 1,920 individual three-foot by six-foot panels created by the loved ones of people who had lost their lives to AIDS. Hundreds of thousands of people viewed the quilt in Washington during the weekend of the Washington March (NAMES Project Foundation, n.d.). While this was a huge success for AIDS visibility, many gay and lesbian activists viewed it as a depoliticized response that also de-centered gay connection to the epidemic (Rofes, 1990; Vaid, 1995; Rimmerman, 2008).

In this context of a broader conversation about the connection between lesbian and gay politics and AIDS politics, the AIDS movement both gave birth to a new, radical part of the LGBTQ movement *and* contributed to the growth and proliferation of a more mainstream lesbian and gay movement. On the mainstream side, AIDS activism, particularly the service provision movement, brought people in who had never been activists before, namely economically privileged gay, white men. This impacted the gay and lesbian movement that followed, in that these "newly activated gay people" brought with them their own values, worldviews, and priorities into their post-AIDS activism (Vaid, 1995, p. 91). Through their active pursuit of treatment, in particular, they also developed relationships with, access to, and knowledge of government agencies, and they maintained these ties when they moved into lesbian and gay civil rights work. AIDS work thus laid the groundwork for a particular kind of mainstream, government-directed, professionalized gay and lesbian activism in the 1980s and 1990s (Altman, 1986; D'Emilio, 1992). Through the 1980s, a number of large, bureaucratic, well-funded "corporate-style non-profit groups" (Fetner, 2008, p. 45) were born or were developed to do lesbian and gay civil rights work. These included Lambda Legal Defense and Education (founded in 1973 but greatly expanded through the 1980s), the National Gay and Lesbian Task Force (NGLTF), the Human Rights Campaign Fund (HRCF), the Gay and Lesbian Alliance Against Defamation (GLAAD), and an expanded Parents and Friends of Lesbians and Gays (PFLAG).

On the radical, liberationist side, ACT UP led to a new, explicitly *queer* movement by training activists in direct action and by drawing on their anger and their sense of urgency for change (Shepard, 2002; Gould, 2009). The new radical groups extended ACT UP's logic of visibility, reclaiming the word "queer," and mobilizing an assertion of difference rather than sameness with straight people (Cunningham, 1992). They believed that visibility for people who were marginalized because of their gender identity and expression or their sexuality was essential to equality and liberation (Berlant & Freeman, 1993).

Queer Nation and Lesbian Avengers were two high-profile queer groups that grew out of radical AIDS organizing. Queer Nation was founded in the spring of 1990 in New York, directly out of ACT UP. At the same time, lesbians, many of whom had become central caretakers, organizers, and activists during the

AIDS crisis, fashioned their own new politics out of the AIDS movement. Founded in 1992 by a group of six lesbian activists, Lesbian Avengers (n.d.) addressed the sexism within the AIDS and gay movements and established a place to explicitly assert lesbian interests and issues. Both organizations quickly grew, with chapters around the country. One estimate counted Queer Nation chapters in more than 60 cities in the group's first year (Cunningham, 1992).[21]

Both organizations were highly visible, coordinating high-profile actions that, like those of ACT UP, were designed to attract media attention. One ACT UP member wrote of this new activism: "Queer Nation is a peculiar mix of outrage and wackiness – you could call it the illegitimate child of Huey Newton and Lucy Ricardo" (Cunningham, 1992, p. 63). Language appropriation and confrontation was an important part of the style. Activists embraced slogans like "Fags and Dykes Bash Back" and "We're here! We're Queer! Get used to it!" (Marcus, 2002, p. 321; Queer Nation, n.d.). Many of Queer Nation's political actions were intended to bring visibility of queer people to typically straight spaces. "[T]hese groups," Bronski observes, "were fueled by a desire to destroy the closet" (1998, p. 78). Just like it had been for gay liberationists two decades earlier, being out and visible was, for these early 1990s radicals, a *political* strategy for changing hearts and minds. Queer nationalists staged protests – for example, sit-ins in Cracker Barrel restaurants, which had an anti-gay employment policy (Cunningham, 1992). They also staged theatrical "nights out" and "kiss-ins" and "mall visibility actions" – such as the Queer Shopping Network in New York and the Suburban Homosexual Outreach Program (SHOP) in San Francisco (Berlant & Freeman, 1993; Gross, 1993; Fetner, 2008).

The politics of visibility took other forms as well. One of the Lesbian Avengers founders, former ACT UP member and lifelong activist and writer Sarah Schulman, said that the "best thing" that the group did was organize a 40,000-person "Dyke March" at the national 1993 March on Washington for Lesbian, Gay, and Bi Equal Rights and Liberation, as a way of asserting radical politics and lesbian interests and visibility (Shepard, 2002, pp. 138–139).

In addition, some activists who were associated with both ACT UP and Queer Nation, like Signorile, led the charge for the controversial practice of "outing" supposedly queer public figures, especially those who had remained silent on or been hostile to AIDS-related and gay/lesbian-related causes (Bronski, 1998).

Radical queer activism burned out fairly quickly. Queer Nation was only active for about two years.[22] But this movement left an important imprint on the broader gay and lesbian movement. This explicitly queer movement extended to other areas of the politics of gender and sexuality at the time – like the academy, with the development of a field of queer theory by the mid-1990s (Angelides, 2001). Politically, Armstrong (2002) notes that the queer movement was younger (also see Gamson, 1995) and more encompassing of the margins of gay and lesbian communities, and that it therefore helped to expand the reach of the broader movement, especially to people who identified as bisexual, transgender, and otherwise. Queer Nation, with its big tent of nonnormative sexuality and gender identity, and its critiques of traditional gender and sexual categories and identities, contributed to a shift in the mainstream movement such that many organizations adopted the acronym "LGBT" by the mid-1990s (Fetner, 2008; Ghaziani et al., 2016).

The Art and Popular Culture of AIDS

Art and popular culture have long been sites of community-building, resistance, and "performing protest" (Rupp & Taylor, 2003, p. 209) for gender and sexual minorities, as we saw in the mid-twentieth century urban bar culture, drag performances, and discos or in the magazines that circulated surreptitiously among closeted gay men and lesbians after World War II. The artistic response to the AIDS crisis of the 1980s and 1990s took a central role in bringing new visibility to and empathy for gay and lesbian people and lives, building on the post-Stonewall "cultural explosion" that was already very much in progress (Vaid, 1995, p. 79).

In his book on theater, performance, and gay male responses

to AIDS, David Román writes that there had been some earlier local theatrical "AIDS interventions," like the Los Angeles-based Artists Confronting AIDS (ACA) organization founded in 1985 (1998, pp. 44, 73). But Larry Kramer's *The Normal Heart*, which opened at the Public Theater in New York's East Village in April of 1985, was one of two plays that year that had the "ability to mainstream AIDS to a wide range of audiences" (1998, p. 59). The play was a barely fictionalized account of Gay Men's Health Crisis, Kramer's contentious relationship with the organization, and the way in which mainstream institutions in New York City and the country – from New York's mayor Ed Koch to the *New York Times* – betrayed gay men by failing to act with urgency in the face of the early AIDS crisis. Román argues that the play can be criticized for a celebration of romantic, desexualized, hetero-normative gay male love and for portraying gay men with AIDS as victims who "simply die pitiful deaths" (1998, p. 63). But, the play also earned substantial mainstream public praise (see, e.g., Rich, 1985), and Shilts wrote that it had an "immediate political impact" in that it prompted Mayor Koch to expand New York City's public support for people with AIDS (2007, pp. 556–557). Kramer himself explained his intention with the play this way:

> I wrote it to make people cry: AIDS is the saddest thing I'll ever have to know. I also wrote it to be a love story, in honor of a man I loved who died. I wanted people to see on a stage two men who loved each other. I wanted people to see them kiss. I wanted people to see that gay men in love and gay men suffering and gay men dying are just like everyone else. (1994, p. 94)

The show resonated broadly and has been revived many times. An acclaimed Broadway version of the show won the 2011 Tony Award for Best Revival of a Play; and in 2014 it was adapted to an HBO movie directed by Ryan Murphy (of the television show *Glee*) and starring a number of A-list actors (Geidner, 2011; Genzlinger, 2014).

Other significant theatrical productions raised awareness of AIDS and AIDS politics. Tony Kushner's two-part Pulitzer- and

Tony Award-winning play *Angels in America* made it to Broadway in 1993, and the Tony Award-winning *Love! Valour! Compassion!* followed in 1995. Jonathan Larson's Pulitzer- and Tony Award-winner *Rent* debuted on Broadway in 1996 and became, for many young people, a touchstone of the power of art, community, and love in the time of AIDS. When the multiracial group of young, struggling, HIV positive and negative artists, musicians, performers, and intellectuals in *Rent* sang about "being an *us* for once, instead of a *them*," they asserted the power of the margins to build a community of love, support, and strength.[23]

The first TV movie about AIDS, *An Early Frost*, aired on NBC in November 1985. Starring acclaimed actors, the film was written by Ron Cowen and Daniel Lipman, the eventual co-creators of the American version of the hit Showtime series *Queer as Folk*. The film's protagonist was a handsome, gender conforming, young, white, gay lawyer who goes home to his parents and grandmother to grapple with their reactions to his coming out as both gay and HIV positive. While adhering to NBC's requirement that the film show no gay physical affection, the show's creators and director had at least two aims in making the film: to convey accurate, up-to-date medical information about AIDS to scared and often-uninformed viewers, and to make a movie that resonated with a mainstream audience. As the gay male director, John Erman, said: "I figured out in my head that I was making that movie for my Aunt Myrtle. . . . I thought, *I want to make this movie so that she will realize that gay people are just as good as anybody else.*" The film was nominated for 14 Emmy Awards and drew more viewers on the Monday night it aired than *Monday Night Football*.[24]

These earlier successes led to other TV and film productions, such as the 1993 movie *Philadelphia*, which was "one of the first big-budget, star-studded Hollywood productions to present the gay individual as a normal, good citizen" (Seidman, 2002, p. 133). Tom Hanks, starring alongside Denzel Washington, played the lead character – for which he won an Academy Award – a young, white, gay lawyer with AIDS who fights the anti-gay, anti-AIDS discrimination he faces at work. On television, another break-through moment came in the third season of MTV's highly popular

The Real World, in which young, Cuban American, HIV positive AIDS educator Pedro Zamora became increasingly ill. The reality formatting of the show and its popularity, plus Zamora's charisma and outspokenness, brought awareness of HIV/AIDS to MTV's young audience. Even then-President Bill Clinton called Zamora during his illness and issued a statement when Zamora died in November 1994 at the age of 22 (Navarro, 1994; Gross, 2001).

Celebrities contributed to public awareness by lending both their names and platforms to AIDS education and fundraising. Some also changed the conversation through their own struggles with AIDS. It was the illness and death from AIDS-related complications of the mostly closeted 1950s film heartthrob Rock Hudson that finally inspired his friend, President Reagan, to end his silence on AIDS and prompted the mainstream media to pay attention to the years-old epidemic. Many believe that Hudson's announcement that he had AIDS and his subsequent death a few months later, in 1985, was a watershed moment in the visibility and media coverage of AIDS (Kinsella, 1989; Gross, 1993; Rotello, 1997; Shilts, 2007). Shilts argued that Hudson's revelation made AIDS both interesting and relatable to a broader American public:

> There was something about Hudson's diagnosis that seemed to strike an archetypal chord in the American consciousness. For decades, Hudson had been among the handful of screen actors who personified wholesome American masculinity; now, in one stroke, he was revealed as both gay and suffering from the affliction of pariahs. Doctors involved in AIDS research called the Hudson announcement the single most important event in the history of the epidemic, and few knowledgeable people argued. (2007, pp. 578–579)

Other high-profile deaths of gay men added to the mainstream visibility of AIDS: activist and artist Keith Haring died of AIDS-related complications in February 1990; the band Queen's lead singer, Freddie Mercury, died in November 1991.

There was a mainstream pop cultural mega-moment in November 1991, when the Los Angeles Lakers basketball player Earvin "Magic" Johnson, who identified as straight, revealed to the world that he was HIV positive and was retiring from the game. Johnson's announcement was particularly important to the mainstream conversation because it refuted the public narrative that AIDS primarily struck gay, white men (Faderman & Timmons, 2009). This high-profile revelation, Cohen argues, "forever changed, at least in terms of quantity, the coverage focused on AIDS among African Americans. ... Suddenly ... there was one black man whom reporters, editors, and media institutions could not ignore" (1999, p. 149). African American tennis star Arthur Ashe, who also identified as straight, followed Johnson's revelation months later with a similar announcement that he had lived with an AIDS diagnosis since 1988. These two straight, African American sports icons substantially increased the attention paid by the mainstream public to HIV in general and, more pointedly, to African Americans with AIDS (Cohen, 1999).

HIV and AIDS after the "Protease Moment"

The year that *Rent* debuted on Broadway – 1996 – was a watershed year for AIDS treatment. By this time, when the AIDS movement, especially the direct action part of it, was in decline, between 650,000 and 900,000 Americans were HIV positive and more than 350,000 had died of AIDS-related causes. Worldwide, more than 21 million people were HIV positive and more than 4 million had died (Román, 1998). Scientists had not yet found a successful treatment drug. The drugs that were available before 1996 were not particularly effective, were extraordinarily costly, and were also highly toxic.

The first drug considered to be effective was AZT, which slowed the replication of HIV in the body. The FDA approved it in March 1987, and it prolonged life by about a year. But its significant drawbacks were that bodies became resistant to it quickly and it was extremely toxic and expensive. Burroughs Wellcome sold it under the name Retrovir for $8,000–10,000 per year. These disadvantages made the drug incredibly controversial (Epstein, 1996; Whiteside, 2008; Byrne, 2015).

Within a few years of the introduction of AZT, scientists came to understand that, like fighting other infections, a "combination therapy" for HIV would be more effective and less poisonous to the body. Antiretroviral therapy (ART) would be a combination of drugs to slow the growth of HIV in the body in various ways. But it was not until 1996, more than 15 years after the first AIDS cases appeared in the United States, that there was a breakthrough in the science of ART. A combination therapy that included a new class of drugs called protease inhibitors was announced at the Eleventh International AIDS Conference in Vancouver, Canada, in July. This new treatment brought a quick and substantial drop in the number of AIDS-related deaths (Whiteside, 2008; Faderman, 2015). Rofes declared, provocatively, referring to the impact of this "Protease Moment": "AIDS, as we have known it, *is* over" (1998, pp. 29, 10; emphasis in original). Yet, the drug combination was still extremely expensive and inaccessible to many (Warner, 1999). One estimate in 2008 was that, in the wealthiest countries, treatment could cost between $850 and $1,500 per patient per month (Whiteside, 2008).

In recent years, the prevention and treatment debate has centered around a new regimen. An antiretroviral drug that has been sold by the brand name Truvada since 2004 was later found to effectively block HIV *transmission*. In 2012, the FDA approved the drug to be used as a preventative measure for those at high risk of exposure to HIV, and Truvada began being used in this way, for pre-exposure prophylaxis, or PrEP. In other words, taking Truvada prophylactically has been shown to prevent new transmission of HIV, and the drug began to be marketed and used for this purpose (Murphy, 2014). The medicine, like many others in the HIV regimen, has a high list price. In 2015, it cost more than $1,500 per month per user (Corbin, 2015).

The use of an antiretroviral drug by HIV negative people for the purpose of HIV prevention is new and very controversial. It has reignited a debate in many gay male circles, as well as in the public conversation, about what this means for safer sex practices. Larry Kramer, for one, who has been living with HIV since the 1980s, jumped into the fray and received a lot of public criticism for his position. He said, in 2014:

Anybody who voluntarily takes an antiviral every day has got to have rocks in their heads. There's something to me cowardly about taking Truvada instead of using a condom. You're taking a drug that is poison to you, and it has lessened your energy to fight, to get involved, to do anything. (Murphy, 2014, p. 44)

Others, in response, have said that PrEP should be celebrated and has the potential to defeat AIDS (Sullivan, 2014).

There is no HIV vaccine yet, and there is not much of an industry impetus to develop one. Jon Cohen notes that "the best hope the world has to thwart this virus is the same weapon effectively used against smallpox, polio, hepatitis B, rabies, and other devastating viruses: a vaccine." Yet this depends on the work of pharmaceutical companies, and they have "largely decided to sit on the sidelines" of this effort (2001, pp. xvi, 104). The work is expensive, time-intensive, and relies on commercial interests finding a value in a project for which "the market is limited and risks are high" (Whiteside, 2008, p. 36).

Yet for many in the United States and around the world, the available treatment and prevention regimens are out of reach and the numbers of people around the globe who have contracted HIV and have suffered from AIDS remain staggeringly high. "The burden of HIV/AIDS," Whiteside writes, "is not borne equally. . . . AIDS is primarily a disease of the poor, be they poor nations or poor people in rich nations" (2008, p. xii). According to the CDC (2016b), in the United States, by the end of 2016, more than 1.2 million people were living with HIV, including 39,513 new HIV diagnoses in 2015 alone. In 2014, more than 6,700 deaths were due directly to HIV/AIDS. Among new cases, men who had sex with men (the CDC measures behavior rather than identity) made up 67 percent of all HIV diagnoses. Among men who had sex with men, African American men had the largest number of new diagnoses. In fact, from 2005 to 2014, while diagnoses dropped substantially for white men who had sex with men, they rose for Latino men who had sex with men by 24 percent and for Black men who had sex with men by 22 percent, though this number has stayed relatively steady since 2010. Among heterosexual groups,

African American women represent by far the largest number of new cases of HIV, with 4,142 in 2015.

Worldwide, the Joint United Nations Programme on HIV/AIDS (UNAIDS, 2016b) finds that approximately 36.7 million people around the world were living with HIV and that approximately 2.1 million people were newly infected in 2015. The same year, approximately 1.1 million people around the world died from AIDS-related causes. Overall, since the beginning of the AIDS crisis, about 35 million people have died from AIDS-related causes.[25] Every *day*, UNAIDS (2016a) estimates, 5,700 adults and children are newly infected with HIV worldwide.

The global fight against HIV and AIDS is far from over.

The Political Legacies of AIDS

AIDS devastated lesbian and gay communities and the movement that was beginning to take national hold by the end of the 1970s. It revealed, again, the deep homophobia of the US government and the extent to which sexual minorities could so readily become scapegoats and outcasts of the state. It also inspired a massive and diverse response: community-building and the development of social services that were self-determined and self-sustaining; a radical AIDS movement that both reviled the state and made massive demands on it; new queer organizing that pushed the mainstream movement to be more inclusive of a broad range of genders and sexualities; a rich artistic response that won hearts and minds and accomplished wide visibility; and a broad, well-resourced civil rights movement that had a seat at the table of mainstream politics.

The political legacy of this early fight against AIDS in the United States was both a new movement – an AIDS-focused one – and new growth and division within what, by the end of this period, was known as the LGBT movement. AIDS and the response to it built new gay community institutions and identities (Padug & Oppenheimer, 1992). It brought gay men and lesbian activists together in different, authentic ways that mended some of the deep divisions of the 1970s (D'Emilio, 1992; Vaid, 1995; *Pride Divide*, 1997; Chauncey, 2005; Faderman, 2015). And while AIDS prematurely took the lives of so many young activists, it also made activists out of many people who had never before joined a political movement (D'Emilio, 1992; Vaid, 1995).

The AIDS movement also demonstrates that we need to look more closely at our understanding of what it means to be either assimilationist or liberationist. Like so many liberationists before them, ACT UP activists, for instance, took a confrontational, direct action approach to their organizing. They had a strong critique of the US government and an unapologetically proud and visible approach to gay and lesbian identity. They also, however, like assimilationists, demanded something of the state, to which they looked for social change. On the other hand, GMHC and other AIDS service organizations drew criticism at the time for not being political enough and for playing into Reagan's small government, conservative approach to the social welfare of Americans by providing a private option for the care of people with AIDS. However, these ASOs were also community-controlled and community-run institutions that did not rely on the state for support. For ACT UP, GMHC, and many other responses to the AIDS crisis, we see simultaneous elements of assimilationist and liberationist approaches. This offers up a more complicated way to view past and future LGBTQ movements.

Finally, the political and cultural response to AIDS during these crisis years provides us with another reminder that the Right can regularly revive the old, worn trope of queer people – especially gay men in this case – as sick, immoral, dangerous people who do not deserve the care and attention of the nation. At the same time, we see a movement fighting back by demanding rights and social welfare from the state and creating cultural responses that unapologetically assert sexuality, love, and community. AIDS brought people, as Russo said, "out of the closet and into the battle" (Marcus, 2002, p. 293), and LGBTQ movements were forever changed because of it.

4

Marriage Politics

This is what victory looks like. It is a beautiful summer day: June 26, 2015. Crowds in the streets and in the bars display utter jubilation. Ben & Jerry's renames an ice-cream flavor "I Dough, I Dough" in celebration. Honey Maid tweets a photo of a map made of graham crackers with the caption "love reigns from coast to coast." Social media sites are awash in rainbow flags. The Supreme Court has issued a much-anticipated ruling: it is unconstitutional to define marriage as simply between a man and a woman. It is an unequivocal moral celebration of marriage, written by the swing vote, a Reagan-appointed Justice Anthony Kennedy. "No union," it says, "is more profound than marriage, for it embodies the highest ideals of love, fidelity, devotion, sacrifice, and family. In forming a marital union, two people become something greater than once they were" (*Obergefell et al. v. Hodges*, 2015, p. 48).

Marriage is, as Chauncey writes in his classic book on the subject, "an emblem of . . . citizenship and equality" (2005, p. 161). Individual marriages can be frivolous and short-lived, but the institution of marriage itself is never politically unimportant. In addition to its symbolic and political importance, civil marriage has substantial *material* consequences. It is an economic, legal, and civic institution, which, in the United States alone, confers at least 1,138 federal benefits to married people that are off-limits to their unwed counterparts (Cahill, 2004). These benefits have been widely recognized by policymakers, courts, scholars, and activists.

They include a whole host of tax, inheritance, and employment benefits; immigration and child care rights; and medical and legal privileges (Wolfson, 2004; Chauncey, 2005; *Obergefell et al. v. Hodges*, 2015). This litany of benefits can come cheap to those who are legally entitled to them: marriage licenses might cost a couple tens of dollars, while hiring an attorney to put this wide range of legal protections in place for unmarried partners – from power of attorney to designating a beneficiary to securing parental rights – would likely cost thousands (Chauncey, 2005).

Like most institutions, marriage is also historically contingent. Marrying for love is a relatively new historical development. Until modern times, and in most places around the world, marriage has been a tightly regulated "system of . . . political and economic advancement" as it created larger families with corresponding "cooperative relations" (Coontz, 2005, pp. 7, 6). In the mid- to late eighteenth century, alongside industrialization, marriage became a state institution (Blank, 2012). The corresponding shift to love as the basis for marriage arose with the development of modern Western capitalism and substantial shifts in the view and role of women in society (Graff, 2004).

For many gay men, lesbians, and bisexual people, marriage has been one of the primary sites of material, legal, and symbolic struggle in recent decades. As we will see in this chapter, marriage politics are not just about the right to a legal union for same-sex couples. They are also about the role of the state in granting legitimacy and benefits to all people and their various kinds of partnerships and the "struggle over the place of lesbians and gay men in American society" (Chauncey, 2005, p. 3). So, too, the fight for marriage equality has raised debates within LGBTQ communities about assimilationist versus liberationist philosophy, strategies, and tactics of social change and social justice, including the limits and possibilities of achieving social change through the law (see, e.g., Ghaziani et al., 2016). The fight for marriage has relied on a "legal rights strategy" that looks to the courts for LGBTQ social change (Rimmerman, 2002) and reflects a broader debate within LGBTQ and a range of other American social movements about "whether rights matter for social movements" and a

benefits to same-sex, unmarried partners and was vocal about its rationale: "We really believe the family is who you love and who you live with . . . the families of all [Ben & Jerry's] workers deserve as a basic human right to live free of the fear that a catastrophic illness or accident could destroy them financially" (Polikoff, 2008, pp. 49–50). These policies proliferated, and by the time the first marriage licenses were being granted to same-sex couples, in Massachusetts in 2004, nearly half of the Fortune 500 companies in the country offered some benefits to their employees' same-sex domestic partners, as did the public offices of ten states and more than 125 localities.[4]

Marriage as a civil institution

But, was marriage *itself* worth fighting for? By the late 1980s, LGBTQ Americans were beginning to grapple with this question in earnest. As with many other social movements of the past century, the debate over marriage equality rested on the question of whether assimilation into mainstream institutions is preferable to the creation of new institutions, and on whether marginalized minorities of any kind should turn primarily to the government to grant them legitimacy. Was marriage an institution worth embracing? And what role should the state play in the intimate lives of its inhabitants?

Seidman argues that the role of the government in private romantic and sexual lives has changed over time. Until the mid-nineteenth century in the US, "[t]he state mostly stayed out of the business of regulating its citizens' intimate affairs" (2002, p. 166). This shifted in the years between 1860 and the first few decades of the twentieth century, when heterosexuals and their families were the target of a new "web of governmental control" around "birth control, abortion, interracial marriage, prostitution, commercial sex, forced sterilization, and public sexual representations" (2002, p. 168). In the decades after World War II, this subsided for *heterosexuals*, but between the 1930s and 1960s, "[f]or the first time in American history, the state mobilized its growing authority and resources to control same-sex behavior" as sexual minorities became "the personification of the bad sexual citizen" (2002, pp. 170, 173).

LGBTQ writers and activists had two responses to the state's new control: some sought the support of the state and recognized its institutions, laws, and policies to be the potential source of change, while others opted out; "[i]n short, assimilationists want homosexuals to be recognized and accepted as good sexual citizens; liberationists challenge the sexual norms associated with this ideal" and do not look to the state as the solution (Seidman, 2002, p. 173). While, as we saw in chapter 2, there was a flourishing strand of liberationism after Stonewall, by the mid-1970s assimilationist politics had won out in the organized lesbian and gay movement. The assimilationist majority "press[ed] America to live up to its promise of equal treatment of all of its citizens; they wish[ed] to be a part of what is considered a basically good nation; this requires reform, not revolution" (2002, p. 175). Still, the fight for marriage equality is one of those key issues, Seidman argues, that engaged both assimilationists and liberationists, as it concerns the proper relationship between the state and LGBTQ people and the cultural question of what counts and gets state-sanctioned as *normal*.

Is marriage too "normal"?

With its historical connections to both heterocentrism and the oppression of women (see, e.g., Blank, 2012), modern Western marriage has been the object of criticism by both feminists and LGBTQ theorists and activists for decades. Many have questioned whether marriage as an institution should be rejected in favor of alternative forms of intimate and family relationships not necessarily based in monogamy or traditional gender roles. The Gay Liberation Front, in 1969, offered this critique: "We expose the institution of marriage as one of the most insidious and basic sustainers . . . of the system" (Stacey, 2011, p. 13).

Yet, by the late 1980s and early 1990s, marriage had gained traction as a civil rights goal and as a matter for debate. One of the earliest clashes over marriage and its political role in the movement took place on the occasion of the 1987 March on Washington, even before marriage became a focus of the mainstream movement. During this second national march, a Los Angeles group called Couples Inc. organized a collective ceremony, dubbed the Wedding, outside of the federal Internal Revenue Service (IRS) building. The event was both a celebration and a political action for, according to the Couples Inc. president, "equal rights to demand recognition of our existing ongoing relationships" (Ghaziani, 2008, p. 120). This was an assertion of the need for rights for lesbian and gay *couples* – not just individuals – and, outside the IRS, it highlighted the fact that the government, in denying same-sex couples access to the institution of marriage, deprived them of rights and benefits. This demonstration – of more than 7,000 people – was "the most controversial event of the march" (Ghaziani et al., 2016, p. 173), because it revealed a philosophical split among lesbian and gay people and activists concerning the value versus the harm of marriage and the question of whether entry into this institution was worth collectively fighting for.[5]

Following the controversy over the 1987 action, the most highly cited early debates about marriage among lesbian and gay activists occurred in a 1989 issue of *Out/Look* magazine between two lawyer-activists: Thomas Stoddard, a gay man who was the executive director for Lambda Legal Defense and Education Fund, and Paula Ettelbrick, a lesbian feminist who was Lambda's legal director. In his contribution, "Why gay people should seek the right to marry," Stoddard noted that marriage was a traditionally stifling institution that had been "oppressive, especially (although not entirely) to women," and that it was not yet a political goal for the movement; marriage should nevertheless be a *right* for gay and lesbian people.[6] Even more, marriage (and all the legal and material benefits that accompany it) should become a *focus* of the current "gay rights movement" (1993, pp. 398, 400). Noting the central and symbolic importance of marriage, Stoddard wrote that it is "the centerpiece of our entire social structure," and that alternatives, like domestic partnership, still demean gay and lesbian people and their intimate relationships. "Gay relationships," he argued, "will continue to be accorded a subsidiary status until the day that gay couples have *exactly* the same rights as their heterosexual counterparts." At the same time, Stoddard's focus on *rights* as the basis for full citizenship included the notion that "enlarging the concept [of marriage] to embrace same-sex couples" would not simply reproduce its oppressive characteristics, but "would necessarily transform it into something new" (1993, pp. 400, 401; emphasis in original).

In her response, titled "Since when is marriage a path to liberation?" Ettelbrick agreed with Stoddard about marriage's cultural centrality. But, she reached a very different conclusion about the relationship that LGBTQ people should have with this institution. She saw gaining the right to marriage as a tempting but problematic goal. "After all," she wrote, "those who marry can be instantaneously transformed from 'outsiders' to 'insiders,' and we have a desperate need to become insiders." Marriage would normalize gays and lesbians in the eyes of their families and friends: "Never again would [we] have to go to a family reunion and debate about the correct term for introducing our lover/partner/ significant other to Aunt Flora. Everything would be quite easy and very nice." But marriage, Ettelbrick wrote, "will constrain us, make us more invisible, force our assimilation into the mainstream, and undermine the goals of gay liberation" (1989, p. 402).

Asserting an explicitly *queer* identity, Ettelbrick argued that "[b]eing queer means pushing the parameters of sex, sexuality, and family and, in the process transforming the very fabric of society." She urged the movement *not* to take up the marriage fight, calling it a "trap" that would stigmatize non-married gay and lesbian people, restrict the range of acceptable intimate and family arrangements, and invite the state in to further regulate and confine queer sex and relationships. It also would put resources and energy toward an issue that resonates most with white, well-off men, centering their experience and their issues. Rather than turning the movement's focus to marriage, she argued that "[w]e must keep our eyes on the goals of providing true alternatives to marriage and of radically reordering society's views of family" (1989, pp. 402–403, 405).

For "normal" and for "queer": the debate continues

As marriage gained some traction politically in the 1990s, the debate continued on the extent to which a civil rights versus a liberationist focus was the most effective means to LGBTQ social justice. The difference in view between two prominent gay writers, Andrew Sullivan and Michael Warner, offers another example of the philosophical and political arguments for and against marriage within the movement at this time.

Sullivan made a strong case for a marriage movement in his 1995 book *Virtually Normal*. Laying out a plan for the future of gay and lesbian politics, Sullivan called for the movement to concentrate entirely on achieving legal and "formal public equality" rather than focusing on broader cultural shifts and arenas; furthermore, "equal access to civil marriage" should be the "centerpiece of this new politics." Because marriage is so symbolically important and *civil* marriage confers deep public legitimacy, "[d]enying it to homosexuals is the most public affront possible to their public equality" (1995, pp. 178, 179). Sullivan firmly staked his claim on marriage on the basis that, "[i]f nothing else were done at all, and gay marriage were legalized, ninety percent of the political work necessary to achieve gay and lesbian equality would have been achieved. It is ultimately the only reform that truly matters." While he left some room for a recognition and celebration of "what is essential and exhilarating about [the] otherness" of lesbian and gay people, he was dismissive of liberationist philosophy and politics (1995, pp. 185, 204). Sullivan (2003; 2004a; 2004b) continued to advocate for marriage in the years to come. For him, civil marriage is a state-sanctioned recognition of full humanity that, by definition, changes gay people's relationships with their families of origin, with their futures, and with their country.

In 1999, academic Michael Warner made a strong case *against* a marriage movement, partly in direct response to Sullivan.[7] On the very first page of *The Trouble with Normal*, Warner plainly wrote of the normalizing institution of marriage: "I argue that marriage is unethical"; to continue focusing movement energy on marriage "represents a widespread loss of vision." He also saw the desire for marriage as merely an attempt to "clean ourselves up as legitimate players in politics and the media." This inherently de-sexing strategy, argued Warner, sent the problematic message that, "if you behave yourself, you can have a decent life as a normal homo – at least, up to a point" (1999, pp. vii, 39-40).

Warner had a few basic problems with marriage. First, a movement focus on marriage seeks validation from the state, bringing it in as an arbiter of legitimate intimate relationships. To say that marriage is simply a private, individual, politically neutral *choice* or *right* that should be available to everyone is to ignore the role that the state plays in sanctifying some relationships and prohibiting or criminalizing others and in conferring hundreds of tangible/ material benefits on people within the institution. Involving the state in same-sex relationships in this way is not a costless political choice. Second, and relatedly, Warner argued that the movement's marriage focus narrows the range of legitimate and acceptable relationships, providing a moral dividing line among LGBTQ people and their relationships. Marriage pares down the "astonishing range of intimacies" that are available to and part of queer lives and communities (1999, p. 116).

Finally, Warner wrote, marriage is the narrow goal of a movement that is bent on a broader "dequeering agenda," one that is increasingly led by and representative of a privileged part of the LGBTQ community: a largely white, well-off, male, gender-conforming, corporate-leaning group that is most interested in public "respectability" above all else politically. "[I]n its newest manifestation," Warner worried, "the lesbian and gay movement threatens to become an instrument for the normalization of queer life. Nowhere is that more visible than in the presentation of the gay marriage issue." Citing Sullivan directly here, Warner wrote that marriage divides the queer community into the "Good Gay," who "would not challenge the norms of straight culture, who would not flaunt sexuality, and who would not insist on living differently from ordinary folk," and the "Bad Queer," who is "the kind who has sex, who talks about it, and who builds with other queers a way of life that ordinary folks do not understand or control" (1999, pp. 139, 78, 80, 113, 114).

This philosophical debate over marriage has continued (Bernstein & Taylor, 2013; Kimport, 2014; Bernstein, 2015; Ghaziani et al., 2016). Some progressives have articulated similar concerns to those of Warner about the institution of marriage and the extent to which the mainstream LGBTQ movement has focused on marriage rights and on privileging a certain narrow set of intimate relationships (Polikoff, 2008; Stacey, 2011). Lisa Duggan argues that the fight for marriage now displays a *"new homonormativity"*: "a politics that does not contest dominant heteronormative assumptions and institutions, but upholds and sustains them . . . a privatized, depoliticized gay culture anchored in domesticity and consumption" (2003, p. 50; emphasis in original). As writer Hugh Ryan lamented in 2014: "Marriage is here, it's not queer, and we've already gotten used to it" (n.p.).

However, some LGBTQ activists and academics who are decidedly progressive and liberationist *have* embraced marriage, illustrating the philosophical and political complexity of this issue within the movement (Rofes, 2002). Other progressives, too, have picked up Stoddard's argument that LGBTQ participation in marriage could and would *change* the institution, and that this was an important project of the movement: participating in existing institutions and changing them from *within*. Sociologist Mary Bernstein, for instance, argues about the potential of same-sex marriage: "the very presence of gay male and lesbian couples, especially those with children, destabilizes the heteronormativity heterosexual people take for granted" (2015, p. 323; also see Graff, 1996).

The Right's "Defense" of Traditional Marriage

The Right's insertion into politics: mobilizing homophobia

As activists and writers debated the philosophical and political implications of marriage through the late 1980s and 1990s, the Religious Right that emerged as a political force at the end of the 1970s gained power and numbers and increasingly demonstrated its influence at the ballot box. Even as mainstream Protestant denominations began to open up a bit to gay rights and to denounce anti-gay discrimination, the Christian Right doubled down on its anti-gay agenda, wielding it to gain political power (Diamond, 1995; Chauncey, 2005). Religious conservatives framed themselves as defenders of Christian morality against a dangerously secularized state. In the name of religious freedom, they called for a "defense" of traditional values and the withholding of protections for lesbian and gay people. They called for the state, instead, to protect *their* freedom as Christians and to do their bidding.

The Religious Right gained new national political presence when Pat Robertson – whom we met in chapter 3 – ran for president in the 1988 Republican primaries. Although he did not win his party's nomination, the 2 million votes he received did help launch the Christian Coalition, a prolific and wildly successful political organization that Robertson founded in 1989 that relied on local, grassroots organizing (Vaid, 1995; Fetner, 2008; Polikoff, 2008). Building power, Robertson and the Christian Right inserted their politics into the 1992 presidential election in unprecedented ways (Diamond, 1995). Herzog writes that 1992 "marked the first time the rights of homosexuals became a major theme in a presidential election" (2008, p. 61). The national Republican Party platform that year opposed nondiscrimination protections on the basis of sexual orientation and opposed same-sex marriage and other family rights, such as adoption (Cahill, 2004). At the Republican National Convention, more than 40 percent of the delegates identified as evangelical Christians, and Christian Right mega-commentator and political strategist Pat Buchanan, who had run that year for president in the Republican primaries, gave the Convention's opening remarks, opining: "[T]here is a religious war going on in this country for the soul of America. It is a culture war as critical to the kind of nation we shall be as the Cold War itself" (Fetner, 2008, p. 80).

In the early 1990s, the Christian Right also continued to work on the local front, building on work that Anita Bryant began in the late 1970s, by supporting local anti-gay ballot initiatives in a number of states across the country. Exemplifying this effort was Colorado's Amendment 2, a statewide ballot initiative approved by 53 percent of voters in November 1992. The proposition amended the state constitution to prevent any municipality, state department, or school district in the state from passing laws that would *protect* gay, lesbian, and bisexual people from discrimination based on their sexual orientation (Rimmerman, 2002). Amendment 2 eventually was ruled unconstitutional, in the 1996 landmark decision of *Romer v. Evans*, in which the Supreme Court was clear that the initiative so egregiously targeted LGB Coloradans that it "classifies homosexuals not to further a proper legislative end but to make them unequal to everyone else. This Colorado cannot do" (quoted in Sullivan, 2004a, p. 104). Despite this gay rights victory, the Amendment 2 initiative signaled the Christian Right's new aggressive insertion into local and national American politics. The Colorado fight was also indicative of the "direct democracy" political strategy that the Religious Right had effectively employed since the Anita Bryant days: the use of local anti-gay ballot measures. Sociologist Amy L. Stone notes that 146 such measures appeared on ballots between 1974 and 2009 (2012, p. xv).

The Right and its broader reach: organizing against marriage

The early 1990s was a time of some initial legal and political progress on marriage equality, as we will see below. This served to further mobilize the Christian Right. The 1996 passage of federal legislation restricting marriage benefits to mixed-sex couples was one direct rightwing response to the possibility of marriage equality. In a presidential election year, and with almost three-quarters of Americans reporting that they opposed same-sex unions, Republicans in Congress introduced the Defense of Marriage Act (DOMA). The bill codified a definition of marriage as solely between a man and a woman, thus denying any federal marriage benefits to same-sex spouses: "[T]he word 'marriage' means only a legal union between one man and one woman as husband and wife, and the word 'spouse' refers only to a person of the opposite sex who is a husband or a wife" (quoted in Sullivan, 2004a, p. 207). DOMA also explicitly established that states were not compelled to recognize same-sex marriages from other states. So, while mixed-sex couples, by virtue of the Full Faith and Credit Clause of the US Constitution, can travel from state to state with the assurance that their marriage will be recognized across the country, DOMA explicitly did not extend this right to same-sex spouses. Same-sex couples who were married in their home state could cross state lines and find themselves suddenly single in the eyes of the law. Congress passed DOMA easily, with votes of 342 to 67 in the House and 85 to 14 in the Senate (Faderman, 2015). Democrat Bill Clinton had been elected president in 1992 in part by making promises about advancing gay and lesbian rights. But when the Defense of Marriage Act arrived on Clinton's desk in September 1996, he signed it – late one night and with no public fanfare.[8]

Just as the federal government had narrowly and explicitly defined marriage, so states began to do the same (Stone, 2012). In early 1995, South Dakota legislators passed a state law explicitly clarifying that "any marriage between persons of the same gender is null and void" (Faderman, 2015, p. 587). Statewide ballot initiatives – popular votes on marriage – began in 1998 in Alaska and Hawaii (Stone, 2012). By the end of the year 2000, 40 states – either by legislative action or popular vote – had passed laws or constitutional amendments explicitly excluding same-sex couples from the institution of marriage (Same-sex marriage laws, 2015).

The Right won a lot of the battles it waged on marriage equality in the late 1990s and the early part of the new millennium. "[T]he first conservative evangelical Republican president," George W. Bush, was elected as US President in 2000, and this "emboldened" the Religious Right (Herzog, 2008, p. 166). And, for this revitalized Right, 2004 was a banner year, as President Bush backed a Federal Marriage Amendment proposal that sought to change the federal Constitution to restrict marriage to a union between a man and a woman.[9] Noting, in February 2004, that an amendment was needed to "protect marriage" for the greater good, Bush counseled: "Marriage cannot be severed from its cultural, religious and natural roots without weakening the good influence of society" (Sullivan, 2004a, pp. 342, 343). This sentiment was reflected in the ballot box. Neither the Democratic Party platform nor the Republican Party platform supported marriage equality in 2004 (Cahill, 2004). And, on the day that President Bush was re-elected on November 2, 2004, 11 states (out of 11 that were considering such initiatives) passed measures that banned same-sex marriage via state constitutional amendments. Eight of these states even banned civil unions (Associated Press, 2004; Chauncey, 2005).

The "homosexual menace" returns

In the Right's crusade against marriage equality, it is worth noting the return of an anti-gay trope that we have seen at least since World War II: this framing of gay and lesbian Americans as threatening to the nation and its young people. Remember Anita Bryant and John Briggs in the 1970s, and their campaign to "save" American youth from ostensible homosexual predators and recruiters and the anti-gay local and state ballot initiatives that followed in the early 1990s (Stein, 2001). Once again, in the marriage fight, the Right trotted out the menacing image of a gay man or gay couple posing a grave danger to innocent children.

As the fight over California's anti-gay Proposition 8 held the future of marriage equality in the balance in the fall of 2008, a highly-effective "yes on 8" television ad began to air in both Spanish and English.[10] The 30-second ad opens with an adorable girl in pigtails running up to her mom, who is sorting mail at a kitchen counter. The girl is holding the children's picture book *King & King*, by Dutch authors Linda De Haan and Stern Nijland. The girl hands the book to her mom as she reports enthusiastically: "Mom, guess what I learned in school today? . . . I learned how a prince married a prince, and *I* can marry a princess!" Pepperdine University School of Law Professor Richard Peterson takes over part of the screen (in the way a used car salesman might in a low-budget, late-night ad) and warns: "Think it can't happen?

It's already happened! When Massachusetts legalized gay marriage, schools began teaching second graders that boys can marry boys." The mom's eyes widen and she considers the book with a look of deep concern. The ad ends as the words on the screen urge: "Protect Our Children. Restore Marriage."[11]

Marriage equality strategist and activist Marc Solomon called this "Princes" ad "diabolically brilliant" (2014, p. 227). Many considered it and its "fear-mongering message that children are in danger" (Fleischer, 2010, p. 49) to be incredibly effective in influencing hundreds of thousands of voters who ultimately voted for Prop 8, including half a million parents with children at home. Overall, the ad's message that legalizing same-sex marriage endangers children was central to the success of the anti-gay Prop 8 campaign (Fleischer, 2010).[12]

Changing Laws, Locally and Nationally

Amassing state-level wins

The earliest marriage equality fighters had to work hard to convince their colleagues that marriage was strategically worth the broader movement's attention. Evan Wolfson was an early believer in the cause of marriage and a tireless champion of it. As early as 1983, as a Harvard Law School student, Wolfson had written a thesis that argued for a focus on marriage equality, writing of its importance to the broader cause of lesbian and gay social justice (Yoshino, 2015). Working as a lawyer for Lambda Legal before movement activists saw marriage equality as viable or desirable, Wolfson had to fight to involve the LGBT legal rights organization in a marriage equality case in Hawaii. He was even briefly fired for pushing back on Lambda's refusal to represent the plaintiffs in that case (Wolfson, 2004; Chauncey, 2005; Solomon, 2014).

In December 1990, as the Religious Right was gaining power and visibility in national politics, three same-sex couples together requested licenses and were denied them in Honolulu. They filed suit, claiming that it was unconstitutional to deny their access to marriage. Two and a half years later, in May 1993, they received a first-of-its-kind favorable ruling by the Hawaii Supreme Court. The ruling, *Baehr v. Lewin*, considered whether the couples had a "fundamental right of marriage" (quoted in Sullivan, 2004a, p. 96), recognizing that marriage comes with many material benefits that same-sex couples are unable to access, and invoking Hawaii's state constitution's equal protection clause. The Court indicated that the lower court could only deny these couples their marriages if it could articulate "compelling state interests" in favor of doing so.

While this was a huge legal victory, particularly evident in the reasoning that same-sex marriage bans denied equal protection on the basis of sex, the ruling did not result in any same-sex marriages in the state. Instead, the Hawaii Supreme Court kicked the case back down to the lower court, which heard it in 1996 and ruled that the state had not, in fact, shown that it had a compelling interest in preventing same-sex marriages. The court declared that the state could no longer deny licenses to same-sex couples, but it stayed its ruling until the case was resolved by a higher court. By November 1998, Hawaiian voters had passed a state constitutional amendment that allowed the state legislature to define marriage as only between a man and a woman – which the legislature promptly did. This initiative passed with 69 percent of the vote and was the focus of a major national conservative campaign (Chauncey, 2005; Polikoff, 2008).

In the end, no same-sex marriages took place in Hawaii in the 1990s, despite the favorable ruling in 1993. But, Hawaii ignited a movement and showed that court rulings in favor of marriage equality were possible (Chauncey, 2005). Marriage equality advocates continued their state-level fights for recognition, while Wolfson continued to be a vocal, enthusiastic, national leader, eventually founding the organization Freedom to Marry. In the early 1990s, after the Hawaii win, a young lawyer, Mary Bonauto, worked on behalf of New England's Gay & Lesbian Advocates & Defenders (GLAD) to adopt the vision for the movement that marriage equality was the way to achieve broader LGBTQ equality.

One of the most important political aspects to understand about the marriage equality movement is that its architects, activists like Wolfson and Bonauto, had a state-by-state strategy in mind all along. They were quite deliberate about the geography of their work. They knew they had a state game to play that would, at some point, result in a battle on the federal front: fighting DOMA and bringing a marriage challenge to the Supreme Court. But, they started in what they believed to be the most hospitable states, and they went from there (*Winning Marriage*, 2005; Solomon, 2014).[13] They had a theory of legal change that relied on this state-by-state strategy.

Turning to New England as a strategic starting point, Bonauto and GLAD led the legal charge for civil equality in Vermont.[14] Their suit filed on behalf of three same-sex couples resulted in a December 1999 Vermont Supreme Court ruling that the benefits of marriage could not be withheld from same-sex partners, although the result was the establishment of a separate-but-equal category of "civil unions" for same-sex partners (Chauncey, 2005; Polikoff, 2008). Civil unions were won in a number of other states, but civil rights groups continued to fight for full marriage. "Comparing marriages to civil unions or domestic partnerships," the Human Rights Campaign wrote, "is a bit like comparing diamonds to rhinestones. One is, quite simply, the real deal; the other is not" (n.d., p. 5).[15]

Just as this state-level strategy was gaining steam, the marriage movement got a bit of help from the Supreme Court. In its June 26, 2003 decision in *Lawrence v. Texas*, the Court finally decriminalized sodomy, overruling the 1986 decision in *Bowers v. Hardwick* that had upheld its criminalization. The 2003 ruling overturned a Texas law, and similar laws against sodomy in twelve other states, where same-sex couples (as well as mixed-sex couples in nine states), could face criminal charges for engaging in adult, private, consensual anal or oral sex (Greenhouse, 2003). This ruling was a huge step forward in the struggle for LGBTQ rights. It decriminalized same-sex sexual practices and, for all intents and purposes, LGBTQ people (Richman, 2009). As Yoshino argued, the criminalization of sodomy in *Bowers* had provided a foundation for further limits on gay people: "*Bowers* caused many courts to rule that gays could not receive any meaningful protection under the Constitution ... These courts reasoned that a Constitution that allowed homosexual conduct to be criminalized could not bar other forms of discrimination against gays" (2015, pp. 37–38). According to Sullivan, overturning *Bowers* therefore removed "[t]he single most serious barrier to recognizing the right to marry" (2004a, p. 106).

On the heels of this Supreme Court victory came the first marriage equality court decision that actually resulted in some marriages, filed by Bonauto in Massachusetts. On November 18, 2003, the Massachusetts Supreme Judicial Court ruled, in *Goodridge v. Department of Public Health*, that "barring an individual from the protections, benefits, and obligations of civil marriage solely because that person would marry a person of the same sex violates the Massachusetts Constitution" (quoted in Sullivan, 2004a, p. 118). The Court gave the state 180 days to begin issuing marriage licenses and was very clear that a separate-but-equal civil unions solution was not acceptable (Cahill, 2004). On May 17, 2004, Massachusetts became the first state in the US to begin legally marrying same-sex couples. On that first day, 752 couples obtained a marriage license (Chauncey, 2005).

In the six-month period between the Massachusetts ruling and the first legal same-sex unions, marriage equality supporters across the US began taking action to secure marriage rights for same-sex couples. Most of these were extralegal acts that, in the end, were undone. For instance, the young, straight, Irish Catholic new mayor of San Francisco, Gavin Newsom, made a remarkable, high-profile move: in defiance of a California ban on same-sex marriage (an earlier one, before Prop 8), and right in time for Valentine's Day, he simply began issuing marriage licenses in his city on February 12, 2004. According to reporter and marriage equality activist Matt Baume (2015), Newsom had been prompted by President Bush's anti-marriage push in his 2004 State of the Union address to take a local stand for same-sex marriage. Newsom's act of civil disobedience in defiance of state law began with the marriage of a lesbian couple – Phyllis Lyon and Del Martin – who had been together for more than 50 years and who had, as you will remember from chapter 2, founded the Daughters of Bilitis. San Francisco officials continued to marry thousands more same-sex couples who, for the most part, lined up for licenses as an act of political protest (Taylor et al., 2009). Within the month, the California Supreme Court stepped in and ordered the city to stop. By this time, approximately 4,000 same-sex couples had been issued marriage licenses in San Francisco. The state Supreme Court ultimately ruled that these marriages were invalid.[16]

Other rogue local leaders who supported marriage equality followed Newsom's path. A day-long action by a clerk in Sandoval County, New Mexico on February 20, 2004, resulted in more than 60 same-sex marriage licenses (Morn, 2013). Jason West, the 26-year-old mayor of New Paltz, New York, presided over 24 same-sex marriages on February 27, 2004, then was stopped by judicial action and charged with misdemeanor counts of "solemnizing marriages without a license" (Rovzar, 2011, n.p.). In early March 2004, the county in Oregon that included Portland issued licenses to same-sex couples for seven weeks, marrying more than 3,000 couples before a judge stepped in (Chauncey, 2005).

By the spring of 2004, same sex marriages – legally licensed and not – were taking place in large number, and marriage equality looked like an ambitious but a potentially viable goal for the LGBT civil rights movement. On the heels of the Massachusetts win, Wolfson, Bonauto, Matt Coles from the American Civil Liberties Union (ACLU), and others convened in Jersey City in May 2005 to devise a plan for national marriage equality. They predicted a win on full marriage in just 10 states by the year 2020 – as well as civil union-like alternatives in another 10 states (Solomon, 2014). Their short-term plan for the next four to five years was marriage in just two or three more states (*Winning Marriage*, 2005, p. 4).

Massachusetts was, as we have seen, the first state to legalize same-sex marriage, in the spring of 2004. The second state to do so, more than four years later, was Connecticut, when that state's Supreme Court overturned the state's marriage ban in October 2008. The third state, right in the heartland, was Iowa, in April

2009. The Iowa Supreme Court decision was significant because it was unanimous and because it was in a part of the country that had a reputation – fairly or not – for conservative social values. The court's reading that denying same-sex couples the right to marry was unconstitutional was, in the words of one Lambda lawyer, "a game-changer" for these reasons (quoted in Witosky & Hansen, 2015, p. 212). These first few states had achieved marriage equality by judicial decision. But the next few states, also in the spring of 2009, took legislative action on behalf of marriage equality for the first time, in Vermont, Maine (later repealed before it was reinstated by voters), and New Hampshire (Solomon, 2014). By November 2012, for the first time, voters went to the polls and *supported* marriage equality, voting in favor of it in each place it was on the ballot: Maryland, Washington state, Minnesota, and Maine. The pace in the states accelerated. In May 2013, within a span of ten days, three new states – Rhode Island, Delaware, and Minnesota – gained marriage equality through legislative action (Solomon, 2014). A series of lower and appellate court decisions in late 2013 and throughout 2014 brought marriage to all but 13 of the remaining states in the country (Yoshino, 2015).

Going federal

As the state battles marched on and marriage equality activists amassed a number of wins, debates began over whether to it was time to pursue a *federal* challenge to marriage bans. An intra-movement disagreement unfolded over the most effective course of action for legal change. Some marriage equality supporters wanted to push forward with a federal challenge to DOMA and California's Proposition 8, with an eye toward undoing the existing state-level bans and bringing a Supreme Court ruling that could make same-sex marriage legal nationwide. Others, including many of the groups and lawyers that had been carefully and strategically fighting the state battles, believed that a federal – ultimately a Supreme Court – challenge was, in the words of a Lambda Legal attorney, "risky and premature" (quoted in Yoshino, 2015, p. 33). By early 2009, after the passage of Proposition 8, just four states had achieved marriage equality. By contrast, as Yoshino points out, when the case challenging bans on interracial marriage was filed, ultimately leading to the Supreme Court's 1967 *Loving v. Virginia* ruling that outlawed any state bans, 33 states allowed interracial marriage. Bringing federal suits, then, meant asking the courts to get ahead of the states, and this worried longtime marriage movement strategists. They believed that they needed to win more states before they could focus on a successful federal suit. They knew that the stakes, if they were to lose at the Supreme Court level, were too high (Solomon, 2014; Yoshino, 2015).

Yet lawyers launched two federal lawsuits that ultimately found their way to the Supreme Court. The first was a direct challenge to Prop 8 in California, brought by a new marriage advocacy organization, the American Foundation for Equal Rights (AFER), and its bipartisan high-profile legal team (the pair of lawyers had been on opposite sides of the *Bush v. Gore* suit in 2000, which ultimately landed the presidency for George W. Bush).[17] In the few years to follow, a federal challenge to DOMA was also shaping up, led by a private attorney who had experience with LGBTQ rights cases and who had been contacted by Edie Windsor, a New York City lesbian in her 80s. Because of DOMA, Windsor stood to owe the federal government more than $300,000 in estate taxes when her wife died, because her marriage was not eligible for federal affordances (Faderman, 2015).

The federal district judge in California found that Prop 8 violated the federal Constitution's Fourteenth Amendment on grounds of equal protection and due process. The appellate court agreed. And on June 26, 2013, the Supreme Court decided, in a 5–4 vote in *Hollingsworth v. Perry*, to let the initial district court level ruling stand. This invalidated Prop 8 itself but avoided a broader and more substantive ruling that might have rendered *all* state marriage bans unconstitutional. On the same day in the summer of 2013, the Supreme Court issued a broad ruling in the *United States v. Windsor* DOMA case. In another 5–4 decision written by Justice Kennedy, the Court ruled that Section 3 of DOMA (the part of the law that defined marriage as solely between a man and a woman) was unconstitutional, in that it "writes inequality into the entire U.S. Code" and "disparages and injures those whom the state, by its marriage laws, sought to protect in personhood and dignity" (quoted in Faderman, 2015, p. 628; also see Yoshino, 2015).

Another important part of the federal marriage story is President Barack Obama's shifting position on marriage and his role in the politics and jurisprudence of marriage. When Obama ran for president in 2008, he had not publicly supported same-sex marriages (though many believed he *was* a supporter – see Faderman, 2015), nor had any of the other front-runners for that office. Obama said that he supported civil unions but that he believed "that marriage is the union between a man and a woman. For me as a Christian, it's a sacred union" (Faderman, 2015, p. 611). As a candidate, Obama worked to thread the needle by supporting LGBTQ rights without alienating a broader public that was, on balance at the time, against same-sex marriage.

During his first term in office, at a time when he said that he was "evolving" on the issue (Faderman, 2015, p. 614), Obama's first major move toward marriage equality was to instruct his Department of Justice to stop defending DOMA, finding that it was unconstitutional. In addition, in the summer of 2011, he supported a bill in Congress to repeal DOMA (Yoshino, 2015). Finally, after Vice President Joe Biden announced on national television that he was "absolutely comfortable" with same-sex marriage (quoted in Solomon, 2014, p. 304), Obama explicitly came out for marriage equality. On May 9, 2012, he did a carefully staged televised interview with popular *Good Morning America* anchor Robin Roberts, in which she asked directly: "Mr. President, are you still opposed to same-sex marriage?" and he responded: "I've been going through an evolution on this issue." He said that he had thought civil unions might be a workable alternative, but that this had changed. "I've just concluded that for me personally, it is important for me to go ahead and affirm that I think same-sex couples should be able to get married" (Solomon, 2014, p. 307; Faderman, 2015, p. 615). When Obama ran for reelection in 2012, he became the first viable candidate to run as a supporter of marriage equality. That year, as well, marriage equality became part of the national Democratic Party platform for the first time (Bolcer, 2012).

Finally, although the Supreme Court declined to provide a broad ruling on marriage in the Prop 8 case, it finished the job exactly two years later, on June 26, 2015 (and 12 years to the day after its ruling in *Lawrence v. Texas*). By that time, after *Perry*, appellate courts across the country had ruled that state bans on same-sex marriage were unconstitutional. One court, however, the Sixth Circuit Court of Appeals with the jurisdiction of the states of Kentucky, Michigan, Ohio, and Tennessee, upheld a marriage ban in its November 4, 2014 ruling. This disagreement among the appellate courts made the need for a national resolution to the constitutional issue of marriage more immediate. In January 2015, the Supreme Court agreed to hear the cases that came out of this Sixth Circuit, under the consolidated name of *Obergefell v. Hodges*. The named plaintiff, James Obergefell, was from Ohio and had a male partner who suffered from Lou Gehrig's disease. As Obergefell's partner was dying, they chartered a plane to Maryland, a state where they could legally wed, and were married as the plane sat at the Maryland airport. After Obergefell's husband died, Ohio denied Obergefell's request to be listed as married on the death certificate (Faderman, 2015; Yoshino, 2015).

On June 26, 2015, in another 5–4 decision penned by Justice Kennedy, the Court ruled unequivocally that, on Fourteenth Amendment grounds, all marriage bans must be lifted and same-sex couples granted the rights to marry in their states. Kennedy wrote:

> The Court, in this decision, holds same-sex couples may exercise the fundamental right to marry in all States. It follows that the Court also must hold – and it now does hold – that there is no lawful basis for a State to refuse to recognize a lawful same-sex marriage performed in another State on the ground of its same-sex character.

Kennedy closed with a soaring statement on the importance of marriage. Of the Court's petitioners, he concluded: "They ask for equal dignity in the eyes of the law. The Constitution grants them that right" (*Obergefell*, 2015, pp. 48, 49).

With this decision, complete civil equality on marriage in all 50 states was achieved. Many ecstatic observers celebrated the marriage movement's rapid and surprising success. Sullivan, for instance, wrote: "I never believed this would happen in my lifetime. ... I never for a millisecond thought I would live to be married myself. Or that it would be possible for everyone, *everyone* in America" (2015, n.p.; emphasis in original).

Popular Culture, Celebrity, and Marriage

Over the past few decades in the US, there has been a dramatic change in public opinion and broad cultural shifts on marriage and LGBTQ rights (Fetner, 2016; Gates, 2017). Chauncey writes of gay and lesbian people: "[I]t is hard to think of another group whose circumstances and public reputation have changed so decisively in so little time" (2005, p. 166). He notes, particularly, that the public attitudes of young Americans have changed considerably and he attributes some of the overall shift to increasing personal familiarity with gay and lesbian people.[18] Chauncey notes that in 1985 more than 50 percent of Americans reported that they did not know a gay person. By 2000 that number had declined to about 20 percent. In 1985, just 22 percent of Americans reported having a close acquaintance or friend who was gay. That number jumped to 43 percent in 1994 and 56 percent in 2000. In just eight years, from 1992 to 2000, the proportion of Americans who reported having a family member who was gay or lesbian rose from 9 to 23 percent. It is clear that, as Chauncey writes, Americans were still quite ambivalent about homosexuality in general – with a "significant majority" still reporting "moral disapproval" by 2000 and 44 percent, in 2002, indicating that "homosexuality was an unacceptable 'alternative lifestyle.'" Yet this moral disapproval did not seem to get in the way of broad support for civil rights laws protecting gay and lesbian people from discrimination. In 2002, 86 percent of respondents believed that gay people should be granted "equal rights in terms of job opportunities" (2005, pp. 48, 55).[19]

On marriage specifically, attitudes also have shifted dramatically. Solomon writes that "support of this cause was historically remarkable." Pollsters had not "seen support grow like this, from 27 percent in 1996 to a solid majority in 2011, on any other social issue" (2014, p. 292). This was even the case in the decade or so between when marriage equality was recognized in Massachusetts and when it was legalized throughout the nation. While 59 percent of Americans had *opposed* marriage equality in 2004, just 10 years later 59 percent *supported* it (2014, p. 343). Solomon writes that this majority held in every region and that support had grown among Republicans and older Americans.

While we do not know much about the definitive reason for the shift in public opinion, and this is quite difficult to study effectively, many analysts and activists believe that some of it can be attributed to the fact that more gay, lesbian, and bisexual people have come out and are known to the people in their lives (Chauncey, 2005; Fetner, 2016). They also believe that some of the change in attitudes can be ascribed to the growing visibility of lesbian, gay, and bisexual people and their allies in pop culture. Historian and journalism professor Rodger Streitmatter, for instance, argues that we can look to popular culture to understand shifting attitudes about LGBTQ people: "The media have not merely *reflected* the American public's shift to a more enlightened view of gay people, but they have been instrumental in *propelling* that change" (2009, p. 2; emphasis in original).

For instance, television has been highly important in bringing familiarity with (at least some kinds of) gay people to viewers who do not necessarily have any out gay friends or family members. Chauncey writes of a new TV visibility from 1989, when the popular drama *thirtysomething* caused controversy and lost advertisers when it hinted at same-sex sex with a quick shot of two men in bed (doing nothing overtly sexual); when Ellen DeGeneres came out as gay on her situation comedy in 1997; and when the hit NBC comedy *Will & Grace* aired in 1998, with its gay title character Will Truman. "It would be hard to overstate," Chauncey writes, "how much this changed the dominant representation of gay people" (2005, p. 54).

The LGBTQ social movements of the past few decades have also opened up a space for celebrity activism on LGBTQ issues. Again, while we cannot show a direct causal link between celebrity involvement and a shift of public opinion, we can say that celebrities have been central in raising the visibility of the marriage movement and bringing it mainstream legitimacy. LGBT rights organizations mobilized celebrities nationally, with, for instance, the Human Rights Campaign's Equality Rocks effort, which relied on "prominent musicians – both American and international – who support committed gay and lesbian couples getting married."[20] In 2012, as Washington state considered a ballot initiative to legalize same-sex marriage, straight Seattle rapper Macklemore wrote, performed, and released an extended video (with Ryan Lewis and featuring lesbian singer Mary Lambert) of his gay rights/marriage equality anthem, "Same Love." Beyond its potential effects in Washington state, the song garnered extensive air play on pop and hip-hop radio stations around the country, reaching number 11 on the Billboard charts (Caulfield and Trust, 2013). Nominated for Song of the Year at the Grammys in January 2014, "Same Love" was performed as 34 same- and mixed-sex couples were legally married during the awards show (*Rolling Stone*, 2014). The song's video, which features a joyous wedding celebration between two men, has attracted more than 173 million views on YouTube to date.[21]

Pro-marriage equality celebrities were particularly visible in California's marriage fight. For instance, a number of high-profile celebrities teamed up to perform in Funny Or Die's video "Prop 8 – The Musical" at the end of 2008, with a commentary on the biblical reading of same-sex relationships, the separation of church and state, and the economic impact of banning same-sex unions (TrueBlueMarjority, 2008). After the passage of Prop 8 and after it had been challenged in court, Academy Award-winning screenwriter and LGBTQ and marriage equality activist Dustin Lance Black wrote a play called 8, which dramatized the trial. The play was performed in New York and in Los Angeles, with star-studded casts. Demonstrating the reach of Prop 8 and the extent to which the marriage fight has also been waged in the cultural realm, *8* was viewed online about 900,000 times within the first year it was made available. It has since been staged hundreds of times around the world, in local theaters and by school groups (Yoshino, 2015).[22]

Athletes, too – especially straight, male athletes in high-profile team sports like football – became vocal advocates for marriage equality. For example, Chris Kluwe, then-punter for the Minnesota Vikings, and Brendon Ayanbadejo, then of the Baltimore Ravens, made short videos in support of marriage equality through their state-level marriage equality organizations.[23] Ayanbadejo also wrote a piece for the *Huffington Post* called "Same sex marriages: What's the big deal?" (2009). He used his own biography, as the son of a Black father and white mother whose marriage was not legally protected until the 1967 Supreme Court ruling that struck down interracial marriage bans, to make the case for the right of same-sex couples to wed. He also actively took advantage of the platform he had as a professional football player on a winning team to raise visibility for the case of marriage equality. After his team, the Baltimore Ravens, made it to the Super Bowl in January 2013, he worked to mobilize the new visibility this success offered for the cause of marriage equality (Bruni, 2013).

Marriage, Privilege, and the LGBTQ Civil Rights Movement

Marriage politics birthed a number of new organizations focused specifically on the issue – such as Freedom to Marry and AFER. It also came to shape – some would say dominate – the agenda of many of the longstanding professional LGBTQ civil rights organizations, like the Human Rights Campaign. A symbol of mainstream organizing, HRC seemed to focus almost exclusively on marriage for a number of years, even bringing in Chad Griffin – California's marriage equality activist and AFER cofounder – as its president in 2012. HRC had long been criticized by movement activists on the Left. Its political agenda has been read by many as an effort to promote, in the words of one prolific HRC critic, "the equal treatment and civil rights of its mostly wealthy, mostly white, mostly straight-looking, mostly gay male major donor base" (Juro, 2004, n.p.; also see Vaid, 1995; Valentine, 2007; Ghaziani, 2008; Spade, 2011; Roberts, 2013). HRC took center stage in the marriage fight and, in the process, attracted a lot of criticism for the way its marriage campaigns seemed to privilege the visibility, experience, and demands of white, gender conforming, well-off gay men and their families. As writer Derrick Clifton (2013) noted critically, HRC "has been lent high legitimacy as the organization representing the entire movement" and, in this role, "has thrown almost the full weight of their strategy, fundraising moolah and public platform on the issue of marriage equality" (n.p.).

Many critics have framed the centrality of marriage in the political agenda of large, professionalized LGBTQ organizations as an effect of privilege that ignores substantial issues faced by less privileged LGBTQ people or that simply concentrates movement resources on an issue that disproportionately benefits privileged people. They view marriage as displacing a focus on issues such as the racism experienced by and perpetuated by LGBTQ communities, homelessness, and transgender justice (for discussion, see, e.g., Stein, 2013). Some also view the centrality of marriage to the mainstream LGBTQ movement as evidence and a symptom of the fact that the movement has become dominated by a few large LGBT civil rights groups that "have become the lobbying, legal, and public relations firms for an increasingly narrow gay, moneyed elite" – an "Equality, Inc." (Duggan, 2003, p. 45). This is both a concern about the substance of the movement's focus on marriage and a critique of the process of inclusion and decision-making around the national agenda, which many see as now being too top-down and dominated by a few players like HRC.[24]

On the limitations on marriage itself, law professor Katherine Franke writes about the complexity of the race politics of the marriage movement. One way in which the movement may have benefited the race/class-privileged is that the backlash against gains in LGBTQ rights disproportionately falls on LGBTQ people who face multiple forms of marginality. The marriage win, she argues, comes with a "price tag":

Gay people in Mississippi, Alabama, Georgia, Louisiana, Idaho, and Montana reported an increase in hostility in their communities that negatively tracked the success of the marriage equality movement nationwide. In their churches, workplaces, and at family dinners they often bore painful witness to religious conservatives' need to hold the line on marriage equality while the rest of the nation went to hell. This climate forced many gay and lesbian people, particularly people of color, even deeper into the closet. (2015, p. 191)

Wins on marriage, then, are not race-, class-, or location-neutral. Urban, white, gay, middle-class men are not, Franke argues, those who tend to suffer the backlash and pay the cost of the marriage movement's victories.

Others, however, have argued that to *reject* the institution of marriage is an expression of privilege. Rofes argues that not all LGBTQ people can afford to turn away the state-given benefits that come with marriage: "Smug middle-class gay activists have the economic and social capital that allow them to hold marriage as a distance, but many poor and working-class LGBT couples understand the legal, economic, and social benefits which would accrue to them once same-sex marriage is won" (2002, p. 151). There is also the finding from recent social science that provides complexity to the argument that marriage politics are just a reflection of privileged gay male interests: the finding that, relative to men, women enter same-sex unions in fairly substantial disproportionate numbers: "Marriage has gendered meanings, and the LGBT movement's campaign for marriage rights resonated especially with women" (Ghaziani et al., 2016, p. 176). Just as it did a generation earlier, before there was a viable marriage movement in the US or elsewhere, so marriage equality raises the larger questions of who benefits from LGBTQ organizing, who speaks for diverse LGBTQ communities, and what role the state should play in movements for social change.

After Marriage

When the nationwide marriage win was in sight, activists, writers, and a number of the mainstream LGBTQ civil rights groups began to ask: what comes next (see, e.g., Montgomery, 2015)? The HRC, for instance, published a lengthy report called *Beyond Marriage Equality*, which made a case for a focus on broad nondiscrimination laws concerning employment, housing, education, and public accommodations, among other domains. The report highlighted that only 18 states plus the District of Columbia have laws that explicitly prohibit public and private employment discrimination on the basis of sexual orientation and gender identity. Three additional states bar discrimination by sexual orientation but do not include gender identity as a category to protect transgender employees (HRC, 2015, p. 31).[25] There is, as of yet, no clear federal protection against workplace discrimination (Wolf, 2017). There has been some recent attention paid to the fact that LGBTQ nondiscrimination laws are not just a feature of large or coastal cities. One March 2017 analysis found that of the approximately 50 towns and cities that adopted nondiscrimination laws since 2015, *all* were in states that handed Donald Trump a victory in November 2016, and more than half had populations of 35,000 people or fewer (Stein, 2017).

Others, looking to a time when the marriage fight would be over, added that transgender rights should be a new priority in the broader LGBTQ movement (see, e.g., Capehart, 2015; Yoshino, 2015). Some on the Left called for the continued advocacy of a more liberationist agenda, one that would not rely on the state for the granting of justice and would celebrate difference and *queerness*, specifically (e.g., Stein, 2015). Historian Timothy Stewart-Winter (2015) wrote in the *New York Times* that queer people should leverage their historical role as outsiders for further social change – like trans rights, support for homeless youth, and Black Lives Matter – rather than abandoning this status once the marriage door had been fully opened: "Betraying our history – forgetting what it has meant to be gay – would be a price too high to pay" (n.p.). Some have urged, simply, that the marriage victory does not mean it is time to pack up the movement and go home to new spouses. Signorile argues that activists and optimistic community members suffered from "victory blindness": "the dangerous illusion that we've almost won" (2015, p. 1).

It remains to be seen where the LGBTQ civil rights movement will next put its energy and resources and how it will connect with the more radical, liberationist strand of the movement or with groups that focus specifically on intersectional identities. We can see, however, that marriage politics are exemplary of the longstanding tensions between liberationists and assimilationists (Ghaziani et al., 2016) and of the longstanding politics of privilege.

Marriage is a necessary civil rights gain. You cannot be free if you do not have the self-determination to love and partner and build a family. There is also some recent research that shows that the very existence of marriage equality laws may bring other societal benefits, like the reduction in suicide attempts among young people (Segal, 2017). But many LGBTQ critics of marriage as an institution and a strategy have noted that the win on marriage comes with costs. As Ettelbrick (1989), Warner (1999), and others have argued for decades, handing over regulation of intimate relationships to the state brings constraints.

In her articulation of this argument about state regulation, Franke writes that marriage carries with it "a new conception of new freedom and equality through a form of state licensure" (2015, p. 11). Divorce, for instance, is a *state*-regulated form of ending a romantic relationship (also see Bernstein, 2015). Married couples are not free to end their relationships any way they want. The state takes an interest in how they part. So, too, marriage also normalizes some kinds of relationships and pathologizes – even *criminalizes* – others. Non-monogamous marriages, for instance, run afoul of adultery laws that might make them illegal (Rhode, 2016). For partners who want to build alternative forms of intimacy not necessarily grounded in monogamy, marriage might bring new forms of criminality and marginalization. "[W]hen you marry," Franke argues, "the state acquires a legal interest in your relationship. Cloaking freedom in state regulation – as the freedom to marry surely does – is a curious freedom indeed, for this freedom comes with its own strict rules" (2015, p. 9).

5

LGBTQ Youth and Social Change

Generations of activists have done the work to open up a diverse and multifaceted space for LGBTQ social change. Since the national marriage win, mainstream LGBTQ civil rights organizations have been stepping up efforts at other forms of legal and policy change, like nondiscrimination efforts in employment, housing, and facilities (see, e.g., the 2015 HRC report discussed in chapter 4). Other LGBTQ activists have committed to intersectional work, through movements like Black Lives Matter (see, e.g., Garza, 2014; Moore, 2014). Still others are turning, like activists have done for decades before them, to other institutions that have a potentially large public reach and constituency. This chapter focuses on two of those institutions through the lens of youth: schools and media.

Teenagers and young adults are already central actors in the stories in this book. They were the soldiers during World War II who found each other and built vibrant lesbian and gay communities. They were catalysts at Stonewall, standing up to police brutality with strength, camp, and courage. They were on the front lines of ACT UP and Queer Nation, pushing the mainstream AIDS and gay and lesbian movements in more radical directions.

This chapter moves the clock forward a bit to focus specifically on young LGBTQ people since the 1990s. It turns to two examples that highlight the theme of this chapter, a theme that has been central to the book: that social movements are often oriented toward culture and changing hearts and minds rather than only changing law and policy. These movements focus primarily on changing *culture* and cultural institutions and on building new communities. In other places in the book, I have talked about the ways in which LGBTQ activists have turned to the law to make change and the ways in which there are limits to what legal and policy shifts can do. I also have highlighted the connection between legal and cultural change, when, for instance, movement activists believe that visibility and pop cultural representation help to pave the way for policy change, as in the case of marriage equality politics. I have also provided examples in which cultural action has been explicitly taken – a play performed, a television show written – in order to build mainstream visibility and empathy and, ultimately, policy change, as was the case with AIDS activism. Finally, we have encountered examples of times when activists have felt so alienated from their country and its mainstream institutions that they have carved out their own cultural spaces and communities, with no immediate hope or desire to impact mainstream change, as was the case with radical lesbian feminists in the 1970s. These relationships between legal/policy and cultural change have always been dynamic and complicated.

This chapter allows us to examine this relationship even further. I focus here on youth-focused and youth-driven social change efforts that have educational and cultural institutions as their starting place and their target of change and that I believe are at the forefront of current LGBTQ social change. The institutions that I focus on here are *schools* and *media*. I illustrate some of the ways that education and culture can be the site and focus of social change. There are so many examples of ways in which young people have organized for social change around gender and sexuality. I have chosen two that are national in scope and that allow me to illustrate in more detail how – in the current educational, technological, and pop cultural moment – LGBTQ social change occurs in and through culture, sometimes with the backing of law and policy, sometimes outside of it.

First, the example of Gay–Straight Alliances (GSAs) shows the connection between the state (in the form of public schooling and the laws that govern public schooling) and culture and community. Here we have an example of the ways in which LGBTQ young people and their allies are more active than ever before not just in their demands for safe spaces, broad tolerance, and equal treatment behind school doors, but also in asserting visibility in school and in youth communities. My second example is the It Gets Better Project, which allows for a discussion of media as a site of increased visibility for LGBTQ young people and young adults and an examination of a kind of community-building that happens outside formal institutions and that relies on modern technology to build visibility and community.

LGBTQ Young People in the US

Before we get to social organizing, we need some context. In August 2016, the federal Centers for Disease Control and Prevention (CDC) released the first nationally representative study to ask high school students about their sexual orientation, practice, and identity. This most recent version of the Youth Risk Behavior Survey found that approximately 8 percent – or about 1.3 million – of high school teens identify as gay, lesbian, or bisexual, and that others reported that they have had same-sex sexual contact but do not identify as L, G, or B (CDC, 2016a; Hoffman, 2016). A recent study estimates that 150,000 – or 0.7 percent of – young people aged 13 to 17 identify as transgender (Williams Institute, 2017). For young adults, the numbers are even larger. A study conducted just before the November 2016 presidential election found that while 12 percent of the total population identifies as LGBTQ, 20 percent of young adults aged 18–34 do so. The study found that 12 percent of young adults also identify as transgender or gender nonconforming (GLAAD, 2017).

For these young people, what is it like to be young and LGBTQ – in and out of school – these days? After more than half a century of activism designed to improve the experience of being a sexual or gender minority in the US, to what extent have young LGBTQ people reaped the benefits of these efforts?

Progress

Some social scientists tell an optimistic story. Among the most prominent is psychologist Ritch C. Savin-Williams. In 2005 he published a controversial and much-discussed book called *The New Gay Teenager*, in which he focuses on what he calls "same-sex-attracted" young people.[1] His argument, grounded in a strong methodological critique of past research on gay-identified young people, is that there has been a generational shift in the way that young LGB people view themselves and are viewed and treated by others. He celebrates the fact that young people today are "not embarrassed by gayness, don't consider it deviant, and see it all around them – on television, in movies, in songs, in cultural icons, among their friends" (2005, p. ix). These young people tend not to identify with the "gay" label:

> The new gay teenager is in many respects the *non*-gay teenager. Perhaps she considers herself to be "postgay," or he says that he's "gayish." . . . They have same-sex desires and attractions but, unlike earlier generations, new gay teens have much less interest in naming these feelings or behaviors as gay. (2005, p. 1; emphasis in original)

It is not that these young people deny or are ashamed of their attractions, Savin-Williams argues. They are, rather, "more resilient than suicidal. . . . They're adapting quite well, thank you" (2005, p. 3). Ultimately, he predicts that gay identity will become obsolete, and that the sheer "*ordinariness*" of same-sex-attracted young people will prevail (2005, p. 216; emphasis in original).

Additional research on the identity of young people finds a kind of flexibility to youth identity and porous gender and sexual boundaries. Psychologist Lisa M. Diamond finds that for young women (teens and young adults), in particular, the development of sexual attraction and orientation are characterized by "dynamic variability," "fluidity," and a nonlinear approach to adopting labels and identities over the course of a young lifetime (2007, pp. 152, 153). In his sociological investigation of current "post-gay" politics and identity, Ghaziani finds that LGBTQ college students may privilege a kind of "building bridges" to straight classmates and a downplaying of their gender and sexual identity, "a strategy of de-emphasis that mutes distinctions between gay and straight" (2011, pp. 117, 114). Recent research also points to the creative complexity of the sexual and gender identity of young people. One study finds that young adults aged 18–34 "appear more likely to identify in terminology that falls outside those previously traditional binaries" of both sexuality and gender (GLAAD, 2017, p. 4).

Some researchers have also argued that schools themselves are changing for the better. A provocative study that has received attention in the US was conducted by English sociologist Mark McCormack. It finds that straight-identified boys and schools in the UK, in particular, have moved beyond the kind of homophobia that may characterize their counterparts in the US. Through a study of three English high schools, McCormack tells a "good-news story" (2012, p. xxv). He finds that the straight-identified boys in his study were affectionate and emotionally demonstrative with each other, that they eschewed blatant homophobia and rarely used homophobic language, and that they generally did not fear being perceived as gay.[2] This behavior in young straight men, McCormack argues, signals the "redefining [of] heterosexuality and masculinity for their generation." Not only are they not homophobic, but these young men are actively "gay friendly – espousing pro-gay attitudes, being inclusive of gay students, condemning homophobia, and having close friendships with gay students," which, in turn, helps to create "gay friendly high schools" (2012, p. 123; emphasis omitted). Like Savin-Williams, McCormack credits pop culture and social media with at least part of this shift.

Others who have examined the experiences of young LGB people have similarly found that things are changing for the better – even if not across the board or all at once. Writer Benoit Denizet-Lewis (2009), for instance, profiled a number of middle school students all over the US who identified as gay, lesbian, or bisexual and were out to friends, family, teachers, and classmates. He notes that these young teens came from all over the country – Oklahoma, Texas, Michigan – not just the more liberal coastal cities. While these young people faced homophobic bullying and ignorance, they also found supportive parents: moms who chaperoned a weekly dance for gay kids in Tulsa or a Midwestern dad who accompanied his son to his first Pride parade.

From the US popular press, we also now hear good news stories of young LGBTQ people who have the support to come out and to thrive in their schools and communities. There is the moving story of the trans guy whose fraternity raised money for his surgery when his insurance would not cover it (D. Collins, 2017). There is the happy story of Brad Taylor and Dylan Meehan, boyfriends from Carmel, New York, whose "cutest couple" yearbook superlatives photo went viral when their friend posted it to her Tumblr (Garcia, 2013). There is the brave story of Mitch Anderson, from small-town Texas, who took the opportunity of his graduation speech to come out publicly to his classmates and their families (Belonsky, 2013). There are the heartwarming stories of young trans women in Massachusetts, California, and Missouri who became prom or homecoming queens of their high schools (LGBTQ Nation, 2013; Steinmetz, 2014; Garner, 2015). There is, too, the inspiring story of a Girl Scout troop in Colorado that admitted a 7-year-old transgender girl, according to the organization's policy of inclusiveness, despite the threat of a Girl Scout cookie boycott from some anti-LGBTQ activists (Hetter, 2012) and the Boy Scouts' change in membership policy in 2017 to become trans-inclusive (Grinberg, 2017). There is the story that seemed to be everywhere of straight-gay male friendships, embodied in the "promposal" story in the spring of 2015 about a straight-identified boy who asked his gay best friend to prom (and earned them both a spot on Ellen DeGeneres's talk show, where they were each presented with a check for $10,000). The straight boy made the invitation by posting a sign in his school hallway that read: "You're hella gay, I'm hella str8, but you're like my brother, so be my d8?" (Ermac, 2015).

Continuing challenges

Despite these promisingly uplifting stories, many still find that schools can be incredibly tough places for LGBTQ young people. Sociologist C.J. Pascoe (2007) found that teachers still fail to correct their students' homophobia and even participate in homophobic joking, banter, and culture-building. Teachers also tend to maintain a heterocentric and heteronormative culture in their classrooms and their school, upholding views of mixed-sex couples as normal and natural and same-sex couples as either deviant or nonexistent (also see Biegel, 2010). For example, a school administrator in the Northern California school that Pascoe studied forced a self-identified lesbian student to cover up a "Nobody Knows I'm a Lesbian" t-shirt because, as the student understood it, the administrator worried that it promoted same-sex sex.[3] At the same time, the school's rituals celebrated and showcased presumably heterosexual sex and sexuality in many ways. Tellingly, no one intervened when a senior boy walked around school in a shirt that read "One of us is thinking about sex. It must be me" (2007, p. 68). Some of the self-identified straight boys Pascoe studied said they would never go to a prom that they thought would be attended by an out gay and gender nonconforming male classmate. Even a well-meaning teacher created a kind of "shrine to heterosexuality" through a prominent classroom photo display of exclusively male/female couples dressed for the school's proms and other formal celebrations (2007, p. 31).

Other academic studies support Pascoe's portrait of schooling (see, e.g., Macgillivray, 2004). In addition, we now have very good national data on the health and school experiences of young people who identify as LGB and T, which reveal that there is still much work to be done. The Gay, Lesbian & Straight Education Network (GLSEN) conducts regular studies of the climate of elementary and secondary schools for LGBTQ youth. GLSEN's most recent survey of elementary school students and teachers found that almost half of elementary school students (46 percent) and teachers (49 percent) reported that they heard phrases like "that's so gay" or "you're so gay" used as epithets at least sometimes in their schools.[4] These young students report that name-calling and bullying that target gender performance and perceived sexual orientation are common in their schools. This bullying has an impact on both the happiness of elementary students at school and also their educational performance.

GLSEN's report of secondary schools is even more grim.[5] The organization's 2015 survey of more than 10,000 LGBTQ-identified young people concluded that, while school climate seems to be slowly improving, "[s]chools nationwide are hostile environments for a distressing number of LGBTQ students, the overwhelming majority of whom routinely hear anti-LGBT language and experience victimization and discrimination at school" (Kosciw et al., 2016, p. xvi). GLSEN found that 57.6 percent of students reported feeling unsafe at school due to their sexual orientation, while 43.3 percent felt unsafe due to their gender expression. Homophobic and transphobic remarks from both teachers and students were common in schools. Of those surveyed, 58.8 percent regularly heard homophobic remarks and 40.5 percent regularly heard transphobic comments. More than half of the students reported that their teachers or other staff at their schools made homophobic remarks (56.2 percent) or transphobic remarks or negative comments about gender expression (63.5 percent). A CDC study confirms the disproportionate levels of bullying for LGB students when compared with their non-LGB peers: 34 percent of LGB students reported that they were bullied at school and 28 percent reported that they were bullied online, compared to 19 percent and 14 percent, respectively, of their straight peers (CDC, 2016a).

The negative school climate created by both young people and adults in schools seriously harms students both academically and emotionally. Students who reported that they were targets in their schools missed more school, had lower grades, and more frequently reported that they did not plan to continue their education beyond high school (Grant et al., 2011; Robinson & Espelage, 2011; Kosciw et al., 2016). The CDC (2016a) reported that more than 10 percent of LGB students had recently (within the previous 30 days) missed school because they feared for their safety.

Breaking down the L, G, B, and T a bit, we see that bisexual students face specific challenges. A 2012 Human Rights Campaign survey of more than 10,000 LGBT-identified young people looked at the 3,808 respondents who explicitly identified as bisexual and at their experiences in and out of school (Andre et al., 2014).

While the report is not broadly comparative, it does indicate that bi-identified young people are comparatively less happy and less likely to indicate that they have a caring or supportive adult in their lives than their gay and lesbian peers. They also tended to be out in smaller proportions to family, peers, and teachers.

For young people who identify as gender nonconforming, genderqueer, and transgender, schools can be especially tough places. These students tend to feel comparatively quite unsafe and more targeted for harassment (Grant et al., 2011; Kosciw et al., 2016). Anti-trans harassment and violence in schools is also more pervasive for trans students of color (Grant et al., 2011). Even when schools do have policies and programs in place to protect and support LGBTQ students, these often focus primarily on sexual orientation and tend not to be geared specifically to trans and gender nonconforming students (McGuire et al., 2010). Anti-trans perpetrators in schools include teachers as well as students. Jenifer K. McGuire and colleagues found that "harassment of transgender youth was pervasive in schools" (2010, p. 1185) and that teachers are just as likely to make problematic comments as they are to intervene when students make these comments. In a national study of transgender Americans, 31 percent of respondents reported that they were harassed by teachers or staff in their schools (Grant et al., 2011).

It is important to understand how other forms of marginality impact the experience of LGBTQ young people in schools. For instance, studies have found that there are some racial/ethnic differences in the way that LGBTQ students experience school. This is an area where more scholarship is needed. Savin-Williams (2005) indicates that young gay people of color may feel more positively toward school than their white gay peers and may not feel any more negatively toward school than their straight peers of color. GLSEN has called for further research on the intersection of racial and sexuality/gender but has found, overall, that, students who identify as Asian/South Asian/Pacific Islander and as Black or African American report feeling relatively safe and feeling victimized less with respect to sexual orientation than students of other racial/ethnic groups (Kosciw et al., 2016). A 2014 study by GSA Network and Crossroads Collaborative, however, found that the intersection of racism and anti-LGBTQ bias means that young LGBTQ people of color face substantial challenges in school and that they perceive that they are targets of disproportionate disciplinary action in school (Burdge et al., 2014; Klein, 2014). Media attention tends to focus overwhelmingly on the harassment, abuse, and suicides of white LBGTQ youth, ignoring the ways in which young people of color are victimized in their schools and how this impacts their engagement with and success in school (Moodie-Mills, 2011). We are also just beginning to focus on how other forms of victimization and marginality, like high rates of homelessness, impact LGBTQ youth (Choi et al., 2015).[6]

No current discussion of the experiences of being young and LGBTQ should ignore the tragic fact that there have been too many suicides to list. The Trevor Project reports that young people who identify as lesbian, gay, or bisexual are four times more likely than straight youth to attempt suicide and these attempts are four to six times more likely to require medical treatment than the suicide attempts of straight peers.[7] The 2016 CDC report found that more than 40 percent of LGB-identified students had "seriously considered" suicide and 29 percent had attempted it in the year prior (CDC, 2016a). This scholarly work supports the public narrative that LGBTQ-identified young people are more likely to consider, and even attempt, suicide than their straight and nontransgender (cisgender) peers.[8] One recent study of 96 transgender young people aged 12 to 22 found that 30 percent had attempted suicide at least once (Peterson et al., 2016; also see Grossman & D'Augelli, 2007).[9] Another comparative study of more than 13,000 middle and high school students in Wisconsin found that bisexual-identified young people, in particular and relative to gay- and lesbian-identified youth, are at high risk of suicide. This study found, for example, that "although less than half of 1% of straight-identified students reported thinking seriously about killing themselves 'almost all of the time,' 5.6% of bisexual-identified students reported doing so" (Robinson & Espelage, 2011, p. 320).

Laws and policies

When it comes to legal protections for young LGBTQ people, progress has been slow, but there have been important gains in this aspect of the LGBTQ civil rights movement. The 1996 federal appellate court ruling in *Nabozny v. Podlesny* was a legal turning point. In this case, Wisconsin student Jamie Nabozny sued his school district for failing to protect him against years of anti-gay abuse by his classmates and his teachers. For the first time ever, at that late date in the mid-1990s, a court ruled that districts and their administrators were responsible for upholding gay students' Fourteenth Amendment rights of equal protection and could be held liable for allowing anti-gay harassment and discrimination (Griffin & Ouellett, 2003; Macgillivray, 2004; Biegel, 2010). Since then, activists have successfully pushed a number of states to pass laws that specifically protect students from bullying, harassment, and discrimination on the basis of sexual orientation and/or gender identity. According to GLSEN's most recent state data, 18 states plus the District of Columbia have anti-bullying and -harassment laws that protect LGBTQ students; 14 states plus DC have anti-discrimination laws that specifically protect LGBTQ students by making it illegal to discriminate on the basis of sexual orientation and gender identity – of these, only Wisconsin does not include gender identity in its nondiscrimination law (GLSEN, n.d.(a); Percelay, 2015).

At the federal level, at the time of writing, a pair of proposed laws – the Student Non-Discrimination Act (SNDA) and the Safe Schools Improvement Act (SSIA) – would protect LGBTQ students. These laws were endorsed by President Obama and a number of advocacy groups but have not yet made much progress in Congress. In April 2014, the US Department of Education clarified that Title IX of the Education Amendments of 1972, the law that makes sex discrimination illegal in education programs that receive federal funding, also applies to gender identity (Percelay, 2015). A letter was issued in May 2016 offering "significant guidance" on policies and best practices for protecting the rights of trans students (US Department of Justice, 2016). The Obama administration also began enforcing Title IX to protect the civil rights of transgender students and transgender student athletes. As we will see in chapters 6 and 7, these protections are severely endangered by Donald Trump's presidency.

States run the gamut in their approach to LGBTQ students and issues in school. Some states maintain and continue to endorse "no promo homo" laws, a general term for laws that prohibit teachers from introducing and discussing LGBTQ issues in public schools in any way that might be construed as positive. Currently, eight states have these laws on the books (GLSEN, n.d.(a)). Other states have taken expansive action to support and protect LGBTQ young people. California, for instance, enacted the FAIR Education Act (also known as Senate Bill 48) in January 2012 to extend the state education code so as to ensure that the social and historical contributions of LGBTQ people are included, alongside those of many other groups, in California's curricula (California Department of Education, n.d.; Equality California, n.d.). In addition, ten states so far – California, New Jersey, New Mexico, New York, Oregon, Illinois, Vermont, Rhode Island, Connecticut, and Nevada – plus the District of Columbia, have taken further steps to protect LGBTQ young people by banning harmful "conversion therapy" (a practice developed by the Religious Right in the 1990s to "cure" same sex-desires) for youth (Avery, 2017). Under President Obama's leadership, there had been momentum to ban this treatment at the federal level by defining such "therapy" as consumer fraud (Ames, 2015). But the future of this federal action may be up in the air, given that the 2016 Republican Party platform has been read as supporting – in a thinly veiled way – such therapy (Stack, 2016b).

Young People Changing Their Schools: GSA Organizing

Gay–Straight Alliances (GSAs) provide one example of the ways in which young people, with the support of school staff, have organized for LGBTQ social change. They also provide an example of the ways in which schools themselves, as organizations, have been shaped by youth leadership and have developed to support the changes that are necessary to become responsive to and inclusive of LGBTQ young people. GSAs are a youth-led response to institutional problems. As we will see, they have yielded some important – albeit sometimes limited – positive results for their members and their schools. Despite their limitations, GSAs are an important and increasingly common example of young people taking the initiative to change the culture of an institution that is so central to their lives. It is also important to situate this form of organizing historically. It is difficult to imagine the existence of an LGBTQ youth movement for changing the culture and institution of schooling without the fights of the previous generations, the movements that began in secret because leaders who acted on behalf of the state depicted gay people as dangerous and sick and passed laws to serve this diagnosis. Anita Bryant worked to "save our children" from, in her view, predatory homosexuals who needed to recruit in order to grow their ranks. Now, young people organize for themselves in schools.

Before GSAs: support in schools

GSAs were not the first form of support for LGBTQ young people or in schools. Parents and Friends of Lesbians and Gays (PFLAG) was started in New York City in 1973 by a small group of parents to support their gay and lesbian kids (Chauncey, 2005). Pat Griffin and Mathew Ouellett identify a few "historically groundbreaking" programs in schools that were founded in the 1980s, before there was much programmatic or policy focus at all on LGBTQ young people (2003, p. 109). New York City's Harvey Milk School, which opened in the mid-1980s as a project of the Hetrick-Martin Institute, was a public school designed specifically to serve gay and lesbian students who chose to attend (also see Marcus, 2002). On the other side of the country, in 1985, Project 10 began in one school in Los Angeles and then grew to serve the entire school district. Project 10 provided counseling and support in schools for gay and lesbian students. The program, founded by teacher and counselor Virginia Uribe, was likely the first in-school support program in the traditional public schools for LGBTQ students (Miceli, 2005).

As Griffin and Ouellett (2003) recount, the end of the 1980s saw an increase in educators' attention to the experience and the needs of gay and lesbian young people. This was prompted in part by the 1989 publication of a US Department of Health and Human Services study of teen suicide. The study did not focus specifically on gay and lesbian youth, but it did indicate that gay- and lesbian-identified young people were two to three times more likely than straight youth to attempt suicide. Advocates used this statistic to urge policymakers and educators to focus directly on supporting gay and lesbian students. In the early 1990s, as educators and academics increasingly turned to the needs of gay and lesbian young people in and out of schools, advocacy took the form of a focus on safety, inclusion, and civil rights.

The first GSAs

One of the first groups in the country to call itself a Gay–Straight Alliance was started in Massachusetts in 1988 at Concord Academy, an elite private school with an unsupportive – even hostile – leader, according to the GSA's co-founder (Jennings, 2006). At the time, GLSEN's eventual founder, Kevin Jennings, was a young gay teacher at Concord. A straight student with a lesbian mom approached Jennings about starting a club to combat homophobia at the school, which she called the "Gay–Straight Alliance." At the same time, Phillips Academy Andover, another elite Massachusetts boarding school, had founded its own GSA under the leadership of teacher Kathy Henderson. Soon Jennings was taking calls from other private schools that were interested in the work he and students were doing at Concord. Within a couple of years, Jennings's partner had founded the first public school GSA, at Newton South High School in the Boston suburbs.

The early GSAs in Massachusetts spread – primarily through teacher exchanges – throughout the state, and they helped to shine a spotlight on the experiences of lesbian and gay students. The work of Jennings and others garnered the attention of policymakers in Massachusetts in the early 1990s and led to hearings, in the fall of 1992, in which students from around the state testified about their experience of being lesbian and gay in their schools and homes. This work also led to the development of a report offering a series of recommendations on how to ensure that these young people would be safe in their schools. In early 1993, the state board of education and the governor of Massachusetts created the first public program of its kind in the country, Safe Schools for Gay and Lesbian Students (Jennings, 2006; Sadowski, 2016). The work of Jennings and his colleagues also resulted in the founding and growth of the national organization that would ultimately become GLSEN (Miceli, 2005). In 1998, GLSEN began registering and connecting GSAs throughout the country. At around the same time, youth worker Carolyn Laub founded the Gay–Straight Alliance Network of California, first in San Francisco in 1998 and then statewide by 2001. The organization now has a national reach (see "Change the Nation," n.d.). Like Project 10 and the early GSAs in Massachusetts, GSA Network grew out of the actions and awareness of students themselves (GSA Network, n.d.; Miceli, 2005).

GSAs and the law

As GSAs began to spread throughout the country, a number of districts attempted to block their formation. Some even argued – before the national decriminalization of sodomy with the 2003 Supreme Court *Lawrence v. Texas* decision – that GSAs promoted an illegal activity (sodomy), and therefore did not have a right to exist. After many legal fights, often helmed by the ACLU and Lambda Legal, students won the right to start these clubs in their public schools, with the same benefits and resources as other student clubs (Miceli, 2005; Biegel, 2010). Their legal argument was that banning some non- or extracurricular student-initiated clubs and not others, for whatever reason, is a violation of the Equal Access Act. This act, a federal law since 1984, had been championed by conservative Christians who wanted to ensure that students' religious clubs could meet on public school campuses. The law requires that any secondary school that receives federal funds must allow *all* or *no* noncurricular student clubs on campus and provide equal access to school resources.

Ultimately, a case brought in Salt Lake City, Utah, on behalf of students who had attempted to start a GSA, resolved the legal issue in 2000. It established that the Equal Access Act clearly mandated that GSAs could *not* be banned in public schools as long as the school or district supported any other noncurricular clubs. The ruling ensures that any such group be student-initiated and student-led. As Jennings explained: "What's very important to understand is that gay–straight alliances have a legal right to exist only if they are formed and led by students. So, you know, if they are organized by an outside group they lose the legal protections granted to them under the Equal Access of 1984" (Miceli, 2005, p. 110).

GSAs in practice and impact

Sociologist Melinda Miceli (2005) writes that the youth-led GSAs are more directly political than Project 10 or other counseling models had been before them. Their focus has been on youth agency, building community within a school, safety, visibility, and changing school culture. She argues that the word *gay* in the group's title is an explicitly political move to increase the visibility of gay students within schools. The explicit inclusion of *straight* students has helped to legitimize and grow the movement by bringing in those who "might otherwise feel that the problems of LGBT students are of no concern to them" (2005, p. 193). Best estimates are that there are now more than 4,000 GSAs across the country (Toomey et al., 2011; Sadowski, 2016). To be more inclusive, some groups now include *transgender* in their name, and some use *queer* rather than *gay* as their umbrella term (GLSEN, n.d.(b)).

Researchers and advocates have found positive, if somewhat limited, impacts of GSAs on young people in schools. These studies tend to find that it is the *presence* of a GSA rather than individual *membership* in the club that impacts student experience. One study found that the presence of a GSA in the school "may increase the subjective experience of safeness" for students, broadly speaking, but may not actually impact the "prevalence of victimization." Students also reported that they had "better grades and were less likely to skip school because of fear" due to GSAs. Specific membership in the GSA, however, did not seem to impact feelings of safety or students' "likelihood of skipping school" (Walls et al., 2010, pp. 325, 326). Another study, which looked at the longer-term impact of GSAs on LGBT young adults, confirmed this positive impact of GSA *presence* on "young adult psychosocial well-being and educational attainment," including college attainment (Toomey et al., 2011, p. 180). GLSEN confirms a range of positive benefits to the presence of a GSA. In general, students in schools with GSAs heard fewer homophobic and transphobic remarks, felt safer and less victimized, felt that school staff and students intervened more when they heard anti-LGBTQ comments, and overall felt a stronger sense of belonging in their schools (Kosciw et al., 2016).

GSAs have also been valuable to young people's political and leadership development, serving as spaces where members can develop a sense of "politicized consciousness" and "activist identity" (Mayberry, 2006, p. 27). Miceli argues that this is an unequivocal achievement of GSAs: "One of the GSA movement's most significant achievements is that it produced a new generation of political activists to fight for the civil liberties of LGBT citizens" (2005, p. 229). For instance, straight participants learn how anti-LGBTQ discrimination impacts their peers and they gain a sense of their own straight privilege through their involvement. And GSA participants also report that the activism that had been nurtured through their GSA involvement would continue beyond high school.

GSA limits and challenges

GSAs also have limitations. A study of 22 Massachusetts high schools with GSAs, for instance, found that the alliances typically operate to promote student "safety" and "tolerance" of student gender and sexual diversity but do not explicitly confront issues of privilege or encourage a "more comprehensive examination of heterosexism and gender oppression and their effects on all members of the school community" (Griffin et al., 2004, p. 21). Miceli's (2005) interview study with GSA student participants and faculty advisors found that GSAs had a limited impact on curbing institutionalized homophobia and heterosexism and that they often failed to attract large numbers of LGBTQ students, who might have feared being labeled with a stigmatized identity by joining their school's club.

Access to GSAs is also a challenge for many students. In the mid-1990s, Salt Lake City employed the tactic of banning all extracurricular student clubs rather than allowing GSAs in the district's schools (Jennings, 2006; Mayberry, 2006; Eckholm, 2011). More recently, other districts have considered this strategy, as well, and 14.1 percent of LGBTQ students surveyed by GLSEN report that they could not freely promote or form a GSA in their schools. GLSEN also found that just over half of the students surveyed had GSA-like clubs at their schools. Access varied greatly by age, with just 14.5 percent of middle schoolers reporting that their schools had GSAs versus 61.2 percent of high schoolers (Sieczkowski, 2013; Kosciw et al., 2016).

GSAs are not equally accessible to all students and do not impact all LGBTQ-identified students in the same way. The GLSEN survey found that students in small towns and rural areas have significantly less access to GSAs, with 31.4 percent of these students (versus 62.6 percent of urban and 63.0 percent of suburban students) reporting the presence of a GSA in their school (Kosciw et al., 2016). Miceli (2005) found that working-class students and students of color do not have as much access to, and do not participate at the same rates in, GSAs as their middle-class and white peers. Participation may be especially low among students of color who attend schools in which they are in a racial majority, while one study of 13 GSAs in Massachusetts found that students of color who are GSA members indicated lower levels of perceived support from their GSA when compared with their white peers (Miceli, 2005; Moodie-Mills, 2011; Poteat et al., 2015). Access to

GSAs may also be lower for immigrant students (Toomey et al., 2011). A study of the school experiences of transgender students found that it was particularly important for trans youth that their GSAs work specifically to be trans-friendly and inclusive (McGuire et al., 2010; also see Sadowski, 2016).

It may also be the case that GSAs are heavy on the "S" students and may not, therefore, be reaching the "G" students and other sexual and gender minorities. Miceli quotes Jennings in 2003 as saying about the GSA space: "I think they've become the kind of place where if you're young and you're different, you go. It's kind of a way of solidarity. I think the majority of young people involved in GSAs are straight-identified" (2005, p. 118; also see Poteat et al., 2015).

These limitations vary by chapter and by organization, and there is still a lot we do not know about the differences between GSAs. Miceli (2005), for example, argues that the GSA Network has provided an explicit focus on youth leadership development and activism, on the inclusion of bisexual and transgender students, and on race/class diversity in GSAs. GSAs are changing with the politics of the time and with student interests. This is clear from the organization's new name and tagline, which it changed in April 2016. The new name became Genders & Sexualities Alliance Network with the new tagline "trans and queer youth uniting for racial and gender justice" (GSA Network, 2016). GLSEN, too, has responded to concerns about access and inclusion. Its online support for GSAs includes resources for trans-inclusivity and awareness about gender nonconformity and gender diversity and resources for the recognition of Black History Month and Native American Heritage Month.[10] Miceli also notes that, dating back more than a decade, GLSEN has responded to concerns about lack of focus on racial diversity and intersectionality by sponsoring programming and providing resources about race and for students of color.

Media, Visibility, and Community: The It Gets Better Project

LGBTQ pop cultural visibility

In the story of LGBTQ social change, art, media, and pop culture have been central and complicated actors. Art has been mobilized for community-building, identity development, and for speaking truth to power, as we have seen in everything from the homophile magazine in the 1950s to the poetry of Audre Lorde in the decades that followed, to *Rent* in the 1990s. Art and popular culture also have been employed to marginalize and pathologize LGBTQ people. As Russo wrote in his groundbreaking book on the subject, looking back at a time when LGBTQ and gender nonconforming characters were either hidden or tragic or truly terrible caricatures: "The history of the portrayal of lesbians and gay men in mainstream cinema is politically indefensible and aesthetically revolting" (1987, p. 325). Lesbians, gay men, and gender nonconforming characters appear in American film through its history as suicidal, homicidal, or as utterly laughable. "[H]omosexuals," Russo observed, "are essentially buffoons who soothe an audience's sense of superiority by portraying gays as weak, powerless sissies" (1987, p. 219). These portrayals have been a way to, as Gamson argues, continually achieve a "redrawing of the lines between the normal and the abnormal" (1998, p. 5; also see Seidman, 2002).

As a result of the social movements of the past few decades and significant changes in general attitudes about gender and sexuality, the mainstream media representation of LGBTQ people has changed substantially (see, e.g., Streitmatter, 2009). Over the past few decades, those in my generation – children of the 1980s and early 1990s – experienced the first real critical mass of positive gay and lesbian characters, storylines, and artists. About TV, in particular, scholar Ron Becker notes that there was a "startling increase of gay-themed programming on prime-time network television in the 1990s" (2006, p. 3).

For me, personally, consuming mainstream and basic-cable pop culture during the 1980s and 1990s meant that I took full advantage of this new lesbian, gay, and gender nonconforming visibility. Prince, in all his purple genderbendiness, provided my soundtrack as I started high school. I adored Rickie Vasquez on *My So-Called Life* in 1994, "primetime's first gay teenager," according to *Entertainment Weekly*.[11] That same year, I mourned the passing of the incredible young AIDS activist, Pedro Zamora, from MTV's *The Real World: San Francisco*. A few years later, I rooted for Jack McPhee on *Dawson's Creek* to get kissed by his handsome prom date. As I was becoming a young adult, Will Truman and his best friend Grace Adler were the hip Manhattan professionals whose work lives, friendships, and romances filled my first apartment with laughter. Moving just slightly out of the mainstream, I found other iconic shows, artists, and characters. I crammed for my Women's Studies finals to the music of the Indigo Girls, Tracy Chapman, Melissa Etheridge, and Ani DiFranco. I became intimately connected to the young queer characters who were moving into adulthood in their various communities and navigating jobs, love and sex, health, their families, and their tight-knit groups of friends. *Rent* debuted on Broadway in 1996 and became my rallying cry. *Queer as Folk* then *The L Word* on Showtime brought the lives of more gay and lesbian young adults into my life through paid premium cable.

These were among the best-known young queer and LGB pop cultural figures of my generation. There were not many of them, their portrayal could be read critically as problematic in a number of ways (see, e.g., Schulman, 1998; Gross, 2001; Seidman, 2002; Becker, 2006), and they did not nearly represent the full diversity of LGBTQ communities. Becker, for instance, argues about TV in the 1990s: "most gay-themed programming was used to appeal to an audience of socially liberal, upscale, white heterosexuals who prided themselves on being gay-friendly" (2006, p. 212). And, as sociologist Suzanna Danuta Walters reminds us in her book about the complexity of LGBTQ visibility, "cultural visibility" is not the same as "inclusive citizenship" and all the civil equality that implies (2001, p. 10). But, these artists were adding their voices, their experiences, and their political points of view to the mainstream. These characters were three-dimensional, loved, and *out*. In this way, they were speaking back to their tragic, tortured, and pathologized counterparts that Russo (1987) wrote so eloquently about a generation before.

Moving ahead by a few years, the television show *Glee*, in my view, is especially noteworthy for its popularity and its reach. I spend a bit of time on it here as an example of the kind of mainstream pop cultural representation of LGBTQ young people – and the critical acclaim it has received – that we encounter these days.

This show, with storylines that revolved around gender and sexual diversity and its universal theme of finding community in shared outsiderness, struck a chord for many and became wildly popular. In its six-year run, *Glee* and its actors were nominated for more than 150 awards, including 17 Primetime Emmys (four of which they won), 10 Golden Globes, 4 Screen Actors Guild Awards, and 6 GLAAD Media Awards (for LGBTQ representation).[12] *Glee* won Golden Globe awards for best comedy twice. Cast members performed for the President of the United States, and *Glee* has been credited with the growth of school arts programs worldwide (Goldberg, 2015). One of the show's central couples, Kurt Hummel and Blaine Anderson, landed the cover of *Entertainment Weekly* in January 2011 for a story called "Gay Teens on TV" (see "This week's cover," 2011). Chris Colfer, the actor who played Kurt, was named one of *Time Magazine*'s 100 most influential people in the world in 2011 (Agron, 2011). That same year, the series spawned a *Glee* movie, which was part concert footage and part testimonials from young people who have felt empowered by the show. The most popular actors from the show – like Darren Criss who played Blaine – have a huge number of fervently devoted social media followers.

Glee gave us the broad story arc of a relatively racially diverse group of suburban, Midwestern misfits who banded together via their school's glee club to take control of their high school experience, to gain self-acceptance, and to triumph over the bullies of the world. The show, which ran from 2009 to 2015, featured a number of LGBTQ characters and storylines. Kurt was tormented by McKinley High's football team, struggled to come out as gay in school, and was being raised by a sweet, supportive, widowed dad. We saw him fall in love over duets and lattes with Blaine, the out gay crooner from the rival glee club who liked sports and who was incredibly self-assured and not at all tortured by his sexual orientation. Kurt and Blaine were physically affectionate. They lost their virginity on the show. They ultimately got married. *Glee* also gave us two gay football players: Dave Karofsky, bully turned bear cub, and Spencer Porter, who described himself as "postmodern gay" and was kind of a jerk until he realized his inner musician. *Glee* also gave us one of the only prominent young bisexual characters on TV, Brittany S. Pierce: cheerleader, dancer extraordinaire, girlfriend to many over the years, and wife, eventually, to lesbian cheerleader Santana Lopez. Over the run of the show, *Glee* also introduced two transgender characters and storylines: Unique Adams, who landed at McKinley after a stint in a rival singing group, and the football team's Coach Beiste, whose story of transition from Shannon to Sheldon became a substantial focus of the show's last season.

Glee portrayed and confronted homophobia and transphobia in a number of ways. The show portrayed it as *individual* and blatant, by depicting multiple incidents of bullying and name-calling; as *subtle*, for instance, in multiple storylines about self-doubt and self-hate; and as *institutional*, by exposing the way that schools like McKinley failed to protect bullied students or neglected to include information about sex and relationships among same-sex couples in their sex education curricula. The show became a vehicle for queer visibility, through a "born this way" message around natural variation and diversity in sexuality and gender; an advocate of marriage equality through its story-lines; and a support for young people struggling with suicidality (see, e.g., Kinser, 2012).

There are now many other groundbreaking mainstream characters, shows, artists, and pop cultural moments for and about young LGBTQ people. In fact, there is no way to write about these without being almost instantly outdated. They include hip-hop and R&B singer Frank Ocean acknowledging that his first love was a man; Lady Gaga, the international phenomenon with (at latest count) more than 69 million Twitter followers, identifying as bisexual and a strong LGBTQ advocate, and penning perhaps *the* pride anthem of recent years: "Born This Way"; young Justin Suarez, on *Ugly Betty* sharing a first kiss with a male friend turned love interest; the straight boy-gay boy and straight girl-lesbian girl best friendships on MTV's *Faking It*; gay R&B singer/songwriter Jamal Lyon from FOX's hit show *Empire*; and one of the only out HIV positive young characters on TV in recent days, Eddie, from HBO's *Looking*. Deserving of special mention is *The Fosters*, a television show that centers around a multiracial family headed by two women. The show has featured two out trans characters (played by trans actors Tom Phelan and Elliot Fletcher) and a wildly popular romance between two 13-year-old boys who had possibly the "youngest same-sex kiss" on television in the spring of 2015 (Mandell, 2015; Ross, 2015).

This representation is by no means perfect. The LGBTQ movement has paid attention to pop cultural representation by doing a regular accounting of the diversity – broadly defined – of TV and film characters over time, under the assumption that more diverse visibility is good for the broad LGBTQ community. When Queer Nation activists engaged in a high-profile and sustained protest of the blockbuster movie *Basic Instinct* in 1991 and 1992, they were objecting to the portrayal of the homicidal lesbian and bisexual characters (Beale, 1992; Cunningham, 1992; Signorile, 2003). These murderous women who loved women were a trope – the kind of narrow LGB characterization that had become standard by that time. With simply *more* LGBTQ characters and with broader diversity – in terms of sexuality, gender, gender identity, race, class, location, age, and ability status – there is simply greater scope to tell more varied LGBTQ stories and to raise the visibility of a broader range of LGBTQ-identified people. This allows for wider identification with characters and in storylines, none of which individually bears the weight of representing an entire LGBTQ identity. The one homicidal lesbian character does not have to stand in for *all* lesbians; she can be just one of a wide range of diverse lesbian characters out there in popular culture. While sheer *numbers* of any one kind of character do not tell the whole story of representation, they do help to reveal the possibility of more varied and complex kinds of characters and storylines.

With this assumption about diversity undergirding its work, the Gay and Lesbian Alliance Against Defamation has been working since 1985 to serve as a media watchdog for the portrayal of LGBTQ people (Faderman, 2015). The organization publishes an annual accounting of LGBTQ characters in TV and film. For the 2016–17 television season, GLAAD's (2016b) latest TV study found that 4.8 percent of series regulars – 43 characters – on scripted primetime network TV were LGBTQ, and 92 series regulars on scripted primetime *cable* were LGBTQ. An additional 28 and 50 LGBTQ characters were in *recurring* roles on broadcast and cable, respectively. LGBTQ representation of regular and recurring characters is weighted toward men: 56 percent and 54 percent of these characters are men on scripted primetime broadcast network and cable respectively. Among these LGBTQ regular and recurring characters, 42 percent are people of color on networks and 25 percent are people of color on cable. In the three forms of television that GLAAD examined – scripted programming in broadcast, cable, and streaming TV – 30 percent of the 278 total LGBTQ regular and recurring characters were bisexual and 6 percent – 16 total characters – were transgender.

While GLAAD indicates that television is making progress with respect to LGBTQ representation, its latest study of films released from major Hollywood studios in 2015 observes that: "Hollywood films lag far behind other media when it comes to portraying LGBT characters, cementing the industry's reputation as [comparatively] outdated" (2016a, p. 4).[13] GLAAD found that there were 126 film releases by the major studios in 2015, and that only 17.5 percent of them included LGBT characters and only one was identified as "trans-inclusive." Of the 47 identifiable LGBT characters in these films, the significant majority was male (77 percent) and white (72.3 percent).[14] GLAAD found, as well, that "[t]he majority of LGBT characters in mainstream films remain minor characters" (2016a, p. 9).

Pop cultural representation provides visibility for LGBTQ

young people. It also provides the opportunity for young people to build identity and community (Driver, 2008; Gray, 2009; Ito, et al., 2010). We see the ways in which young people interact with these old forms of media – television, music, and film – in innovative ways through new media that allow them to actively make and maintain connections via shared passions and identities. It just takes a quick check of Twitter, Tumblr, and any number of old or new media platforms in recent years to realize how connected young people have become to these stories, characters, and pop cultural figures and how readily young fans have built online communities to share their reactions to their favorite characters and storylines. This is particularly true now, in this age of social media, when fans have relatively easy access to building virtual communities around their shared fandom. This "participatory approach toward new media" both "provide[s] a site for kids to exercise agency and authority" and "provide[s] kids with a space to negotiate issue of identity and belonging within peer cultures" (Ito et al., 2010, pp. 10, 9).

The It Gets Better Project

The It Gets Better Project is an important example from recent years of the mobilization of pop culture and media for LGBTQ social change. In the fall of 2010, in response to a number of high-profile suicides of both teens who self-identified as gay and teens who had been bullied because they were perceived to be gay, author and activist Dan Savage created the It Gets Better Project. Savage noticed that, while he was an invited speaker to many college campuses, he was never invited to middle and high schools. "[S]chools," he wrote, "would never invite gay adults to talk to kids; we would never get permission." He realized, though, that he did not need the approval of school gatekeepers because he could reach young people directly through social media: "[I]n a world with YouTube and Twitter and Facebook – I could speak directly to LGBT kids right now. . . . I could look into a camera, share my story, and let LGBT kids know that it got better for me and it would get better for them too. I could give 'em hope" (2011, p. 4).

Savage enlisted his husband, Terry Miller, in making an eight-minute video for the project, with the simple message that life gets better after high school and that suicide is too permanent a solution to the temporary problems of youth. The video tells Savage's and Miller's own stories: how they were both mercilessly picked on and bullied at school, but how they later grew into productive and happy adults, husbands, and fathers. They talked about their happy moments as dads – snowboarding with their son, being with him as the sun came up over Paris on a family vacation – and they urged young people to survive high school so that they could get to joy and fulfillment in adulthood. Savage urged: "However bad it is now, it gets better. . . . Your life can be amazing. But you have to tough this period of it out, and you have to *live* your life, so that you're around for it to get amazing. And it can and it will." Miller counseled: "If you can live through high school . . . you're going to have a great life. . . . So just stick it out. It's painful now, but it's going to get so much better." They did not claim to have a universal story, but they believed that telling their individual stories might have an impact on young people who could not see beyond their current pain.[15]

Savage writes that the traffic generated by responses to his video crashed his computer within hours of its posting. That video has now been viewed on YouTube more than two million times. A second video followed within a day and, within a week, one thousand It Gets Better videos had been posted, following Savage's model. Within a month, Savage's computer crashed again after then-President Obama posted his own It Gets Better contribution. Savage wrote optimistically of the project's impact: "The It Gets Better Project didn't just crash my computer. It brought the old order crashing down" (2011, p. 5):

[T]he old order . . . fell apart when the It Gets Better Project went viral. Suddenly, gay, lesbian, bisexual, and transgender adults all over the country – *all over the world* – were speaking to LGBT youth. . . . Soon straight people – politicians and celebrities – were talking to LGBT youth, too, delivering the same message: It gets better, there's nothing wrong with you, and we're working to make it better. (2011, p. 6; emphasis in original)

The campaign gave some evidence to young people, who might be feeling isolated in their own lives, that they were not alone.

The It Gets Better movement has become a mainstay in the LGBTQ movement for youth. Users have created more than 50,000 videos, which have been viewed more than 50 million times.[16] A wide range of videos have been posted by LGBTQ and ally politicians and political leaders, performing artists, activists, staffs of major brands and companies, sports teams (including baseball's Tampa Bay Rays and the athletic department of New York University[17]), everyday people, and a huge number of celebrities – including those associated with many of the LGBTQ-friendly television shows of recent years. In 2011, Savage and Miller edited *It Gets Better*, a book that includes a collection of essays, a resource guide, and a series of testimonials designed to speak to and support young people.

Tragic moments in the It Gets Better Project's history underscore that whatever pop culture can offer, it may have a limited ability to change the conditions of people's individual lives. Some of the young people who created It Gets Better videos later took their own lives: bullied 19-year-old EricJames Borges, for example (Grindley, 2012) and bullied 14-year-old Jamey Rodemeyer (Hughes, 2011), who, quoting Lady Gaga, mentioned the support he had received on his video.[18]

There also has been criticism of the project. Walters writes that some see it as a glossy and "trendy" celebrity campaign that is simultaneously too pessimistic and too optimistic:

> On the one hand, it posited gay youth as inherently in crisis, always on the brink of abuse or self-annihilation. So, in that sense, it painted an overly *gloomy* picture of what it is like to live as gay (or trans or bi) in the world as we know it. And on the other hand, it painted an overly *rosy* picture of adult queerness, fully embraced, successful, freed of the ugliness of anti-gay animosity. (2014, pp. 254–255; emphasis in original)

Walters further notes that the project does not fully confront the privilege inherent in Savage and Miller's story and the message that "it gets better." The many privileges of two white, urban, cisgender, American, professional men afforded them options that many others could not count on in their own lives. However, Walters's overall assessment is that the project is "mercifully more expansive and complicated than its originator, Dan Savage" (2014, p. 255), in that the forum it provides allows the space for the telling and dissemination of *many*, varied stories, not only those of Savage and Miller.

In his work, Savage regularly argues that coming out is one of the most radical things that LGBTQ people can do, and that visibility changes both public opinion and creates connection with friends and family members who might otherwise hold a negative abstract view of LGBTQ people. As Signorile has said: "Everyone must come out of the closet, no matter how difficult, no matter how painful. . . . If they [the people in our lives] don't know that we're queer – if they think only the most horrible people are queer – they will vote against us" (2003, p. 364).

The It Gets Better Project is a form of organizing in this vein. It is a pop cultural, media-reliant response to social inequality – a form of organizing that depends on new media for coming out, community-building, visibility, and changing the way that LGBTQ people feel about themselves and experience their lives. In this form, celebrities work to leverage their platform to promote self-acceptance and to provide role models, and non-celebrities tell their stories for their own healing and celebration and to reach across the ether to make connections to others. Project organizers do their work in the hope that isolated young people will seek out and find others like them across the globe to assuage their sense that they are alone in their experience. They hope that communities will develop to steel themselves against despair and that an intergenerational conversation will allow young people to look beyond their immediate experience to imagine possible futures.

Hearts and Minds

In this chapter, we have seen how young people engage in nonstate-focused forms of mobilization. We have seen how pop cultural representation for visibility and community has increased; and we have seen examples of self-determined forms of organizing, in GSA and in online communities built around fandom and around social media campaigns like It Gets Better.

LGBTQ movements have long focused on opening up the state, changing laws, and increasing protections for people who have been historically demonized as dangerous outsiders. These movements also have been about building alternative communities, outside the reach of the state. And, they have been about changing hearts and minds, where the stakes are both personal and political. Art and popular culture have been there in each of these endeavors. As Rupp and Taylor argue, forms of art and culture that can be understood to be intentionally political "are capable of winning a hearing for serious political purposes precisely because of their entertainment value" (2003, p. 3). Drag shows – in their case – and so many other forms of entertainment and pop culture attract an audience that might *not* participate in a political rally or visit a political site online and that certainly might not share a marginalized identity with those on stage or on screen. They buy a ticket or turn on the screen for entertainment, and they come to have an emotional connection and reaction to the entertainment they are consuming. In the process, by connecting with the cultural work, their identities and values around gender and sexuality are challenged and often changed.

January 8, 2017 was the last Broadway performance of the Tony Award-winning musical, *The Color Purple*. The show is based on Alice Walker's 1982 novel by the same name. Celie is a young, poor, African American woman in rural Georgia at the beginning of the twentieth century who has been repeatedly sexually and otherwise physically abused by the men in her life, including her stepfather and her husband. The show is a story of her growing independence and ability to fight back. It is also a story of her love for Shug Avery, the glamorous singer who is Celie's husband's longtime girlfriend. Shug and Celie share an intimate friendship that is, at least for Celie, also a romantic and sexual connection. The musical includes many numbers that are triumphant and soaring celebrations of the strength, kinship, and beauty of the show's Black women protagonists. One of Celie's show-stoppers, sung by a performer so talented that words really cannot do her justice, Cynthia Erivo, is the song "I'm Here" in which she asserts her power, humanity, and perseverance. She belts the ending of the song, singing "I'm beautiful" and "I'm here," and it brings audiences to their feet.

At the musical's last performance, Hillary Rodham Clinton and her family were in the audience. As they walked to their seats in the theater, they were met with a spontaneous, sustained, joyous standing ovation and applause that delayed the show by a number of minutes. Audience members in the diverse crowd screamed "I love you, Hillary!" and "thank you, Hillary!" Her presence in the audience was, of course, a reminder of the recent presidential election. It also primed the audience to experience the show as a form of collective grieving for the election, a reaffirmation of strength in a time of fear and anger over the Trump presidency, and the building of community through art – even if just temporarily at the Bernard B. Jacobs Theatre on 45th Street. The numerous standing ovations during the show (I was there, seeing the show for the third time), and the feeling of utter electricity in the theater could be attributed to the fact that it was the last performance of an incredible production. It could also be understood as a reflection of what Clinton's presence meant to the audience, and what it meant to respond to Clinton's loss with a show like *The Color Purple*. This healing and reassertion of power, too, for a community that feels besieged – this confirmation of *being here* and *being beautiful* – is also what art and popular culture can do.

6

The "B" and the "T"

These days, we use "LGBTQ" as a pan-identity label, and we often do not think about the unique politics, history, and experience of each of the individual "letters." In this chapter on the "B" and the "T," we turn to the people of the broad label who are most frequently left out of the politics and the history of the mainstream movement. It is here – in trans politics, bi politics, and the challenges these pose to the broader, mainstream movement – that we can see the LGBTQ movements going in new directions but also coming out of and building in response to longstanding tensions and divisions among activists and their politics. Politically, these two identity groups by no means *necessarily* share political interests, and there are both important intersections and fraught historical relationships between bisexual and transgender people and politics (Eisner 2013; Burleson 2014). But bi- and trans-identified people and communities *do* share the experience of being erased, marginalized, and sometimes completely abused by lesbian and gay movements of the past half-century. In this chapter, we see the ways in which *exclusion* and *privilege* have operated within the broad movement. We also see, in most recent years, the ways in which trans politics, in particular, have become more of a focal point for the mainstream LGBTQ movement and a target of the Right.

Just a note about definitions in this "B" and "T" discussion: First, it is important to note that gender categories – like *transgender* – and sexual categories – like *bisexual* – are not mutually exclusive. Bisexuality refers to sexual orientation, while transgender refers to gender identity. And people vary widely in the way they understand and make meaning of the various parts of their identity, and definitions of social categories are historically specific and change with time. So, of course, a person can identify as both bisexual *and* transgender. My separation of these identities for this chapter is for the purpose of discussing politics and efforts for social change that have been mobilized around one of these identities or another.

A good working understanding of bisexuality comes from Robyn Ochs, a bisexual activist and writer, who offers a popular definition that has been widely adopted among bi writers and activists: "I call myself bisexual because I acknowledge in myself the potential to be attracted, romantically and/or sexually, to people of more than one sex, not necessarily at the same time, not necessarily in the same way, and not necessarily to the same degree" (2009b, p. 9). This definition recognizes that gender may be multiple, not just binary, and that bisexuality can mean the capacity for a range of romantic and sexual attractions over the course of a lifetime. It also recognizes that one's relationship to people of different genders – capacity for sexual attraction or romantic connection – may not be equal. Another recent reinterpretation of the "bi" in bisexual is the attraction to one's *own* gender and *other* genders.

The meaning of *transgender* can be complicated and quite varied. The Latin prefix "trans" means *across* or *through*, and "transgender" has become "a catchall term for gender variation" (Stryker & Currah, 2014, p. 6). It has been in broad use as a political and identity term since the early to mid-1990s (Valentine, 2007; Stryker, 2008; Williams, 2014a). As with any broad identity marker, some people appreciate the power and collective nature of the umbrella label, while some feel it skates over too many differences and complexities (for discussion, see Davidson, 2007; Valentine, 2007).[1]

A number of other identity markers either fall under the trans umbrella or exist in relationship to it. *Transsexual* is still sometimes in use and generally refers to a trans person who has undergone medical (often surgical) transition of some kind. It is less broad than the "transgender" umbrella term (see, e.g., Meyerowitz, 2002). In addition, many people prefer not to identify with the binary male/female gender designations or even the "trinary" male/female/transgender model (Beemyn & Rankin, 2011, p. 166). For example, 6 percent of the sample of respondents in the 2008 National Transgender Discrimination Survey identified as genderqueer (Harrison et al., 2011/2012) and 35 percent of respondents on the 2015 National Center for Transgender Equality's national survey identified primarily as *non-binary* or *genderqueer* (James et al., 2016).[2] Genderqueer is an identity that challenges the male/female binary as well as what some see to be the maintenance and reproduction of the binary by some trans people themselves. These identity labels are often set against the term *cisgender* (from the Latin prefix meaning "on this side of"). Cisgender refers to people who are not transgender and whose gender identity matches the sex they were assigned at birth. Use of the term cisgender is a way to depathologize trans identity and to denaturalize cis identity and experience (see, e.g., Aultman, 2014). It calls attention to the social privileges that come with the alignment between birth-identified sex and gender identity.

The Historical Fight for Bi Inclusion and Visibility

In the late 1940s and early 1950s, when noted biologist and sex researcher Alfred Kinsey developed a scale along which to measure human sexual attraction and sexual behavior, he moved the understanding of human sexuality from a *binary* (hetero/homosexual) to a *spectrum*. As noted in chapter 2, his finding that many more people than had previously been assumed had had same-sex sexual experience made headlines and turned his books into bestsellers. He famously wrote of the sexual binary for men: "Males do not represent two discrete populations, heterosexual and homosexual . . . The world is not to be divided into sheep and goats" (Carey, 2005, n.p.; also see Garber, 2000; Angelides, 2001). But while there was relatively widespread bisexual *practice*, there was not yet widespread bisexual *political identification*, and bisexuality as an identity was largely left out as the full-fledged movement for gay and lesbian equality grew through the middle of the twentieth century. In fact, bisexual identity may even have been an early casualty of the post-Stonewall movement. As one scholar recently noted: "One of the byproducts of the gay liberation movement is this . . . solidifying of the [sexual] binary" (quoted in Allen, 2017, n.p.).

Bisexual exclusion worked differently and held different meaning for men and women in the post-Stonewall era. While there is little written about this, some posit that, historically, the political relationship between gay and bisexual *men* has not been particularly fraught. One explanation for this, as Armstrong offers, is that for gay men, generally, their identity has not been strongly connected to the *rejection* of women and women's spaces. So, "when gay men are with women it poses less of an identity threat" (1995, p. 209).

The political rift between lesbian women and bisexual women had its roots, in part, in the homophobic exclusion of lesbians from mainstream feminist organizing in the 1960s and early 1970s, as we saw in chapter 2, and in the sexism of the general American culture and of the gay rights movement. Some theorize that, in response to their exclusion, some lesbian feminists developed the assumption that lesbianism – more specifically, women in intimate relationships with *each other* rather than with men – was *better* feminist practice and was an important response to both a mainstream feminism that excluded lesbian-identified women and the sexism of mainstream American culture (Armstrong, 1995; Udis-Kessler, 1995). From some lesbian feminist perspectives, particularly white radical feminist lesbians, bisexuality represented a problematic connection to men and male privilege. For some, it connoted a wavering commitment to both feminism and queer women's liberation (for discussion, see Armstrong, 1995; Rodríguez Rust, 2000a; Rust, 2000). From this point of view, at a time in the 1970s when lesbian feminists were developing "women's culture" and turning to "cultural feminism" in the form of alternative institution-building (Echols, 1989; Stein, 1997), bisexual women and their potential intimate connection to men represented a threat to the entire community (Udis-Kessler, 1995).

This negative view of mixed-sex love, desire, and connection was not the case, however, for everyone within the burgeoning social justice movements of the 1960s. Historian Paula Giddings argues that Black women activists during the 1960s, for instance, generally did not feel the need or desire to separate from men in their activist work and did not see Black men as a primary source of oppression in the way that many white feminists viewed white men and patriarchy. Their analysis of racism, Giddings writes, generally drew them to collaborate with Black men and to view men as generally being more victimized by the intersection of racism and sexism than they themselves were (1984, ch. 17; also see hooks, 1984).

During the heady post-Stonewall moment of the 1970s, bisexual organizing began – and flourished – with the founding of groups like the National Bisexual Liberation Group in New York City, the Bisexual Center in San Francisco, and Chicago Bi-Ways (Donaldson, 1995; Trnka with Tucker, 1995; Udis-Kessler, 1995; Yoshino, 2000; San Filippo, 2013; Burleson, 2014).[3] Early social and political bi organizing accompanied a 1970s pop cultural focus on bisexuality in the popular press. In May 1974, *Newsweek* ran a story called "Bisexual chic: Anyone goes," which noted the American Psychiatric Association's recent removal of homosexuality from the Diagnostic and Statistical Manual of Mental Disorders (DSM), quoted folk singer Joan Baez on her relationship with a woman, and obliquely referenced Rolling Stones front man Mick Jagger. Such coverage raised bisexuality as a popular *trend*, separating it from and possibly even working *against* a political understanding of it, but raising the visibility of bisexuality as an identity and a practice. The article quoted a Vassar sophomore who had previously had relationships with women and who sounded as if she could just as easily have been talking about the rising popularity of bell-bottom jeans or Birkenstocks: "Coming out into the straight world blew my mind . . . But everybody does bisexuality now. It's really big" ("Bisexual chic," 1974, pp. 554–555).

While singers David Bowie and Janis Joplin and other pop cultural icons gave bisexuality a new popular cache in the mainstream, when the 1970s gave way to the horrible days of the AIDS crisis in the 1980s, the narrative blaming bisexual men for the spread of AIDS to heterosexual people dramatically changed the status of bisexuality. Within straight America, a prevalent narrative was that bisexual men had been the conductors of HIV and AIDS to straight women and communities, the "'gateway' through which HIV could spread from the gay population into the heterosexual population" (Rodríguez Rust, 2000c, p. xiv). Just as gay men had been framed as the menacing dangers of the McCarthy era and of Anita Bryant's campaign to take away civil rights protections, so bisexual men emerged as the demonized other in the age of AIDS.[4]

Gamson cites an example of this 1980s narrative, describing how activists protested the proposed script of an episode of an NBC television series, *Midnight Caller* for a storyline that played to this portrayal of bisexual men: "In that script a bisexual man with AIDS purposely infects others and is shot and killed in the end by one of his female partners. It was objected to by ACT UP members as playing on 'the great fear of the "killer queer"'" (1989, p. 360). AIDS, as we saw in chapter 3, was largely ignored as long as it was identified primarily with gay men, for whom mainstream media, policymakers, and the general public showed little concern. But a narrative of the virus crossing over to heterosexual people featured the image of menacing bisexual men.

Both biphobia within the broader movement and the vilification of bisexual men in mainstream American culture that accompanied the early days of AIDS provided a catalyst for the growth of the bisexual movement in the 1980s. As one bisexual activist who was also an HIV/AIDS educator said: "As horrible as it is, I think AIDS brought bisexuality out of the closet" (quoted in Tucker, 1995, p. 54). The possible role of bisexuality in the spread of AIDS, however problematic this narrative, also increased *academic* focus on bisexuality and bi identity through the 1980s (Rodríguez Rust, 2000d; Burleson, 2014). On the activist front, bi political organization continued to thrive, with a focus on visibility and community-building. In the mid- and late 1980s, activists founded hundreds of local and college-based bi-specific groups (Hutchins & Ka'ahumanu, 1991; Trnka with Tucker, 1995; Serano, 2010).

The growth of a national lesbian and gay movement in the late 1980s and early 1990s, as we saw in chapter 3, also provided an important political opportunity for bisexual activists. The 1987 National March on Washington for Lesbian and Gay Rights was a turning point in bi visibility and political organizing (Udis-Kessler, 1995). A statement by two organizers of a bi contingent of march participants asserted the need to articulate an *explicitly* bisexual identity and presence: "We can't let gays represent us in D.C. We have to go there ourselves, as bisexuals, to speak openly and vociferously as a separate and vital contingent. We must achieve some visibility on our own terms instead of passing as heterosexuals or gays. It's a matter of pride, and survival" (quoted in Hutchins & Ka'ahumanu, 1991, p. 365). The occasion of the march and the failure to include bisexuality in its name led to unprecedented national and international bi organizing. By 1993, when the next national march took place in the capital city, bisexuality had gained a place at the national political table. Bi activists and their supporters made a successful case for a name change for the upcoming march: it was ultimately called the March on Washington for Lesbian, Gay, and Bi Equal Rights and Liberation. By the mid-1990s, as well, campus organizing had become central to bi organizing, and there were more than 1,000 bi-focused groups (campus and otherwise) in the US.[5]

The Historical Fight for Trans Inclusion and Visibility

People who exhibit gender nonconformity or complicate the gender binary have long been the subject of derision and harassment and have suffered as targets of medical, psychological, and legal intervention.[6] For instance, a number of nineteenth- and early twentieth-century American laws made cross-dressing illegal. One 1863 San Francisco law made it a misdemeanor for a person to appear in public "in a state of nudity, or in a dress not belonging to his or her sex, or in an indecent or lewd dress" (Stryker, 2008, p. 32). Like gay and lesbian people who fought against being defined as "sick" after World War II, so transgender and gender nonconforming people have fought against medical and psychiatric pathologizing.[7]

"Gender scientists" (Califia, 1997, p. 52) have played a complicated role in relation to gender nonconforming people for generations – from the earliest advocacy and medical practice of German sexologist Magnus Hirschfeld, who introduced the term "transvestite" in 1910; to the development, in mid-century, of expansive treatment in the United States by German endocrinologist Harry Benjamin, who had worked with Hirschfeld in Germany and moved to the US in 1913; to the debate among experts in the middle of the twentieth century about the role that surgery and psychotherapy should play in the diagnosis, treatment, and support of transgender people (Meyerowitz, 2002; Stryker, 2008).

Christine Jorgensen inspired a cultural turning point in American transgender visibility and the politics of medicine/psychiatry (Stryker, 2008). The ex-soldier, who had been assigned male at birth, commanded international media attention in the early 1950s after her medical transition. The *New York Daily News* first reported Jorgensen's story in December of 1952, under the headline "Ex-GI Becomes Blond Beauty." The then-performer drew more attention in 1959 when she applied for a license to marry her male fiancé, which was denied in New York City because she could not adequately satisfy concerns that she was, in fact, female. As historian Joanne Meyerowitz wrote: "With the Jorgensen story, the floodgates broke. A torrent of new stories on other transsexuals made sex change a constant feature in the popular press" and popular culture (2002, pp. 52–53).

It was around this time, in the 1960s, that scientists began to separate *gender* variation and *transsexuality*, a term developed at this time, from both homosexuality and forms of intersex. An early focus on *gender identity* came from the "rise of university-based sex change programs during the late 1960s and early 1970s" (Stryker, 2008, p. 93). The term Gender Identity Disorder (GID) was added to the American Psychiatric Association's DSM in its fourth edition in 1980. Among its diagnostic criteria is the following: "A strong and persistent cross-gender identification" and "persistent discomfort" with one's birth sex "or sense of inappropriateness in the gender role of that sex" (quoted from the 2000 DSM update, in Stryker, 2008, pp. 14–15). In 2013, the fifth edition of the DSM replaced GID with the designation *gender dysphoria*, a diagnosis that signifies "a marked difference between the individual's expressed/experienced gender and the gender others would assign him or her" (quoted in Engdahl, 2014, p. 267).[8] Associated with these designations, protocols and standards of care developed that have informed the medical and psychiatric treatment of trans people since Dr. Benjamin's time in the mid-twentieth century.[9]

Within the political movements of the time, new gay and lesbian organizations in the post-Stonewall years confronted the politics of gender identity and the existence of trans- and gender nonconforming people, as well. In one particularly evident case of privilege and intra-movement division, some radical feminists – lesbian and otherwise – came to articulate and defend a particularly exclusionary politics. Within the broader feminist and lesbian movements, those who practice personal and political transphobia and transmisogyny[10] have come to be known as "trans-exclusionary radical feminists," or TERFs. In the late 1970s, the TERFs built their feminism and lesbian activism around what critics would identify as a very narrow definition of what it meant to be a woman. Julia Serano (2007) and Susan Stryker (2008) both relate this important history; Stryker writes that some feminists in this period perpetuated the "'transsexual rapist' trope" (2008, p. 105). This trope represented trans women as nefarious, conniving false women who used their purported male privilege and their bodies to figuratively "rape" women by taking their bodies. Janice G. Raymond's 1979 *The Transsexual Empire: The Making of the She-Male* (reissued in 1994) remains the exemplary and foundational TERF text (Califia, 1997). Raymond completely discounted transgender women and their authenticity, labeling them "male-to-constructed-females" throughout the book and writing: "Rape, of course, is a masculinist violation of bodily integrity. All transsexuals rape women's bodies by reducing the real female form to an artifact, appropriating this body for themselves" (1994, pp. 103–104).[11]

The example of TERF politics that I want to spend some time on here is the Michigan Womyn's[12] Music Festival – Michfest – an iconic annual gathering in the Michigan woods. I include this example not because I believe that feminists have been historically any *worse* in their treatment of trans-identified people than others who are outside these political movements, but because I believe this offers a well-known and highly contentious example of the ways in which privilege and exclusion work *within* the broader LGBTQ movement.

In 1976, Michfest became a center of lesbian feminist culture and community building (Taylor & Rupp, 1993). Founded and organized by Lisa Vogel, the festival, in Vogel's words, "has been the crucible for nearly every critical cultural and political issue the lesbian feminist community has grappled with for four decades" (Ring, 2015, n.p.). For decades, Michfest continued to draw thousands of women and a wide range of performers (Greenfield, 2006). It was, according to Vogel, "a space to gather in celebration and exploration of the experiences of females . . . a welcoming space for revolutionary womyn and girls who personify a broad spectrum of gender" (2014, n.p.). This kind of community – emblematic of the kind of alternative cultural institutions that the lesbian and gay movement produced in the 1970s – developed out of a felt need for safe space, separate community, self-determination over bodies and relationships, and celebration of a kind of culture that was not represented in the American mainstream or in the male-centered gay movement at the time.

Michfest always was exclusive to women and was intentionally a women's space, even designating separate childcare for boys between 5 and 10 years of age and separate camping areas for women who brought their boy children (who must not be older than 10) (Michfest, n.d.). Vogel demonstrated her view that there is a fixed essence to womanhood by signing on to an open letter in 1977 that read, in part: "We do not believe that a man without a penis is a woman any more than we would accept a white woman with dyed skin as a Black woman" (Williams, 2014b, n.p.).

In a high-profile incident in August 1991, trans woman Nancy Burkholder was near-forcibly removed from Michfest under cover of night. She was told that the festival was for "natural, women-born-women" only and that trans women were not allowed or welcome, for their own safety and for the safety of other festival attendees (Williams, 2013, n.p.). This became a "catalyzing moment" in the movement to oppose TERF practices and to support trans inclusion in feminist spaces, both within and outside the festival (Valentine, 2007, p. 180; also see Stryker, 2008; Beemyn, 2014). One local response in the following years was Camp Trans, a camp set up by trans people and their allies across the road from Michfest that worked to build awareness among Michfest attendees that this beloved festival was excluding trans women. Camp Trans participants' slogan became: "Camp Trans: For Humyn-Born Humyns" (Serano, 2007; 2013; Williams, 2014b).

In addition to the Michfest example, intra-LGBTQ movement trans exclusion has taken many forms over the years. Lesbians, bisexual people of all genders, and transgender people of all sexual orientations have long condemned the mainstream LGBT rights movement for marginalizing gender politics. Critically coined the "GGGG" movement by Eisner (2013), the name refers to the movement's focus on just the Gay Gay Gay Gay in its aim to be palatable to mainstream people and voters. In particular, the critique highlights the lack of attention to gender and gender identity politics. For example, even as bisexual activists were beginning to claim a place in the national LGBT movement in the early 1990s, winning the right to be included by name in the 1993 national march, transgender activists were still explicitly excluded (Ghaziani, 2008). Even just including trans people explicitly by name was controversial. The march's organizing committee voted down a proposal for trans inclusion in the march's title (Stryker, 2008).

In another central example of intra-movement trans exclusion, the behemoth LGBT civil rights organization, the Human Rights Campaign, has long been criticized for casting aside trans people in the legal fight for nondiscrimination legislation and hate crimes protections. The controversy around HRC's relationship to trans people and politics centered for years on the proposed Employment Non-Discrimination Act (ENDA), a federal bill targeting workplace discrimination that had been stalled almost every year in Congress since 1994. Iterations of the bill, until 2007, focused on sexual orientation and did not include protection for gender identity (National LGBTQ Task Force, n.d.). By 2007, as trans-inclusivity became more of a norm in the broader movement, hundreds of LGBT groups supported a trans-inclusive ENDA, making HRC an outlier (Heywood, 2008; Stryker, 2008; Roberts, 2013). Instead, HRC was willing to support a bill that was gaining traction in the House but explicitly left gender identity protections out. The then-president of HRC, Joe Solmonese, claimed that political expediency was called for in the name of incremental gains: "What was best for our community was that the bill pass rather than fail. Sometimes it is hard for people to see the whole picture, but sometimes you are faced with choices" (Heywood, 2008, n.p.; also see Juro, 2013). In this case, we see a mainstay of the LGBT civil rights movement willing to make political gains at the expense of continued trans exclusion, to make civil rights headway on sexual orientation protections while leaving gender identity discrimination firmly in place.

Current Bi Marginalization and Response

But what about now? Does the broader American LGBTQ movement still exhibit cisgender privilege and a kind of monosexual privilege by excluding, erasing, or marginalizing bisexual and transgender people? And does mainstream American culture erase, ignore, or devalue the "B" and the "T" more than the "L" and the "G"?

The numbers vary, but bi-identified people make up a sizable proportion of the broader LGBTQ community. The Williams Institute, compiling data from five US-based surveys conducted in recent years, found that approximately 1.8 percent of US adults identify as bisexual, while 1.7 percent identify as lesbian or gay.[13]

The numbers are much higher for those US adults who report any experiences of "same-sex sexual behavior" (8.2 percent) or same-sex attraction (11 percent) (Gates, 2011, p. 1). An early 2016 report on recent national survey data of adults ages 18 to 44 found that the proportion of both men and women who explicitly identified as bisexual has risen in recent years: from 3.9 percent of women and 1.2 percent of men in 2006–10 to 5.5 percent of women and 2.0 percent of men in 2011–13 (Copen et al., 2016).[14] A recent study of young people under the age of 30 in the US puts these numbers even higher: 31 percent of respondents indicated that they were not "100% heterosexual" (Cruz, 2015, n.p.).

Yet, despite these numbers, there is evidence that bisexuals may experience more invisibility, prejudice, and discrimination (than their gay and lesbian peers) from both gay and straight people (Denizet-Lewis, 2014). In part, at least, because bi identity can be stigmatized in both straight and gay and lesbian communities, bi people also are less likely than gay men and lesbians to be out to anyone in their lives (Movement Advancement Project et al., 2014). A Pew study found that only 28 percent of those surveyed responded that "all the important people in their life know they are bisexual," while 71 percent of lesbians and 77 percent of gay men reported they were out to the same core group (cited in Movement Advancement Project et al., 2014, p. 2). This holds for visibility in the workplace as well: 92 percent of lesbians and 86 percent of gay men – yet only 48 percent of bisexuals – are out to colleagues at work (Mize, 2016).[15] This disparity in coming out to family, friends, and others also exists for bi teenagers (Andre et al., 2014).

The San Francisco Human Rights Commission (2011) report identifies bi invisibility as the cause of a wide range of negative economic, health, and mental health outcomes for bi-identified people. Sociologist Trenton Mize notes that another cause of negative outcomes for bisexuals are the "assumptions of choice to their sexual orientation" – the misperception that bisexuals, because they can experience love and attraction for more than one gender, have *control* and responsibility over their sexual orientation in a way that gay men and lesbians do not (2016, p. 1137).

Many studies report higher negative outcomes in physical and mental health for bisexuals as compared to gay men and lesbians, and higher again as compared to the general population (see, e.g., San Francisco Human Rights Commission, 2011; Movement Advancement Project et al., 2014; Mize, 2016). We do not have a lot of data, yet, on the experiences of bisexual people. A national Canadian study found that men who identified as gay were 4.1 times more likely than their straight male peers to attempt or seriously consider suicide in their lifetime, while bisexual men were 6.3 times more likely to do so.[16] In this study, lesbians were 3.5 times more likely, while bisexual women were 5.9 times more likely to consider or attempt suicide when compared with straight women. A recent study of US respondents found that rates of diagnosed depression were higher for bisexual people than for gay, lesbian, or straight respondents (MentalHelp.net, 2016).

There is also evidence that rates of sexual violence are higher among bisexual women than they are among straight- or lesbian-identified women. One study of 2010 US national data indicates that bisexual women experience rape at much higher rates than their lesbian and heterosexual female peers: 46.1 percent of bisexual women have experienced rape by any perpetrator in their lifetime, compared with 13.1 percent of lesbians and 17.4 percent of straight women (Walters et al., 2013).[17] Intimate partner violence also occurred at higher rates for both bisexual women and men. Reporting lifetime incidents of rape, physical violence, and/or stalking by a partner were 61.1 percent of bisexual women, 43.8 percent of lesbians, and 35.0 percent of straight women; 37.3 percent of bisexual men, 26.0 percent of gay men, and 29.0 percent of straight men (Walters et al., 2013).[18]

Concerning economic issues, one national study of wages indicates that "bisexual men and women face broad disadvantages in the labor market" (Mize, 2016, p. 1152). And one California study indicates that bisexual workers in the state earn less than both their straight peers and their gay and lesbian peers. Gay men earned 2–3 percent less than straight men, while bisexual men earned 10–15 percent less; lesbians earned 2.7 percent less than straight women, while bisexual women earned almost 11 percent less. Furthermore, two studies of California data indicate that poverty levels are much higher among bisexual men and women when compared with their gay and lesbian counterparts: 17.7 percent of bisexual women versus 7.8 percent of lesbians and 9.7 percent of bisexual men compared with 6.2 percent of gay men lived in poverty (for discussion of these studies, see San Francisco Human Rights Commission, 2011, p. 27) Other studies (of national data) have found poverty levels not to differ statistically by sexual orientation (Badgett et al., 2013).[19]

Bisexuals continue to face and to fight against continued invisibility and scorn, both inside and outside the broader LGBTQ movement. Bisexuals have suffered from two myths: the first is that everybody is at least a little bit bisexual. The second is that bisexuality does not exist. These myths erase bisexual identity by claiming that it is either universal or nonexistent. Bisexuals continue to confront pop cultural tropes and everyday presumptions that they are promiscuous, indecisive, in a transitional phase, or not fully committed to the lesbian and gay community.[20] Bluntly put by two bisexual writers and activists, "bisexual people face the apolitical sexually insatiable swinger stereotype" (Hutchins & Ka'ahumanu, 1991, p. 220). Bisexual men may also still be suffering from the "HIV stigma" trope of the 1980s: that they are the carriers of HIV and AIDS to straight people (Allen, 2017).

We can see an example of bisexual invisibility in one of the most visible national conversations about LGBTQ politics in our lifetime. As late as the summer of 2015, when the Supreme Court ruled that same-sex marriage was a constitutional right, there was a broad, enthusiastic embrace of the new nationwide right to "gay marriage." By using this term, this new marriage right is framed in a way that assumes that people in same-sex relationships are necessarily gay, rather than (among other sexual identities) possibly bisexual instead. With this one important legal step forward, the public discourse – in this case tied to the legal discourse, and including gay and lesbian activists and allies – further cemented bi invisibility (Cruz, 2014b). This is not just obscure semantics. It is leaving bisexuals out of the discussion, the celebration, and the politics of current LGBTQ civil rights.

It is this issue of invisibility – and its more active framing as *erasure* (as something that is actively being *done to* bisexuals) – that is a substantial focus of bisexual advocacy and activism today, alongside a focus on *coming out* to help increase bi visibility and build bi community (e.g., RichardsFink, 2013). In the twenty-first century, just as it is for gay and lesbian efforts, pop culture is a central arena for bi politics (Eisner, 2013; San Filippo, 2013). In part, this means a focus on increasing visibility through the coming out of celebrities. A number of high-profile people have come out as bisexual or have become part of the conversation about bisexual visibility by acknowledging that they have had relationships with people of more than one gender, even if they do not embrace a bi identity. These celebrities include the über-visible Lady Gaga; the hip-hop/R & B singer Frank Ocean; actors Alan Cumming, Evan Rachel Wood, Cynthia Nixon, and Anna Paquin; British Olympic diver Tom Daley; and Chirlane McCray, the wife of New York City's mayor Bill de Blasio (Schulman, 2014).

Some of these pop cultural actors actively use their platform to increase bi visibility and respond to the pervasive misconceptions of bisexuality in the broader culture. For example, in 2014, on CNN, a seemingly perplexed interviewer Larry King asked bi actor Anna Paquin about her sexuality and whether she was a "non-practicing bisexual." The actor, who is married to a man with whom she co-starred on HBO's campy vampire show *True Blood*, had to explain to King that just because she is married to a man does not mean that her bisexuality is a "past-tense thing" (Cruz, 2014a, n.p.): bisexuality as an identity is not contingent on the gender of one's current partner.

Inside the broader LGBTQ movement, bi activists work to combat erasure and assert identity, as well. Bi-identified LGBTQ sports activist and athlete Anna Aagenes wrote that identifying as bisexual was not always easy within the broader LGBTQ community, and that it required a "double coming out" to both gay/lesbian and straight people:

Many bisexual people can relate to my experience of finding that many of my gay and lesbian friends harbor a lot of biphobic beliefs, consciously or subconsciously, and make hurtful statements about the "B" in "LGBT." Finding the LGBT community was like joining a new club that I (technically) belonged to, but when I arrived to pick up my towel and complimentary gym pass, my membership was called into question. (2013, n.p.)

In another example, young bi activist Eliel Cruz works specifically on LGBTQ inclusion in faith-based communities. He has an active social media presence, particularly on bi issues. He writes, in his Twitter bio, that he is – among other things – a "Professional Bisexual" and has spoken about the importance of positive bi representation and visibility in pop culture.[21] These two examples of young activists illustrate the ways in which bi activism today can both sit in the broader pan-identity LGBTQ movement *and* assert the importance of explicitly bisexual visibility both within the movement and in the general American culture.

Current Trans Exclusion and Response

The Williams Institute finds that 0.6 percent of US adults – or approximately 1.4 million people – are transgender, a number that has doubled since the early 2000s (Flores et al., 2016). The National Center for Transgender Equality's latest national survey of 27,715 transgender adults found that survey respondents were twice as likely to be living in poverty than the general US population and three times as likely to be unemployed. Attempted suicide rates were tragically high: 40 percent among survey respondents versus 4.6 percent of the general US population over the course of a lifetime.[22] So, too, were transphobic assault rates: 9 percent of respondents reported that they had been physically attacked in the previous year (James et al., 2016).

Respondents to this national survey revealed discrimination in every facet of their lives (James et al., 2016; also see Schilt, 2010). In the workplace, 30 percent of respondents who had been working in the previous year reported some form of mistreatment due to their gender identity or expression. In housing, 23 percent of respondents reported facing discrimination in the past year. In public accommodations, 31 percent had been mistreated and a full 59 percent reported that they had avoided using a public restroom in the past year for fear of how they would be treated. Public attention has been drawn recently to the fact that trans women and trans women of color are particularly vulnerable to fatal violence. In 2015, for instance, 23 trans women were reported victims of transmisogynistic murders in the US, prompting the advocacy and attention of high-profile trans women like Laverne Cox, Janet Mock, and Caitlyn Jenner (Blumm, 2015; Kellaway & Brydum, 2015; Mock, 2015). Of these victims, 21 were women of color and 13 were under the age of 25 (Tourjee, 2015a; 2015b).

Trans people and activists have made some significant progress in confronting exclusion within the broader LGBTQ movement, as trans issues have become more mainstream. In cultural spaces, for example, prominent cisgender lesbian allies began to take note of the trans exclusion at the Michigan Womyn's Music Festival. The Indigo Girls – the legendary feminist, lesbian, activist singing duo of Amy Ray and Emily Saliers – had been enthusiastic, A-list performers at Michfest for years. But they eventually publicly indicated that they could no longer abide by the trans-exclusiveness of Michfest. They made their protest known in an open letter:

> Although we are playing the festival, we honor the current protest against MWMF and hope that it will help move the community towards change. Any money that we make playing the Festival will go towards Trans Activism. We will make a statement from stage at the Festival in support of Trans Inclusion. We have made it clear that this will be our last time at the Festival until MWMF shows visible and concrete signs of changing their intention. . . . We love Michigan Womyn's Music Festival and hope for it's [*sic*] continued presence and power in our lives. (2013, n.p.)

The Indigo Girls presented their view from the stage, as promised, and the next year, with no change in Michfest policy, they dropped out of the festival completely (Malloy, 2014b). Other allies joined in calling for a change to Michfest's practice (Kim, 2013; Ring, 2015). In 2014, Lea DeLaria, the self-identified butch lesbian actor and activist behind one of the most iconic lesbian roles of recent years, Big Boo of *Orange Is the New Black*, also said that she would no longer participate, because "[w]e queers need to find a way to stop this fighting and work together towards our common goal. . . . I truly look forward to the time when all LGBTQ stand as one" (Brydum, 2014, n.p.).

For her part, Michfest organizer Lisa Vogel maintained that the "womyn-born-womyn" requirement at Michfest was an "intention" that relied on self- and community-policing rather than a hard and fast exclusionary policy (Malloy, 2014b):

> We have said that this space, for this week, is intended to be for womyn who were born female, raised as girls and who continue to identify as womyn. This is an intention for the spirit of our gathering . . . It is not a policy, or a ban on anyone. . . . [W]e trust the greater queer community to respect this intention. (Vogel, 2014, n.p.)

The issue of this rule or norm became increasingly divisive. Finally, in 2015, amid growing attention to its trans-exclusion but not citing this as a direct cause, Michfest announced that it would be ending its 40-year run (Vogel, 2015).

Elsewhere in the movement, particularly in the more high-profile civil rights world, at least nominal trans inclusion in the LGBTQ mainstream civil equality agenda has become more common. Throughout the 1990s, as trans politics gained traction in the mainstream LGBT movement, protections for transgender people were added to more than two dozen local nondiscrimination ordinances across the country (Stone, 2009). The Human Rights Campaign, for its part, has sought to repair its past negative reputation on trans issues. In 2014, its president, Chad Griffin, publicly acknowledged that "HRC has done wrong by the transgender community in the past, and I am here to formally apologize." Griffin promised that his organization would fight for an inclusive ENDA and, beyond that, would "lead the campaign for a fully-inclusive, comprehensive, LGBT civil rights bill" (quoted in Juro, 2014b, n.p.; also see Bernstein, 2015).

Within the broader LGBTQ movement today, the cultural and political conversations about the inclusion of trans women and men in historically women-only spaces is taking place in a number of sites, from lesbian softball leagues to women's colleges (Travers, 2006; Quart, 2008; Padawer, 2014). Within feminist movements, as well, pro-choice and longstanding women's health advocacy groups and service providers are beginning to work through how to become trans-inclusive in their language and their practice: to recognize that trans men may become pregnant, need abortions, and seek out a range of health services typically associated with cisgender women and to advocate and provide health care for people who were assigned female at birth but who do not identify as women (Carmen, 2014a; Hempel, 2016).

From outside of the LGBTQ movement, there have been important and unprecedented federal transgender civil rights gains in recent years. In 2014, President Obama signed an executive order barring employment discrimination by sexual orientation *and* gender identity in federal contracting, and he granted gender identity protections to all federal employees, covering about 20 percent of the American workforce (Stern, 2014). Also in 2014, Obama's Justice Department reinterpreted federal sex discrimination protections to include gender identity and "transgender status" (Geidner, 2014). The administration also reinterpreted Title IX, which bars sex discrimination in schools, to protect transgender students, as discussed in chapter 5. The Obama administration also took affirmative steps to ensure that federal employees have the right to use the bathrooms that correspond with their gender identity (Avery, 2016).

At the federal legislative level, as well, lawmakers have considered trans-inclusive nondiscrimination efforts. In 2015, the Employment Non-Discrimination Act was replaced with a much more comprehensive federal bill, the Equality Act. Reclaiming the name of a broad nondiscrimination bill that was originally proposed in 1974, the Equality Act covers not just employment but also protections in housing, public accommodations, education, among other areas of public and private life. In these new iterations of federal protections, "[r]emoving gender identity," writes National Center for Transgender Equality Executive Director Mara Keisling, "is now completely unthinkable" (2015, n.p.).

While the Equality Act is not yet law – a new iteration of it was introduced in May 2017 by more than 200 senators and US representatives (O'Hara, 2017b) – it seems that trans inclusion in these broad civil rights politics has been secured.

Along with these civil rights gains, and connected to them, transgender visibility has gone mainstream and has been building in popular culture for almost a decade (Stryker, 2008). In 2011, Chaz Bono, the already-famous only child of singers Cher and Sonny Bono, wrote a bestselling book about his experience and his transition (Bono, with Fitzpatrick, 2012; also see Wilson, 2011). In 2013, Fallon Fox told her widely publicized story as a trans woman professional mixed martial arts (MMA) fighter (Hunt, 2013; Zeigler, 2013); and almost 50,000 people signed on (albeit unsuccessfully) to a petition for Victoria's Secret to hire former *RuPaul's Drag Race* contestant Carmen Carrera as the store's first trans model (Rodriguez & Santana, 2013).[23]

By 2014, *Time* magazine had declared a "transgender tipping point" in pop culture and politics (Steinmetz, 2014). Laverne Cox, the trans actress who plays trans character Sophia Burset in the celebrated Netflix show *Orange Is the New Black*, was the first out trans woman to be nominated for a Primetime Emmy Award (Malloy, 2014d) and became the face of trans visibility on the *Time* cover story. That same year, *Time* included a well-known trans teen girl, Jazz Jennings, on its list of the 25 Most Influential Teens of 2014 (Ennis, 2014). Also that year, author and trans activist Janet Mock published her memoir, became a contributing editor to *Marie Claire* fashion magazine, spoke widely in the press about her experience and her advocacy work, and urged a conversation about trans women of color and the race and class politics of LGBTQ visibility (Juro, 2014a). In the world of fashion, Barneys New York introduced a widely publicized spring 2014 campaign featuring 17 trans models (Carmen, 2014b), and models Andreja Pejic and Geena Rocero came out as trans women (Dominus, 2014; Zarrella, 2014). Also in 2014, the acclaimed Amazon show *Transparent* and the high-profile role of trans woman Rayon, in the film *Dallas Buyers Club*, for which Jared Leto won an Oscar, opened up an active and heated conversation about trans representation in mainstream popular culture, including the question of whether cisgender actors should play transgender characters (Addams, 2014; Brodesser-Akner, 2014; Keegan, 2014; O'Donnell, 2014; Zeigler, 2014).

Transgender pop cultural visibility reached even greater heights when Caitlyn Jenner came out in print and on television news (*People Magazine, Us Weekly, Vanity Fair*, and ABC TV's *20/20*), and became a seemingly omnipresent media figure in the spring and summer of 2015.[24] Although she has not been an active athlete for decades, the coming out and celebration of Jenner, the former college football player and 1976 Olympic gold medal decathlete who, for years, was "one of the icons of American masculinity" (Talusan, 2015, n.p.), has significantly raised trans visibility and prompted an unprecedented national conversation about what it means to be transgender (Kahrl, 2015; Zirin, 2015).[25]

Jenner aside, athletics has become an important part of the current pop cultural conversation about transgender inclusion and visibility. Chris Mosier is the most celebrated and recent example as the first out transgender man, in 2015, to make a US men's national team, Team USA, for the sprint duathlon (a run-bike-run event). Mosier is an advocate and activist for LGBTQ sports inclusion and equity. He is currently vice president of the You Can Play Project, an organization dedicated to sports inclusion, and founder of TransAthlete.com, the most comprehensive resource for information about trans athlete policies, participation, and best practices. He also served as executive director of a national LGBTQ student athlete network, GO! Athletes. After he qualified for his national competition, he was unsure about whether he was going to be able to compete as a member of Team USA in his June 2016 World Championship event in Spain, because the team followed the International Olympic Committee (IOC) guidelines about trans athlete participation. At the time, these were restrictive, including a requirement (that was not always enforced) for both trans men and trans women to have undergone a series of gender confirmation surgeries, including internal and external genital reconstruction. Yet these surgeries are both inaccessible and undesired by many trans people and have no bearing on athletic performance (Malloy, 2014a; O'Hara, 2014).[26] Mosier challenged these guidelines and, in January 2016, the IOC announced a change that no longer included the surgery requirement, and Mosier was able to compete. In the summer of 2016, Mosier's visibility crossed over even further, when he became the first transgender athlete to be included in the *ESPN The Magazine*'s "Body Issue" and to be featured in a Nike commercial. The 30-second Nike spot, called "Unlimited Courage," ran during primetime coverage of the 2016 Summer Olympics.[27]

In theory, the transgender politics of recent years rests on a broad understanding of transgender identity that not only includes people who have physically or socially transitioned from one binary gender designation to another, but also those who are genderqueer or nonbinary or who in some other way do not identify with the gender that they were assigned at birth. But there are some ways in which policy conversation has kept the binary in place. For instance, Title IX and more local protections for transgender students do not abolish the binary gender segregation of bathrooms. The pop cultural explosion of recent years also has primarily focused on trans-identified people who have transitioned physically and/or socially. But, it is in the pop cultural space that I believe we are seeing signs of increasing diversity of trans identity and politics, especially connected with the complex ways in which young people tend to understand their sexual and gender identity. Australian model and *Orange Is the New Black* actor, Ruby Rose, for instance, identifies as "gender fluid" and "gender neutral" and has spoken publicly about her gender identity and how it has changed over time (see, e.g., Jarvis, 2015; Molloy, 2015). Actor Asia Kate Dillon, of *Orange Is the New Black* and, more recently, *Billions*, self-identifies as "nonbinary gender." Their *Billions* role was the first gender nonbinary character on a major television show.[28] They made headlines in April 2017 when they petitioned the Television Academy to reconsider the binary, segregated awards categories used for the Emmys. The Academy responded that Dillon was "free to choose the category they wish to enter." While this did not eliminate the gender-designated categories, it did raise the issue of why these categories are necessary and how gender is defined for purposes of these awards (Wong, 2017, n.p.).

Beyond cultural visibility and inclusion, trans activists and advocates have articulated a broad political agenda for the future that includes a focus on changing laws to secure basic human and civil rights as well as changing hearts and minds. These issues include access to facilities and public accommodations, prison justice, Medicaid/Medicare and private health insurance coverage, gender-affirming health care, standing up against racist and transmisogynistic violence, military inclusion, sports inclusion, combatting poverty and homelessness, marriage and family rights, educational trans equality in K-12 schooling and higher education, and addressing the role of the state in defining gender through state-issued identification like drivers licenses and passports.[29]

Trans in the Age of Trump

The recent significant uptick in trans pop cultural and celebrity visibility does not connote political or human rights progress, per se, or stem the epidemic of anti-trans violence (Malloy, 2014e; Mock, 2015; Rodriguez, 2015). And, in fact, with mainstream visibility and some policy progress has come a new onslaught of anti-trans campaigns. Despite – and perhaps because of – some significant political and cultural gains, transgender Americans have found themselves victimized by the Right in recent years. In addition, it seems that, with Donald Trump's election, transgender people have become one of many early targets of a fortified conservative movement.

Even before Trump's win, after taking a loss on marriage, the anti-LGBTQ Right has turned to vitriolic anti-trans campaigns and laws, mostly at the state level, that generally seek to block and even roll back broad nondiscrimination measures (Peters, 2016). These campaigns paint transgender people as dangerous, particularly portraying trans women as deceptive men in women's clothes who seek access to women's bathrooms for nefarious purposes like rape and pedophilia.[30] This narrative mobilizes the assumption that trans women are really men who identify as trans because they are interested in violating women's spaces.

In one notorious example, in March 2016, the North Carolina legislature passed HB2, which the Republican then-Governor Pat McCrory signed into law.[31] The ACLU called HB2 the "most extreme anti-LGBT measure in the country" (quoted in Gordon et al., 2016, n.p.). The law negated a Charlotte anti-discrimination ordinance passed the month before and went much further to *prohibit* public entities in the state from passing nondiscrimination laws that would explicitly protect LGBTQ people on the basis of sexual orientation and gender identity (Epps, 2016). In addition, the law, also dubbed a "bathroom bill," explicitly indicated that people must use the multiple-occupancy, single-sex bathrooms that correspond with the sex that is listed on their birth certificates.[32] This bars many trans people from using the bathroom that corresponds with their gender identity and their gender presentation (Skinner-Thompson, 2016). Debate about this law relied on the narrative that these broad anti-discrimination laws are really about protecting menacing men who would use women's facilities in order to prey on women and girls. In fact, there are exactly *no* reported cases of violence in a public bathroom when trans people are the *perpetrators*, and too many to count when they are the *victims* of transphobic violence (Michelson, 2016). Forcing trans people to use bathrooms that do not correspond with their gender presentation and identity will put them further in harm's way.

The anti-trans North Carolina law and the controversy it stirred up has been the occasion for celebrities and other high-profile people and businesses, once again – as many did with marriage – to use their public platform and their resources for LGBTQ support. PayPal announced that it would not go forward with its planned expansion to North Carolina because of HB2, and many issued economic boycotts of the state. New York State, for instance, became one of a number of municipalities to ban work-related, publicly funded "non-essential" travel to the state. The NBA pulled the 2017 All-Star Game out of Charlotte, noting: "[W]e do not believe we can successfully host our All-Star festivities in Charlotte in the climate created by HB2" (Bontemps, 2016, n.p.).

In addition, entertainers like Pearl Jam and Bruce Springsteen canceled concerts in the state, and Seattle Seahawks quarterback Russell Wilson and his fiancée, singer Ciara, moved their wedding from North Carolina to London because of their opposition to the law (Heller, 2016; Kapadia, 2016; Berman, 2017). Forbes estimated that the law cost North Carolina approximately $630 million in lost business revenue (Jurney, 2016).

The legal future of these state-level anti-trans laws is up in the air. The Obama administration issued a strongly worded directive, followed by a lawsuit, indicating that states should allow students to use the locker rooms and bathrooms that correspond with their gender identity, as doing otherwise would be a violation of civil rights (US Department of Justice, 2016). Trump, however, has reinterpreted this Title IX directive, indicating that instead of providing federal protections for trans people, public facilities access decisions should be left up to the individual states (Peters et al., 2017). As many as 15 states have recently introduced anti-trans bills of this kind, many focusing specifically on young people's access to school facilities (O'Hara, 2017a). The Supreme Court – which passed up an opportunity to rule on an interpretation of Title IX when it decided not to take up trans student Gavin Grimm's case – will eventually need to settle the matter (Farias, 2017).

As the new president and the emboldened Right that elected him turn their attention increasingly to anti-trans efforts – from removing safeties for trans young people, to considering trans-exclusive health care policy, to flippantly announcing a policy (via Twitter) to ban transgender people from the US military (Lubold, 2017; Ring, 2017) – we will have the opportunity to see if and how the mainstream LGBTQ movement mobilizes around the transgender people and politics that it has historically marginalized.

7

Conclusion

Remember back to the years after World War II, when the very first homophile groups in the US furtively built a collective response to the state-sponsored demonization of sexual minorities. At this time, the federal government was working to expel known homosexuals from its offices, depicting same-sex sex and the people who had or desired it as dangerous to the state and its citizens. At the end of 1950, a Senate committee charged with investigating the matter of whether and to what extent the government employed homosexuals wrote of their damaging impact: "These perverts will frequently attempt to entice normal individuals to engage in perverted practices. . . . One homosexual can pollute a Government office" (D'Emilio, 1998, p. 42).

We have seen this echoed in many places in our narrative on LGBTQ social movements of the past few generations. Over and over again, LGBTQ people have been portrayed as dangerous threats to children and country. If we wonder if this narrative is outdated, we just have to look to the "bathroom bill" debates of recent years, in which transgender women are portrayed as menacing pedophiles trolling women's bathrooms for young girls. If we think these anti-trans maneuvers are an outlier, we should look at the 2016 Republican Party platform, the document behind the election of Donald Trump. We can see here evidence that the political party in power has *withdrawn* protection for LGBTQ Americans, in the form of a defense of what it calls the "natural marriage" (Republican National Committee, 2016, p. 31) between one man and one woman: "Traditional marriage and family, based on marriage between one man and one woman, is the foundation for a free society and has for millennia been entrusted with rearing children and instilling cultural values" (2016, p. 11).

This political platform has a constituency. Recent studies find that while acceptance of LGBTQ people has been growing and is fairly high, "nearly a third of Americans remain uncomfortable with their LGBTQ family members, coworkers, and neighbors" (GLAAD, 2017, p. 7). Another national survey conducted in January 2017 found that 25 percent of LGBT respondents reported that they had experienced discrimination in the past year due to their gender identity or sexual orientation (Singh & Durso, 2017). Thus, despite the undeniable shift in public opinion concerning LGBTQ people, including their rights, and the fact that there are unprecedented levels of acceptance of out gay, lesbian, and bisexual people in urban neighborhoods, small towns, and suburbs across the US, this "post-gay" moment, as Ghaziani notes, "may not translate to post-discrimination" (2011, p. 120; also see Stein, 2001; Gray, 2009).

The story of LGBTQ social change in the US has told of the complicated relationship that this demeaned and marginalized group has with its country and its institutions. Some LGBTQ activists have fought their way into existing institutions and have put their lives on the line for the country to protect them and let them in. Others have all but given up, distrustful that the state could ever serve their interests or value them as human beings. They, instead, have put their energies toward broad critiques of the state and its norms and toward building alternative cultures and communities. At stake in these politics is American belonging and democracy – who gets to call themselves American (Bronski, 1998; Seidman, 2002).

We are, in the US, at a turning point in the state's relationship with LGBTQ people. President Obama, especially in his second term, used his power and pulpit to advance LGBTQ civil rights. He spoke out for marriage equality and pulled the state back from defending laws that threatened it (for example, the Defense of Marriage Act). He used executive powers to enhance federal protections, particularly for transgender adults and children. We do not yet know the full extent of how, but we do know that the Trump administration is using the state in very different ways.

The emboldened Religious Right – now with an enthusiastic, loud, and unpredictable ally in the White House – will assert itself in its old ways, via fundamentalist Christianity and homophobic, transphobic politics. One of the cornerstones of the Republican agenda now is so-called religious freedom. This is a movement that has been building at the state level for years, in direct response to state-level marriage equality gains (Ghaziani et al., 2016). Over the past few years, the Right has fought marriage equality laws with claims that they impinge on the religious liberty of those who, for ostensibly religious reasons, oppose same-sex marriage and LGBTQ people. A number of states have considered or passed Religious Freedom Restoration Acts, which allow individuals to cite religious beliefs as justification for refusing to provide their services to particular clients or customers. While a federal RFRA has been on the books since 1993 and has nothing to do with LGBTQ rights, these newer state-level laws are clearly tied to the Religious Right's growing concern over LGBTQ freedom and marriage equality (Fausett & Blinder, 2015; Franke, 2015). These "turn away the gay" bills – from a high-profile law in Indiana in March 2015, to a 2016 Mississippi law named the Protecting Freedom of Conscience from Government Discrimination Act, to bills that were vetoed by the governor of Arizona in February 2014 and the governor of Georgia in March 2016 – have been vigorously opposed by the mainstream American business, sports, and entertainment communities as being bad for business, mean-spirited, and unjust (Terkel, 2015; Signorile, 2016).

During the 2016 presidential campaign, the Trump administration and the Republican Party indicated support for a federal version of these religious freedom laws called the First Amendment Defense Act (FADA). This would, like its state-level counterparts, give very broad leeway to people, businesses, and services to discriminate against LGBTQ people on religious grounds. By putting this in the language of protection from religious *discrimination*, the party sets religious rights against LGBTQ rights; the law would "bar government discrimination against individuals and businesses for acting on the belief that marriage is the union of one man and one woman" (Republican National Committee, 2016, p. 11). This is not simply about bakers refusing to make cakes for two grooms; the law would give broad protections for refusal to provide health and social services to LGBTQ people. It endangers marriage equality, too, by giving state and local officials a tool to refuse access to marriage licenses and certifications (Michaelson, 2016). The political future of these federal religious liberty protections is still up in the air (E. Collins, 2017). So far, amid massive mobilization against it, Trump's focus on religious freedom has not yet included a federal "license to discriminate" against LGBTQ people (Grindley & Ring, 2017).

Trump is already rolling back other protections for LGBTQ people that had been put in place by President Obama. This he can do relatively easily through executive action and executive re-readings of existing federal laws. For instance, in February 2017, his administration reinterpreted Title IX in a narrow way that no longer protects transgender students, revoking Obama's interpretation. Trump's administration sees civil rights issues – like transgender facilities access – as *local* rather than federal concerns. This leaves students in many states and districts unprotected (Ford, 2016; Somashekhar et al., 2017). Leading the charge may be Trump's vice president, former Indiana Governor Mike Pence, whom many view as "one of the most extreme opponents of gay, lesbian and transgender people in the nation" (Boylan, 2016, n.p.; Stack, 2016b).

With Trump's election, the *progress* narrative on LGBTQ civil rights – which has been bolstered in recent years by the federal win on marriage and the substantial, relatively quick shift in public opinion in favor of LGBTQ people and rights – has been interrupted, and the future of LGBTQ social justice is even more uncertain than before. Trump's election – coming months after the tragic Pulse massacre, when 49 people were fatally shot in an Orlando gay nightclub on Latin Night one weekend in June 2016 – is a time when progressive people have reminded each other in countless Facebook and Twitter posts of the Martin Luther King,

Jr. exhortation that "the arc of the moral universe is long, but it bends toward justice."

With this longer look at justice struggles in mind, we remember the themes that have structured this look at LGBTQ social movements in the US since World War II and that can help us make sense of what comes next. First, the *debate between assimilationism and liberationism as strategies for equality and social justice* can be found in almost every example in the book, from the early tensions in the Mattachine Society in the early 1950s, to the varied approaches between second wave feminists and radical lesbian alternative community-builders, to the philosophical and tactical differences between Human Rights Campaign Fund advocates and Queer Nationalists in the 1990s. We see examples, too, of the ways in which this distinction between assimilationism and liberationism has been complicated, as in the example of ACT UP activists who fought with direct action, confrontational tactics, and a sense of urgency, while, at the same time, aiming their demands for treatment at the government. They had a radical analysis of the homophobia that turned the state away from them, but they did not give up on the same government that had ignored and maligned them for years.

Second, and relatedly, we have seen activists throughout the decades struggle with *the limits and possibilities of law and policy for social change.* Some have geared their work to the law and the state, in search of legal defense against discrimination, the freedom to marry, and state-funded AIDS treatment research. These civil rights fights have grown the movement, built the mainstream mainstays like HRC, and drawn in allies who have a strong sense that American law should at least be applied fairly. Others, like radical lesbian feminist groups in the 1970s or the founders of the Gay Men's Health Crisis in the 1980s, have either never trusted the state to provide them with protection or have simply looked elsewhere for change when the state seems beside the point. Instead of focusing on the law or the government, they have built alternative cultural and political institutions and relied on the community to fund and support their work.

Third, we have seen the many ways in which *art and popular culture have been mobilized for social change*, to change hearts and minds and build community when laws and public policy cannot. The earliest discretely disseminated homophile movement publications filled this role, as did the much louder discos of the 1970s, the stage lit mourning of the first AIDS survivors, and the online communities that young people have built around their identities and their pop cultural consumption. We also see the ways in which art, media, and celebrity are mobilized in order to change policy, as has been the case with athletes and hip-hop artists coming out for marriage equality and transgender rights. Culture, in this way, has been and is central to political mobilization for LGBTQ social change.

Fourth, we have seen the *interconnectedness of social movements*, in many places in the ways in which the LGBTQ movement and the Religious Right have fueled each other, building strength and visibility in their reaction to one another. The Right grew substantially when Anita Bryant's anti-gay campaign in the late 1970s developed in response to a growing anti-discrimination movement across the country. For the LGBTQ movement's part, the AIDS movement grew out of the shameful neglect of the Reagan administration when American citizens were dying in droves. In recent years, the anti-LGBTQ Right has gained momentum from marriage equality wins and has made anti-trans politics its next focus. We have also seen the ways in which the LGBTQ movement has drawn from other social movements of its time, like civil rights and Black Power in the 1960s and early 1970s, gaining a language to talk about pride and a set of strategies of protest and organization.

Finally, we have seen the many ways in which *privilege plays a role in movement organizing*, from the continued erasure of bisexual people and politics in the movement, to the marginalization of – if not outright disregard for – transgender people and experiences, to the many ways in which privileged white gay men have often set the agenda and the tone of the mainstream LGBTQ movement through its history. We have seen a number of ways in which activists who have some amount of structural power (by race, class, and gender, for instance) universalize their interests and set movement agendas on their own interests, while ignoring the ways in which these interests might overlook or directly clash with others in the broad and diverse LGBTQ community.

The discussion in these pages is incomplete. My hope is that there is enough here to prompt you to learn more and to inspire you to ask illuminating questions about social change. As you grapple with these questions, remember that LGBTQ movements come in many forms. In the pages of this book, we have stories of people asserting difference, stressing sameness, pushing the country and its institution to change for them, entering these institutions and changing them from the inside, starting their own communities for safety and power and togetherness. Activists in LGBTQ movements will continue to do what marginalized people have always done – some combination of demanding protections from their state and not relying on the state: making communities, making art, and finding ways for self-determination and love.

Notes

Chapter 1 Introduction

1 For an important recent treatment of global LGBTQ history and politics, see Altman & Symons, 2016; also see Adam, 1995; Pierceson, 2016, ch. 8.

2 I do not focus on this pre-mid-twentieth-century period in the book. For those interested in this earlier history, see, as a start: Faderman, 1991; Katz, 1992; 2007; Adam, 1995; Meyerowitz, 2002; Rupp, 2009; Bronski, 2011; Blank, 2012; Stein, 2012.

3 For a useful synthesis and discussion of social movement theory as it has developed in political science and sociology, see, e.g. Rimmerman, 2002; Staggenborg, 2016.

4 Synthesizing sociological theory on a meaning of culture, in the service of a discussion of LGBTQ social activism, Ghaziani writes: "Culture is now more narrowly conceived as discourse, symbols, boundaries, frames, cognitive schema, narratives and stories, identities, values, works of art, ways of life, and institutional codes, among others" (2008, p. 21).

5 For a recent introductory treatment of LGBTQ movements in the US that is grounded in political science and relies on more of an analytical separation of culture and politics and that focuses primarily on legal and policy change, see Pierceson, 2016.

Chapter 2 Before and After Stonewall

1 I use "Christian Right" and "Religious Right" interchangeably throughout the book, as they have been employed by many historians and political commentators of this period and this topic. For a short discussion of the term "Religious Right" in this context, see Fetner, 2008.

2 These early gay and lesbian cultures, identities, and communities intersected with gender performance and identity in ways that will be discussed below.

As for bisexuality in the pre-Stonewall days, scholars have noted that while it existed as a practice, and the term had been introduced, it was not specifically articulated as an *identity* or organized around until the years immediately following Stonewall (Donaldson, 1995; Udis-Kessler, 1995).

3 See Chauncey, 1994; Adam, 1995; Faderman & Timmons, 2009; Stein, 2012; Ghaziani, 2014; Stewart-Winter, 2016.

4 And, in the case of Rupp (2009), well before this time.

5 See Bérubé, 2010; Faderman, 1991; D'Emilio, 1998; Rupp, 1999; Faderman & Timmons, 2009; Ghaziani, 2014.

6 On a similar project in Canada, see Kinsman & Gentile, 2010.

7 See Shilts, 1982; White, 2009; Stein, 2012; Faderman, 2015.

8 Also see Stewart-Winter (2016) for an important argument about the decades-long connection between the gay and lesbian movement in Chicago, urban politics, and African American civil rights that began in the 1960s.

9 See D'Emilio, 1992; Duberman, 1993; Marcus, 2002; Armstrong & Crage, 2006; Faderman & Timmons, 2009; Hirshman, 2013.

10 For these details on Stonewall, see Duberman, 1993; Rivera, 2001; Carter, 2004; Armstrong & Crage, 2006; Faderman, 2015.

11 Black Panther Party co-founder Huey Newton was publicly railing against this homophobia by 1970. The Puerto Rican nationalist group, the Young Lords in New York City, too, embraced trans activist Sylvia Rivera and her organization (Feinberg, 1998; Carter, 2004).

12 GLF, itself, was not immune to the politics of privilege. See the TransGriot's note about the transphobia of the GLF, for instance (Roberts, 2007). On race, class, and gender in the gay liberation movement, see Stein, 2012.

13 See Duberman, 1993; Carter, 2004; Faderman, 2015. Especially on the origins of pride marches, see Armstrong & Crage, 2006.

14 For an excellent discussion of the complexity and range of feminisms of the 1960s and 1970s, from the *liberal feminism* of NOW to the *radical feminism* of the late 1960s and early 1970s, to the *cultural feminism* of the 1970s, see Echols, 1989.

15 Also see a discussion of the race and class limitations of Friedan's analysis in hooks, 1984.

16 Faderman and Timmons (2009) write, by contrast, that the Los Angeles chapter of NOW was much more inclusive and supportive of lesbians and the politics of intersectionality.

17 Like other parts of the LGBTQ movement, lesbian feminist organizing suffered from racism, classism, and ideological divides that are important to recognize (Faderman, 1991).

18 See Duberman, 1993; Marcus, 2002; Malloy, 2014c; Faderman, 2015; Stewart-Winter, 2016.

19 See Gengle, 1976; Combahee River Collective, 1977; D'Emilio, 1992; Chauncey, 2005; Faderman & Timmons, 2009.

20 As was not unusual at the time, Milk used the word "gay" as an ostensibly gender-neutral term and did not explicitly include lesbians.

21 For these details on Harvey Milk, see Shilts, 1982; Faderman, 2015.

Chapter 3 Activism in the Early Days of AIDS

1 As I will discuss below, while gay and bisexual men were more extensively and directly struck by HIV and AIDS than were lesbians, the politics of AIDS impacted gay men *and* lesbians, as well as bisexuals and transgender people of all sexual orientations. The movement language at the time, however, only really added "lesbian" in the 1980s and consistently left out the "B" and the "T" until the 1990s (Highleyman, 2002). I will use "gay" or "gay and lesbian" throughout much of my discussion of the politics in this chapter, since it most accurately reflects the framing of the time.

2 I recommend Jacques Pepin's (2011) account of the origins of HIV and its transmission to the US over the course of the twentieth century.

3 Rotello writes that while the June 5, 1981 *MMWR* issue is generally considered to be the first report on the AIDS phenomenon, Dr. Lawrence Mass had actually published an article in the May 18, 1981 issue of the *New York Native*, called "Disease Rumors Largely Unfounded," which mostly dismissed rumors of a new disease appearing among gay men (1997, pp. 92–93).

4 For useful and thorough discussions of the press coverage of AIDS in the mainstream, gay, and African American media, see Kinsella, 1989; Cohen, 1999.

5 The very first mainstream stories about the *MMWR* reports ran after the June report, in short pieces in the *Los Angeles Times* and the *San Francisco Chronicle* (Kinsella, 1989).

6 For the complicated saga of its discovery, see, in particular, Epstein, 1996; Shilts, 2007.

7 For more information about how HIV works, Whiteside (2008) is a very accessible introduction.

8 For a useful timeline of the first 10 years of the politics and science of AIDS, see Kinsella, 1989.

9 There is a lot of variation in the numbers that are reported by various sources. It is likely – based on a look at CDC data of the time (2001) – that Shilts's are an underestimate. But, I could not verify a number for the exact month of Reagan's speech, so I have left Shilts's data in place, using the rationale that this would have been what he introduced into the public conversation at the time.

10 For this perspective on Reagan, see Padug & Oppenheimer, 1992; Kayal, 1993; Shilts, 2007; Fetner, 2008. For a counterpoint, a view that is less critical of the Reagan administration, see Engel, who writes that, "[t]he government did prioritize AIDS as both a research and treatment challenge within two years of the CDC identifying its existence" (2006, p. 22).

11 See Kinsella, 1989; Patton, 1996; Shilts, 2007; Rimmerman, 2008; Whiteside, 2008.

12 See Altman, 1986; Kayal, 1993; Marcus, 2002; Fetner, 2008; Faderman, 2015.

13 Kayal notes that, in 1986, 83 percent of GMHC's staff and volunteers were white gay men (1993, p. 102).

14 Gould (2009) offers a useful set of possible explanations for why Kramer's 1983 article did not have this impact.

15 This debate about sex positivity has continued through the decades, as HIV/AIDS politics and treatment have changed. For those who are interested in this topic, see a debate about former ACT UP activist and writer Gabriel Rotello's controversial book, *Sexual Ecology: AIDS and the Destiny of Gay Men*, in which he urged: "A sustainable gay culture will not be easy to attain. To achieve it will require a reversal, or at least a modification, of many of the core tenets of gay liberation as they were expressed in the years after Stonewall. People will have to accept the fact that the unlimited, unstructured pursuit of absolute sexual freedom, whether it was psychologically good, bad, or indifferent, was biologically disastrous for gay men" (1997, pp. 290–291). Many read Rotello's work as problematically blaming gay men themselves, as well as gay male sexual practice, for the spread of AIDS and for presenting one unified – and critical – view of gay male culture and community (see, e.g., Rofes, 1998).

16 See Kramer, 1987; Vaid, 1995; Marcus, 2002; Faderman, 2015; France, 2016.

17 See Kramer, 1994; Vaid, 1995; Northrop, 2003; Signorile, 2003; Rimmerman, 2008; Faderman, 2015.

18 Jim Eigo wrote: "When ACT UP began in 1987 its message was unwaveringly sex positive. One reason the group took off so quickly was because its weekly meeting was the sexiest space in the city for a gay guy to be on a Monday night. Urban gay men had seen their community sex spaces erode in the age of AIDS. ACT UP would be a first stand in reclaiming that space, in asserting our right to it" (2002, p. 184).

19 See Gamson, 1989; Vaid, 1995; Epstein, 1996; Marcus, 2002; Signorile, 2003; Faderman & Timmons, 2009.

20 Roth adds an important recent analysis of the complex politics of privilege – particularly with respect to gender – and the role they played in hastening the end of ACT UP. Through a focus on ACT UP/LA, Roth argues that a more nuanced analysis is needed: "the gender dynamics that led to the deaths of individual ACT UPs by the mid- to late 1990s were local stories about gender, but were also about other lines of social cleavage, like race and sexuality" (2017, p. 20).

21 See Berlant & Freeman, 1993; *Pride Divide*, 1997; Shepard, 2002; Rimmerman, 2008.

22 For an explanation as to why this might have been the case, see Armstrong, 2002; Ghaziani et al., 2016.

23 For this paragraph, see Román, 1998. With this visibility came the critique that the cultural work that was bringing HIV and AIDS to the mainstream was a form of commodification and depoliticization that was ultimately detrimental to queer communities (Harris, 1997; Schulman, 1998; and for commentary on this point, see Román, 1998).

24 For this paragraph and its quotes, see Blotcher, 2010, n.p.; emphasis in original.

25 By contrast, the CDC (2013) estimates that, in the US, 636,000 people who have been diagnosed with AIDS have died, but it is unclear how many of these deaths can be attributed directly to AIDS-related causes.

Chapter 4   Marriage Politics

1 As the world changes and marriage movements make their way across the globe, an excellent way to keep track of worldwide progress is via the Pew Research Center's list: http://www.pewforum.org/2015/06/26/gay-marriage-around-the-world-2013/.

2 For the implication of these gendered marriage restrictions for transgender people, see Ring, 2012.

3 These property-based claims sound as if they might only benefit the relatively wealthy. But, they included things like whether a same-sex partner of a deceased tenant in a rent-controlled apartment in New York City had the right – as a family member would – to remain in the apartment at the rent-controlled rate (Chauncey, 2005; also see Polikoff, 2008).

4 See Chauncey, 2005; Polikoff, 2008; Cherlin, 2009.

5 See Marcus, 2002; Taylor et al., 2009.

6 His framing, like much of the marriage equality conversation, is bi-erasing. See chapter 6 for more discussion.

7 For another important liberationist critique of Sullivan, see Duggan, 2003.

8 For an illuminating post mortem analysis of Clinton's approach to gay rights during this time, see Socarides, 2013.

9 Cahill notes the severity of this proposal: "In 214 years, our Constitution has been amended only 17 times since the original Bill of Rights in 1791. . . . The Federal Marriage Amendment would represent the first time a restriction of the rights of a group of people was written into our Constitution since it was ratified in Philadelphia in 1789" (2004, pp. 11–12).

10 The ad can be found here: https://www.youtube.com/watch?v=0PgjcgqFYP4.

11 For transcripts, descriptions, and discussions of this ad, see Biegel, 2010; Fleischer, 2010; Stone, 2012; Yoshino, 2015.

12 Proposition 8, like many other initiatives across the country, proposed to change California's constitution to encode a narrow definition of marriage.

It read: "Only marriage between a man and a woman is valid or recognized in California" (Yoshino, 2015, p. 21). On November 4, 2008, Prop 8 passed with 52.3 percent of the vote (also see Stone, 2012). For a detailed and careful look at Prop 8 and the eventual challenge to it, see Yoshino, 2015.

13 For those interested in understanding the state-by-state story, Freedom to Marry provides an excellent map resource: http://www.freedomtomarry.org/pages/winning-in-the-states.

14 There were some early cases outside the region, as well. In 1998, an Alaskan court ruled that the state constitution requires marriage equality, but the state quickly amended its constitution to define marriage explicitly as between a man and a woman (Polikoff, 2008).

15 For details on how civil unions and marriages are not equal before the law, see Wolfson, 2004, ch. 7.

16 See Taylor et al., 2009; Kimport, 2014; Solomon, 2014; Harkinson, 2015; Yoshino, 2015.

17 For a discussion of the origins of and politics of this challenge to Prop 8, see Becker, 2014; Solomon, 2014; Faderman, 2015; Yoshino, 2015.

18 Chauncey does not write specifically about trans familiarity or civil rights here. And, he uses "gay" in what I believe to be inclusive of gay men and lesbian women.

19 Chauncey attributes this seeming contradiction to a "growing ethos of tolerance" that seemed to lead many people to support rights for people who they may still disapprove of on moral grounds (2005, p. 55).

20 See http://www.hrc.org/campaigns/equality-rocks.

21 See https://www.youtube.com/watch?v=hlVBg7_08n0.

22 The play can be found at: https://www.youtube.com/watch?v=qlUG8F9uVgM.

23 For one of Ayanbadejo's video's through Marylanders for Marriage Equality, see https://www.youtube.com/watch?v=VRh_wMrbLZI&feature=youtu.be; and see one of Kluwe's through Minnesotans for Equality: https://www.youtube.com/watch?v=NSix0NnVNJ0&feature=youtu.be.

24 See, for example, the controversy over the fourth national march, the Millennium March on Washington for Equality, in April 2000 (Ghaziani, 2008, ch. 9).

25 For updates to these civil rights laws, the work of the Movement Advancement Project is an excellent resource. See, for instance, this map: http://lgbtmap.org/equality-maps/legal_equality_by_state.

Chapter 5 LGBTQ Youth and Social Change

1 He did not specifically study gender identity.

2 Also see a study by Anderson and McCormack, which draws on interviews

with 40 straight-identified male college athletes in England. It found that most "engage in a range of cuddling behaviors with close friends, including cuddling and 'spooning'" without a loss of a sense of "heteromasculine identity" (2015, p. 215). They attribute this shift, in large part, to what they identify as a decline in "homohysteria," or "fear of being socially perceived as gay" (2015, p. 217).

3 This is not an isolated or outdated example. In the fall of 2015, for instance, two students – one in Northern California and one in South Carolina – were similarly barred from wearing their "Nobody Knows I'm a Lesbian" shirts to school (Quinlan, 2015).

4 Elementary school findings are based on a fall 2010 survey of 1,065 3rd through 6th grade elementary school students and 1,099 kindergarten through 6th grade elementary school teachers (GLSEN, 2012).

5 Secondary school findings are based on a 2015 survey of 10,528 LGBTQ-identified students nationwide ages 13 to 21 in grades 6 through 12 (Kosciw et al., 2016).

6 For attention to the experience of LGBTQ students outside the US, see, for example, the resources of the International Lesbian, Gay, Bisexual, Transgender and Queer Youth and Student Organisation (http://www.iglyo.com/) and The Global Alliance for LGBT Education (http://www.lgbt-education.info/). Also see the very helpful 2012 report by UNESCO, *Education Sector Responses to Homophobic Bullying*.

7 Family acceptance matters a lot here. The Trevor Project reports: "LGB youth who come from highly rejecting families are 8.4 times as likely to have attempted suicide as LGB peers who reported no or low levels of family rejection" (n.d., n.p.).

8 See chapter 7 for a more extensive definition and political discussion of the term *cisgender*.

9 A much larger study based on National Transgender Discrimination Survey data of trans and gender nonconforming *adults* found that they are much more likely to attempt suicide in their lifetimes than their cisgender straight and LGB peers. While 4.6 percent of the US population in general and 10–20 percent of LGB-identified adults attempt suicide, 41 percent of trans and gender nonconforming adults report such an attempt (Haas et al., 2014).

10 See http://www.glsen.org/gsa.

11 *Entertainment Weekly* writes in its timeline of "Gay Teens on TV" that, while Rickie was the first primetime young gay character, 1992 saw the first gay teen on network television: daytime soap opera character Billy Douglas from *One Life to Live* on ABC. See this timeline for other notable characters during the 1990s and early 2000s.

12 See http://www.imdb.com/title/tt1327801/awards.

13 Russo gives one explanation for why television may be ahead of film here: "Television programming, scheduled for nearly twenty-four hours a day, was

in constant need of social issues with which to deal, homosexuality among them. A film may have to be a hit, but when a television show flops, there is always next week and another subject, so experimentation was encouraged" (1987, p. 221).

14 GLAAD does not measure class representation, though I believe that we need more data about the way in which TV and film over-represent professional and middle-class people.

15 See https://www.youtube.com/watch?v=7IcVyvg2Qlo.

16 See http://www.itgetsbetter.org/pages/about-it-gets-better-project/.

17 See http://www.itgetsbetter.org/video/entry/6528/ and https://www.youtube.com/watch?v=MriTHFvYZVc.

18 See https://www.youtube.com/watch?v=-Pb1CaGMdWk.

Chapter 6   The "B" and the "T"

1 There are many variations and nuances of this broad term. An old form – in standard use just a few years ago – was transgender*ed*, with an -ed suffix. This has fallen out of use. Some people, as well, use an asterisk as a kind of suffix, referencing the internet catch-all search strategy: trans* (Tompkins, 2014). Others use a hyphen: trans- (Stryker et al., 2008). Both the asterisk and the hyphen are meant to connote an openness and breadth to the term. Others, however, do not like the addition of the asterisk, arguing that the term "trans" itself should be a spacious one and that adding anything after it implies that just the word alone is not open enough or that some nonbinary people are "not trans enough" to use the word "trans" (without the asterisk) to define themselves (The Rogue Feminist, 2013; Gabriel, 2014).

2 For more discussion of terminology and the politics of language, the 2014 *Trans Bodies, Trans Selves* is an incredible resource for trans-focused terminology, as well as for history, health, law, and politics (Erickson-Schroth, 2014). Another excellent resource is a special issue on key concepts of *Transgender Studies Quarterly* (Currah & Stryker, 2014). GLAAD (2014) has a helpful online *Media Reference Guide* designed to help members of the press write about LGBTQ issues in updated, informed, inclusive, LGBTQ-positive ways (for other online language guides, see, e.g., Asher, 2010; Ginelle, 2015).

3 For a useful timeline of bisexual organizing from the late 1960s through the mid-1990s, see Raymond & Highleyman, 1995.

4 See Hutchins & Ka'ahumanu, 1991; Garber, 2000; Rodríguez Rust, 2000c; Ochs, 2009a; San Francisco Human Rights Commission, 2011; Allen, 2017.

5 See Raymond & Highleyman, 1995; Trnka with Tucker, 1995; Udis-Kessler, 1995; Ghaziani, 2008.

6 I recommend a number of accessible and fascinating historical discussions of the broad lived, political, and psycho-medical experience of gender variation

and nonconformity. See Feinberg, 1996; Califia, 1997; Meyerowitz, 2002; Stryker, 2008; Beemyn, 2014.

7 With respect to sexuality since the late 1960s, activists had mobilized to depathologize homosexuality in medicine and psychiatry (D'Emilio, 1998). They were finally successful in December 1973, when the American Psychiatric Association's Board voted to eliminate homosexuality as a mental disorder in the *Diagnostic and Statistical Manual of Mental Disorders* (DSM), where it had been listed since the first DSM in 1952 (Marcus, 2002; Faderman, 2015).

8 Note the maintenance of the gender binary in the DSM designation here, as well.

9 See Serano (2007) for a critical discussion of these standards of care.

10 The concept of *transmisogyny* calls attention to the fact that trans men and trans women have different experiences with transphobia based in part on their gender (along with a whole host of intersecting identities). Transmisogyny is transphobia and sexism (Serano, 2007).

11 These trans-exclusionary "gender panics" can be understood as instances "where people react to disruptions to biology-based gender ideology by frantically reasserting the naturalness of a male–female binary" (Westbrook & Schilt, 2014, p. 34).

12 A spelling that has been adopted by some feminists because it removes the *man* in *woman*.

13 A more recent national Gallup poll found that 4.1 percent of US adults, or more than 10 million people, self-identified as LGBT in 2016 – up from 3.5 percent in 2012. The survey did not break the question down further into individual identities within the pan-identity label (Gates, 2017).

14 In all studies cited here, numbers were only reported in this binary way with respect to gender. Unless indicated here, as well, these studies do not indicate whether and when respondents identify as trans or cisgender.

15 Another recent national survey found that this varies by race, as well. The Center for American Progress found that, in general, "LGBT people of color were more likely to hide their sexual orientation and gender identity from employers" (Singh & Durso, 2017, n.p.).

16 This study, while based on Canadian data, has been widely cited by US advocates.

17 Numbers for men were too small to estimate.

18 The overwhelming majority of perpetrators of intimate partner violence for bisexual and heterosexual women were men (89.5 percent and 98.7 percent, respectively), while 76.4 percent of lesbian women had only female perpetrators. For men, 78.5 percent of bisexuals and 99.5 percent of heterosexuals only had female perpetrators, while 90.7 percent of gay men only had male perpetrators of intimate partner violence (Walters et al., 2013).

19 We would, of course, need more research to make sense of what these

statistics mean and how we can understand the connection between class and sexual identity.

20 For discussion of these presumptions and myths, see Garber, 2000; Yoshino, 2000; Angelides, 2001; Savin-Williams, 2005; Ochs, 2009a; Eisner, 2013; San Filippo, 2013; Burleson, 2014.

21 See https://www.youtube.com/watch?v=XU7Ka_F5cYo.

22 Recent discussions about transgender mental health have focused on transphobia and its impact on trans mental health: E.g., "transgender young people experience higher rates of mental health challenges . . . but the mounting evidence indicates that it's not because they are transgender, but because of how they are treated for being transgender" (Ford, 2015. n.p.).

23 See https://www.change.org/p/victoriassecret-make-carmen-carrera-the-first-trans-vs-model.

24 See, for example, Caitlyn Jenner accepting the prestigious 2015 Arthur Ashe Courage Award at ESPN's ESPY Awards: http://abcnews.go.com/GMA/video/espy-awards-caitlyn-jenner-accepts-arthur-ashe-courage-32482615.

25 Trans writer Meredith Talusan claims of Jenner's story: "Perhaps there hasn't been a coming out this monumental since 1985, when Rock Hudson, one of the iconic male movie stars of the 1950s, announced he had AIDS, and essentially outed himself as gay. That, too, confronted the public assumption of what it meant to be an iconic American man, and showed how a virile body could harbor a secret that was associated with deviance and illness" (2015, n.p.).

26 The 2011 National Transgender Discrimination Survey found that, according to Parker Malloy, "only 33 percent of transgender people have reported undergoing some form of gender-confirming surgery, with 14 percent of transgender women and 21 percent of transgender men not interested in ever having genital surgery" (2014a, n.p.).

27 On Mosier and his work, see Shapiro, 2015; Harding, 2016; Rinkunas, 2016; Stack, 2016a; Steele, 2016; Wilson, 2016. The Nike ad can be found at https://www.youtube.com/watch?v=_gq8PO9XK2Y&sns=em, and has been viewed more than 3 million times on YouTube. The ESPN "Body Issue" can be found at http://www.espn.com/espnw/video/16558267/chris-mosier.

28 Dillon, like many other people (see Guo, 2016), uses singular *they* pronouns.

29 For some exemplary resources on these issues, see Biegel, 2010; Spade, 2011; Erickson-Schroth, 2014; Stryker & Currah, 2014.

30 For an example, see this ad, which ran in Houston when voters considered Proposition 1, the Houston Equal Rights Ordinance (HERO), a broad nondiscrimination bill in November 2015: https://www.youtube.com/watch?v=D7thOvSvC4E.

31 In March 2017, the law was overturned in a controversial compromise that left in place the ban on the passage of new local nondiscrimination laws that would protect LGBTQ people in North Carolina cities

and towns (in the form of a three-year moratorium on these laws) (Fausset, 2017).

32 State laws vary on the requirements necessary to change sex designation on a birth certificate. In North Carolina, "sex reassignment surgery" – or gender confirmation surgery – is necessary to make this change, though the specific nature of the required surgery is unspecified in the law (Lambda Legal, 2015).

References

Aagenes, A. (2013, October 18). Being bi: Coming out to both LGBT and non-LGBT communities. *Huffington Post*. Retrieved October 10, 2016 from http://www.huffingtonpost.com/anna-aagenes/being-bi-coming-out-to-bo_b_4117805.html.

Adam, B. D. (1995). *The rise of a gay and lesbian movement*. Rev. edn. New York, NY: Twayne Publishers.

Addams, C. (2014, March 5). Op-ed: In defense of Jared Leto. *Advocate.com*. Retrieved October 10, 2016 from http://www.advocate.com/commentary/2014/03/05/op-ed-defense-jared-leto.

Agron, D. (2011, April 21). Chris Colfer: Song-and-dance man. *Time*. Retrieved June 9, 2015 from http://www.time.com/time/specials/packages/article/0,28804,2066367_2066369_2066418,00.html.

Allen, S. (2017, January 4). Why bisexual men are still fighting to convince us they exist. *Fusion.net*. Retrieved January 8, 2017 from http://fusion.net/story/378760/bisexual-men-prejudice-aids/.

Altman, D. (1986). *AIDS in the mind of America*. Garden City, NY: Anchor Press.

Altman, D., & Symons, J. (2016). *Queer wars: The new global polarization over gay rights*. Cambridge, UK: Polity.

Ames, S. (2015, May 26). Op-ed: How we'll end "conversion therapy" in four years flat. *Advocate.com*. Retrieved June 3, 2015 from http://www.advocate.com/commentary/2015/05/26/op-ed-how-well-end-conversion-therapy-four-years-flat.

Anderson, E., & McCormack, M. (2015). Cuddling and spooning: Heteromasculinity and homosocial tactility among student-athletes. *Men and Masculinities*, 18(2), 214–230.

Andre, A., Brown, J., Delpercio, A., Kahn, E., Nicoll, A., & Sherouse, B. (2014). *Supporting and caring for our bisexual youth*. Washington, DC: The Human Rights Campaign Foundation.

References

Angelides, S. (2001). *A history of bisexuality*. Chicago, IL: University of Chicago Press.

Armstrong, E. A. (1995). Traitors to the cause? Understanding the lesbian/gay "bisexuality debates." Pp. 199–217 in N. Tucker (ed.), *Bisexual politics: Theories, queries, and visions*. New York, NY: The Haworth Press.

Armstrong, E. A. (2002). *Forging gay identities: Organizing sexuality in San Francisco, 1950–1994*. Chicago, IL: University of Chicago Press.

Armstrong, E. A., & Crage, S. M. (2006, October). Movements and memory: The making of the Stonewall myth. *American Sociological Review*, 71(5), 724–751.

Asher. (2010, November 26). Not your mom's Trans 101. Retrieved January 8, 2016 from http://www.tranarchism.com/2010/11/26/not-your-moms-trans-101/.

Associated Press. (2004, November 3). Voters pass all 11 bans on gay marriage. *NBCnews.com*. Retrieved April 28, 2016 from http://www.nbcnews.com/id/6383353/ns/politics/t/voters-pass-all-bans-gay-marriage/#.VyI-O3AvFY4.

Aultman, B. (2014, May). Cisgender. Pp. 61–62 in P. Currah & S. Stryker (eds.), Postposttransexual: Key concepts for a twenty-first-century transgender studies. Special issue of *Transgender Studies Quarterly*, 1(1–2).

Avery, D. (2016, August 15). New federal mandate says bathroom access "a must" for trans employees. *NewNowNext.com*. Retrieved October 13, 2016 from http://www.newnownext.com/transgender-bathroom-obama/08/2016/.

Ayanbadejo, B. (2009, April 23). Same sex marriages: What's the big deal? *Huffington Post*. Retrieved July 2, 2015 from http://www.huffingtonpost.com/brendon-ayanbadejo/same-sex-marriages-whats_b_190591.html.

Badgett, M. V. L., Durso, L. E., & Schneebaum, A. (2013, June). *New patterns of poverty in the lesbian, gay, and bisexual community*. Los Angeles, CA: The Williams Institute, UCLA School of Law.

Baume, M. (2015). *Defining marriage: Voices from a forty-year labor of love*. Seattle, WA: Self-published.

Beale, L. (1992, March 15). Homosexuals in film: The controversy gay activists say "Basic Instinct" opening Friday, is a perfect example of what is wrong with Hollywood's vision. *Philadelphia Inquirer*. Retrieved September 29, 2016 from http://articles.philly.com/1992-03-15/entertainment/26018983_1_gay-activists-gay-community-national-gay.

Becker, J. (2014). *Forcing the spring: Inside the fight for marriage equality*. New York, NY: Penguin Books.

Becker, R. (2006). *Gay TV and straight America*. New Brunswick, NJ: Rutgers University Press.

Beemyn, G. (2014). US history. Pp. 501–536 in L. Erickson-Schroth (ed.), *Trans bodies, trans selves: A resource for the transgender community*. New York, NY: Oxford University Press.

Beemyn, G., & Rankin, S. (2011). *The lives of transgender people*. New York, NY: Columbia University Press.

References

Belonsky, A. (2013, June 11). Texas teen comes out in high school graduation speech. *Out*. Retrieved March 12, 2015 from http://www.out.com/entertainment/popnography/2013/06/11/texas-teen-comes-out-high-school-graduation-speech.

Berlant, L., & Freeman, E. (1993). Queer nationality. Pp. 193–229 in M. Warner (ed.), *Fear of a queer planet: Queer politics and social theory*. Minneapolis, MN: University of Minnesota Press.

Berman, M. (2017, March 27). North Carolina's bathroom bill cost the state at least $3.7 billion, new analysis finds. *Washington Post*. Retrieved July 12, 2017 from https://www.washingtonpost.com/news/post-nation/wp/2017/03/27/north-carolinas-bathroom-bill-cost-the-state-at-least-3-7-billion-new-analysis-finds/?utm_term=.ad4bec4bd050.

Bernstein, M. (2015, June). Same-sex marriage and the future of the LGBT movement: SWS Presidential Address. *Gender & Society*, 29(3), 321–337.

Bernstein, M., & Taylor, V. (2013). Marital discord: Understanding the contested place of marriage in the lesbian and gay movement. Pp. 1–35 in M. Bernstein & V. Taylor (eds.), *The marrying kind? Debating same-sex marriage within the lesbian and gay movement*. Minneapolis, MN: University of Minnesota Press.

Bernstein, M., Marshall, A., & Barclay, S. (2009). The challenge of law: Sexual orientation, gender identity, and social movements. Pp. 1–17 in S. Barclay, M. Bernstein, & A. Marshall (eds.), *Queer mobilizations: LGBT activists confront the law*. New York, NY: New York University Press.

Bérubé, A. (2010). *Coming out under fire: The history of gay men and women in World War II*. 20th anniversary edn. Chapel Hill, NC: University of North Carolina Press.

Biegel, S. (2010). *The right to be out: Sexual orientation and gender identity in America's public schools*. Minneapolis, MN: University of Minnesota Press.

"Bisexual chic: Anyone goes." (1974, May 27). *Newsweek*. Reprinted pp. 554–555 in P. C. Rodríguez Rust (ed.), *Bisexuality in the United States: A social science reader*. New York, NY: Columbia University Press, 2015.

Blank, H. (2012). *Straight: The surprisingly short history of heterosexuality*. Boston, MA: Beacon Press.

Blotcher, J. (2010, November 10). An Early Frost 25 years later. *Advocate.com*. Retrieved December 15, 2016 from http://www.advocate.com/arts-entertainment/television/2010/11/10/early-frost-25-years-later#article-content.

Blumm, K. C. (2015, July 28). Caitlyn Jenner mourns the murder of two transgender women. *People.com*. Retrieved July 29, 2015 from http://www.people.com/article/caitlyn-jenner-mourns-murdered-transgender-women-india-clarke-kc-haggard.

Bolcer, J. (2012, September 4). Democrats approve marriage equality platform. *Advocate.com*. Retrieved June 8, 2016 from http://www.advocate.com/politics/election/2012/09/04/democrats-approve-marriage-equality-platform.

References

Bono, C., with Fitzpatrick, B. (2012). *Transition: Becoming who I was always meant to be.* New York, NY: Plume.

Bontemps, T. (2016, July 21). NBA will move 2017 All-Star Game from Charlotte over HB2 law. *Washington Post.* Retrieved October 13, 2016 from https://www.washingtonpost.com/news/sports/wp/2016/07/21/report-nba-will-move-2017-all-star-game-from-charlotte-to-new-orleans-over-hb2-law/?tid=a_inl.

Bowers v. Hardwick. (1986). Retrieved December 17, 2016 from https://www.law.cornell.edu/supremecourt/text/478/186.

Boylan, J. F. (2016, December 2). Really, you're blaming transgender people for Trump? *New York Times.* Retrieved January 6, 2017 from http://www.nytimes.com/2016/12/02/opinion/really-youre-blaming-transgender-people-for-trump.html.

Brodesser-Akner, T. (2014, August 31). Can Jill Soloway do justice to the trans movement? *New York Times Magazine.* Retrieved October 10, 2016 from http://www.nytimes.com/2014/08/31/magazine/can-jill-soloway-do-justice-to-the-trans-movement.html.

Bronski, M. (1998). *The pleasure principle: Sex, backlash, and the struggle for gay freedom.* New York, NY: St. Martin's Press.

Bronski, M. (2011). *A queer history of the United States.* Boston, MA: Beacon Press.

Bruni, F. (2013, January 22). Carrying a cause to the Super Bowl. *New York Times.* Retrieved July 10, 2017 from https://bruni.blogs.nytimes.com/2013/01/22/carrying-a-cause-to-the-super-bowl.

Brydum, S. (2014, May 7). *Orange Is the New Black*'s Lea DeLaria withdraws from Michfest. *Advocate.com.* Retrieved October 30, 2015 from http://www.advocate.com/arts-entertainment/2014/05/07/orange-new-blacks-lea-delaria-withdraws-michfest.

Burdge, H., Licona, A. C., & Hyemingway, Z. T. (2014). *LGBTQ youth of color: Discipline disparities, school push-out, and the school-to-prison pipeline.* San Francisco, CA: Gay–Straight Alliance Network and Tucson, AZ: Crossroads Collaborative at the University of Arizona.

Burleson, W. E. (2014). *Bi America: Myths, truths, and the struggles of an invisible community.* New York, NY: Routledge.

Byrne, M. (2015, March 21). A brief history of AZT, HIV's first "ray of hope." *Motherboard.* Retrieved December 17, 2016 from http://motherboard.vice.com/read/happy-birthday-to-azt-the-first-effective-hiv-treatment.

Cahill, S. (2004). *Same-sex marriage in the United States: Focus on the facts.* Lanham, MD: Lexington Books.

Califia, P. (1997). *Sex changes: The politics of transgenderism.* San Francisco, CA: Cleis Press.

California Department of Education. (n.d.). Frequently asked questions: Senate Bill 48. Retrieved April 17, 2015 from http://www.cde.ca.gov/ci/cr/cf/senatebill48faq.asp.

References

Capehart, J. (February 9, 2015). The internal challenges facing the LGBT movement. *Washington Post*. Retrieved June 8, 2016 from https://www. washingtonpost.com/blogs/post-partisan/wp/2015/02/09/the-internal-challen ges-facing-the-lgbt-movement/.

Carey, B. (2005, July 5). Straight, gay or lying? Bisexuality revisited. *New York Times*. Retrieved August 12, 2015 from http://www.nytimes.com/2005/07/05/ health/straight-gay-or-lying-bisexuality-revisited.html?_r=0.

Carmen. (2014a, January 27). #ProTransProChoice: Launching a new reproductive rights movement. *Autostraddle.com*. Retrieved October 16, 2015 from http://www.autostraddle.com/protransprochoice-launching-a-new-reproduc tive-rights-movement-219937/.

Carmen. (2014b, February 21). Portrait of a community: Inside Barneys' groundbreaking campaign featuring 17 trans* models. *Autostraddle.com*. Retrieved January 15, 2016 from http://www.autostraddle.com/portrait-of-a-commu nity-inside-barneys-groundbreaking-campaign-featuring-17-trans-models-224 202/.

Carter, D. (2004). *Stonewall: The riots that sparked the gay revolution*. New York, NY: St. Martin's Griffin.

Caulfield, K., & Trust, G. (2013, September 17). Macklemore & Ryan Lewis' "Same Love" & other no. 11 hits. *Billboard.com*. Retrieved May 26, 2016 from http://www.billboard.com/articles/columns/chart-beat/5695277/mackle more-ryan-lewis-same-love-other-no-11-hits.

CDC. (2001, June 1). HIV and AIDS – United States, 1981-2000. *MMWR*, 50(21), 430-434. Centers for Disease Control and Prevention. Retrieved December 17, 2016 from https://www.cdc.gov/mmwr/preview/mmwrhtml/ mm5021a2.htm.

CDC. (2013, November). HIV in the United States: At a glance. Centers for Disease Control and Prevention. Retrieved December 17, 2016 from www.cdc. gov/hiv/pdf/statistics_basics_factsheet.pdf.

CDC. (2016a). Health risks among sexual minority youth. Centers for Disease Control and Prevention. Retrieved September 30, 2016 from http://www.cdc. gov/healthyyouth/disparities/smy.htm.

CDC. (2016b, December 2). HIV in the United States: At a glance. Centers for Disease Control and Prevention. Retrieved December 17, 2016 from https:// www.cdc.gov/hiv/statistics/overview/ataglance.html.

"Change the nation." (n.d.). GSA Network. Retrieved August 7, 2016 from https://gsanetwork.org/get-involved/change-nation.

Chase, C. (1998). Portrait. Excerpted in L. Feinberg, *Trans liberation: Beyond pink or blue*. Boston, MA: Beacon Press.

Chauncey, G. (1994). *Gay New York: Gender, urban culture, and the making of the gay male world, 1890–1940*. New York, NY: Basic Books.

Chauncey, G. (2005). *Why marriage? The history shaping today's debate over gay equality*. New York, NY: Basic Books.

References

Cherlin, A. J. (2009). *The marriage-go-round: The state of marriage and the family in America today*. New York, NY: Vintage Books.

Choi, S.K., Wilson, B.D.M., Shelton, J., & Gates, G. (2015). *Serving our youth 2015: The needs and experiences of lesbian, gay, bisexual, transgender, and questioning youth experiencing homelessness*. Los Angeles, CA: The Williams Institute with True Colors Fund.

Clifton, D. (2013, March 29). What's behind criticisms of those red equal signs in your Facebook feed? *HuffPost Queer Voices*. Retrieved June 2, 2016 from http://www.huffingtonpost.com/derrick-clifton/human-rights-campaign-same-sex-marriage_b_2973131.html?utm_hp_ref=fb&src=sp&comm_ref=false.

Cohen, C. J. (1999). *The boundaries of Blackness: AIDS and the breakdown of Black politics*. Chicago, IL: University of Chicago Press.

Cohen, J. (2001). *Shots in the dark: The wayward search for an AIDS vaccine*. New York, NY: W.W. Norton & Company, Inc.

Collins, D. (2017, April 21). My life as a trans fraternity bro. *Vice*. Retrieved April 29, 2017 from https://www.vice.com/en_us/article/my-life-as-a-trans-fraternity-bro.

Collins, E. (2017, April 24). Republicans in Congress push for religious liberty executive order. *USA Today*. Retrieved April 29, 2017 from https://www.usatoday.com/story/news/politics/2017/04/24/republicans-congress-push-religious-liberty-executive-order/100842590/.

Combahee River Collective. (1977). The Combahee River Collective Statement. Retrieved July 25, 2016 from http://circuitous.org/scraps/combahee.html.

Coontz, S. (2005). *Marriage, a history: How love conquered marriage*. New York, NY: Penguin Books.

Copen, C. E., Chandra, A., & Febo-Vazquez, I. (2016, January 7). Sexual behavior, sexual attraction, and sexual orientation among adults aged 18-44 in the United States: Data from the 2011–2013 National Survey of Family Growth. *National Health Statistics Report*, No. 88. US Department of Health and Human Services, CDC.

Corbin, S. (2015, February 19). The truth about Truvada. *LGBT Weekly*. Retrieved December 17, 2016 from http://lgbtweekly.com/2015/02/19/the-truth-about-truvada/.

Crimp, D. (1993). Right on, girlfriend! Pp. 300–320 in M. Warner (ed.), *Fear of a queer planet: Queer politics and social theory*. Minneapolis, MN: University of Minnesota Press.

Cruz, E. (2014a, July 31). Larry King is confused by Anna Paquin's "non-practicing" bisexuality. *Advocate.com*. Retrieved October 8, 2015 from http://www.advocate.com/bisexuality/2014/07/31/larry-king-confused-anna-paquins-non-practicing-bisexuality.

Cruz, E. (2014b, August 26). When bisexual people get left out of marriage. *Advocate.com*. Retrieved January 15, 2016 from http://www.advocate.com/bisexuality/2014/08/26/when-bisexual-people-get-left-out-marriage.

References

Cruz, E. (2015, August 20). STUDY: 1 in 3 American young adults identify on bisexual spectrum. *Advocate.com*. Retrieved April 29, 2017 from http://www. advocate.com/bisexuality/2015/08/20/study-1-3-american-young-adults-identi fy-bisexual-spectrum.

Cunningham, M. (1992, May/June). Queer/straight. *Mother Jones*, 17(3), 60-68.

Currah, P., & Stryker, S. (eds.) (2014, May). Postposttransexual: Key concepts for a twenty-first-century transgender studies. Special Issue of *Transgender Studies Quarterly*, 1(1–2).

Davidson, M. (2007, December). Seeing refuge under the umbrella: Inclusion, exclusion, and organizing with the category *transgender*. *Sexuality Research & Social Policy*, 4(4), 60–80.

Decker, J. S. (2014). *The invisible orientation: An introduction to asexuality*. New York, NY: Carrel Books.

D'Emilio, J. (1992). *Making trouble: Essays on gay history, politics, and the university*. New York, NY: Routledge.

D'Emilio, J. (1998). *Sexual politics, sexual communities: The making of a homosexual minority in the United States, 1940–1970*. 2nd edn. Chicago, IL: University of Chicago Press.

Denizet-Lewis, B. (2009, September 27). Coming out in middle school. *New York Times Magazine*. Retrieved February 20, 2015 from http://www.nytimes. com/2009/09/27/magazine/27out-t.html?pagewanted=all&_r=0.

Denizet-Lewis, B. (2014, March 23). Bisexual male seeking like-minded friends . . . and legitimacy. *New York Times Magazine*, 20–29+.

Diamond, L. M. (2007, June). A dynamical systems approach to the development and expression of female same-sex sexuality. *Perspectives on Psychological Science*, 2(2), 142–161.

Diamond, S. (1995). *Road to dominion: Right-wing movements and political power in the United States*. New York, NY: Guilford Press.

Dominus, S. (2014, August 14). Transgender model Geena Rocero tells Glamour why she had to share her true story. *Glamour*. Retrieved January 15, 2016 from http://www.glamour.com/inspired/2014/08/glamour-exclusive-model-geena-rocero-on-being-transgender.

Donaldson, S. (1995). The bisexual movement's beginnings in the 70s: A personal retrospective. Pp. 31–45 in N. Tucker (ed.), *Bisexual politics: Theories, queries, and visions*. New York, NY: The Haworth Press.

Driver, S. (2008). Transforming political activism. Pp. 217–222 in S. Driver (ed.), *Queer youth cultures*. Albany, NY: State University of New York Press.

Duberman, M. (1993). *Stonewall*. New York, NY: Penguin Books.

Duggan, L. (2003). *The twilight of equality? Neoliberalism, cultural politics, and the attack on democracy*. Boston, MA: Beacon Press.

Echols, A. (1989). *Daring to be bad: Radical feminism in America 1967–1975*. Minneapolis, MN: University of Minnesota Press.

Eckholm, E. (2011, January 1). In isolated Utah city, new clubs for gay stu-

References

dents. *New York Times*. Retrieved January 5, 2017 from http://www.nytimes. com/2011/01/02/us/02utah.html.

Eigo, J. (2002). The city as body politic/the body as city unto itself. Pp. 178–195 in B. Shepard & R. Hayduk (eds.), *From ACT UP to the WTO: Urban protest and community building in the era of globalization*. London, UK: Verso.

Eisner, S. (2013). *Bi: Notes for a bisexual revolution*. Berkeley, CA: Seal Press.

Engdahl, U. (2014, May). Wrong body. Pp. 267–269 in P. Currah & S. Stryker (eds.), Postposttransexual: Key concepts for a twenty-first-century transgender studies. Special issue of *Transgender Studies Quarterly*, 1(1–2).

Engel, J. (2006). *The epidemic: A global history of AIDS*. New York, NY: Smithsonian Books/HarperCollins.

Ennis, D. (2014, October 14). *Time* names transgender teen one of 25 most influential. *Advocate.com*. Retrieved January 19, 2016 from http://www.advocate. com/politics/media/2014/10/14/time-names-transgender-teen-one-25-most-influential.

Epps, G. (2016, May 10). North Carolina's bathroom bill is a constitutional monstrosity. *The Atlantic*. Retrieved June 7, 2016 from http://www.theatlan tic.com/politics/archive/2016/05/hb2-is-a-constitutional-monstrosity/482106/.

Epstein, S. (1996). *Impure science: AIDS, activism, and the politics of knowledge*. Berkeley, CA: University of California Press.

Equality California. (n.d.). *FAIR Education Act*. Retrieved April 17, 2015 from http://www.eqca.org/site/pp.asp?c=kuLRJ9MRKrH&b=6451639.

Erickson-Schroth, L. (ed.) (2014). *Trans bodies, trans selves: A resource for the transgender community*. New York, NY: Oxford University Press.

Ermac, R. (2015, May 5). You'll cry when you see what happened during that gay-straight prom date. *Advocate.com*. Retrieved May 7, 2015 from http:// www.advocate.com/youth/2015/05/05/watch-you-ll-cry-when-you-see-what-happened-during-gay-straight-prom-date.

Ettelbrick, P. (1989). Since when is marriage a path to liberation? *OUT/LOOK*. Reprinted pp. 401–406 in William B. Rubenstein (ed.), *Lesbians, gay men, and the law*. New York, NY: The New Press, 1993.

Faderman, L. (1991). *Odd girls and twilight lovers: A history of lesbian life in 20th-century America*. New York, NY: Columbia University Press.

Faderman, L. (2015). *The gay revolution: The story of the struggle*. New York, NY: Simon & Schuster.

Faderman, L., & Timmons, S. (2009). *Gay LA: A history of sexual outlaws, power politics, and lipstick lesbians*. Berkeley, CA: University of California Press.

Farias, C. (2017, March 6). Supreme Court ducks big transgender rights case – thanks to Trump administration. *Huffington Post*. Retrieved April 29, 2017 from http://www.huffingtonpost.com/entry/supreme-court-gavin-grimm_us_58bd7527e4b0b9989418d80a.

References

Fausset, R. (2017, March 30). Bathroom law repeal leaves few pleased in North Carolina. *New York Times*. Retrieved May 7, 2017 from https://mobile. nytimes.com/2017/03/30/us/north-carolina-senate-acts-to-repeal-restrictive-bathroom-law.html.

Fausset, R., & Blinder, A. (2015, March 5). States weigh legislation to let businesses refuse to serve gay couples. *New York Times*. Retrieved June 7, 2016 from http://www.nytimes.com/2015/03/06/us/anticipating-nationwide-right-to-same-sex-marriage-states-weigh-religious-exemption-bills.html?_r=1.

Feinberg, L. (1996). *Transgender warriors: Making history from Joan of Arc to Dennis Rodman*. Boston, MA: Beacon Press.

Feinberg, L. (1998). *Trans liberation: Beyond pink or blue*. Boston, MA: Beacon Press.

Fetner, T. (2008). *How the religious right shaped lesbian and gay activism*. Minneapolis, MN: University of Minnesota Press.

Fetner, T. (2016, Spring). Attitudes toward lesbian and gay people are better than ever. *Contexts*, 15(2), 20–26.

Fleischer, D. (2010, August 3). *The Prop 8 report: What defeat in California can teach us about winning future ballot measures on same-sex marriage*. Retrieved February 19, 2015 from www.prop8report.org.

Flores, A. R., Herman, J. L., Gates, G. J., & Brown, T. N. T. (2016, June). *How many adults identify as transgender in the United States?* Los Angeles, CA: The Williams Institute, UCLA School of Law.

Ford, Z. (2015, March 10). Allowing transgender youth to transition improves their mental health, study finds. *Think Progress*. Retrieved January 19, 2016 from http://thinkprogress.org/lgbt/2015/03/10/3631788/letting-transgender-kids-transition-is-for-their-own-good/.

Ford, Z. (2016, October 7). Pence confirms once and for all that Trump will be an anti-LGBT president. *Think Progress*. Retrieved January 6, 2017 from https://thinkprogress.org/trump-pence-transgender-students-aa32ee93cdb7#. r6pmxc3r4.

France, D. (2016). *How to survive a plague: The inside story of how citizens and science tamed AIDS*. New York, NY: Alfred A. Knopf.

Franke, K. (2015). *Wedlocked: The perils of marriage equality. How African Americans and gays mistakenly thought the right to marry would set them free*. New York, NY: New York University Press.

Friedan, B (1963). *The feminine mystique*. New York, NY: Dell Publishing.

Gabriel (2014, August 25). The trans asterisk and why we need to stop using it. Retrieved January 19, 2016 from http://www.thepulpzine.com/the-trans-asterisk-and-why-we-need-to-stop-using-it/.

Gamson, J. (1989, October). Silence, death, and the invisible enemy: AIDS activism and social movement "newness." *Social Problems*, 36(4), 351–367.

Gamson, J. (1995, August). Must identity movements self-destruct? A queer dilemma. *Social Problems*, 42(3), 390–407.

Gamson, J. (1998). *Freaks talk back: Tabloid talk shows and sexual nonconformity.* Chicago, IL: University of Chicago Press.

Garber, M. (2000). *Bisexuality and the eroticism of everyday life.* New York, NY: Routledge.

Garcia, A. (2013, June 2). Meet Brad Taylor and Dylan Meehan, winners of their high school's "cutest couple" award. *Gaily Grind.* Retrieved March 12, 2015 from http://www.thegailygrind.com/2013/06/02/meet-brad-taylor-and-dylan-meehan-winners-of-their-high-schools-cutest-couple-award/.

Garner, G. (2015, October 6). Students chase Westboro Baptist Church away from their school. *Out.com.* Retrieved January 7, 2016 from http://www.out.com/news-opinion/2015/10/06/watch-students-chase-westboro-away-their-school.

Garza, A. (2014, October 7). A herstory of the #BlackLivesMatter movement. *Feminist Wire.* Retrieved May 5, 2017 from http://www.thefeministwire.com/2014/10/blacklivesmatter-2/.

Gates, G. J. (2011, April). *How many people are lesbian, gay, bisexual, and transgender?* Los Angeles, CA: The Williams Institute, UCLA School of Law.

Gates, G. J. (2017, January 11). In US, more adults identifying as LGBT. *Gallup.* Retrieved April 14, 2017 from http://www.gallup.com/poll/201731/lgbt-identification-rises.aspx.

"Gay Teens on TV." (n.d.). *Entertainment Weekly.* Retrieved June 9, 2015 from http://www.ew.com/gallery/gay-teens-tv-timeline.

Geidner, C. (2011, November 3). An angry heart. *Metro Weekly.* Retrieved August 26, 2016 from http://www.metroweekly.com/2011/11/an-angry-heart/.

Geidner, C. (2014, December 18). Justice Department will now support transgender discrimination claims in litigation. *BuzzFeed.* Retrieved January 19, 2016 from http://www.buzzfeed.com/chrisgeidner/justice-department-announces-reversal-on-litigating-transgen#.gpApyrByD5.

Gengle, D. (1976). Gay American Indians (GAI). Reprinted pp. 332–334 in J. N. Katz (ed.), *Gay American history: Lesbians and gay men in the USA.* 2nd rev. edn. New York, NY: Meridian, 1992.

Genzlinger, N. (2014, May 22). Raging amid tears in a gathering storm. *New York Times.* Retrieved December 11, 2016 from https://www.nytimes.com/2014/05/23/arts/television/mark-ruffalo-stars-in-larry-kramers-the-normal-heart.html?_r=0.

Ghaziani, A. (2008). *The dividends of dissent: How conflict and culture work in lesbian and gay marches on Washington.* Chicago, IL: University of Chicago Press.

Ghaziani, A. (2011, February). Post-gay collective identity construction. *Social Problems,* 58(1), 99–125.

Ghaziani, A. (2014). *There goes the gayborhood?* Princeton, NJ: Princeton University Press.

Ghaziani, A., Taylor, V., & Stone, A. (2016). Cycles of sameness and difference in LGBT social movements. *Annual Review of Sociology*, 42: 165–183.

Giddings, P. (1984). *When and where I enter: The impact of Black women on race and sex in America*. New York, NY: William Morrow.

Ginelle, L. (2015, September 8). Real talk with trans people: How to be an ally. Retrieved January 8, 2016 from https://medium.com/matter/real-talk-with-trans-people-57b9aa3b91a8#.9w7vcnbtd.

GLAAD. (2014, August). *Media reference guide*. 9th edition. Retrieved August 13, 2015 from http://www.glaad.org/reference.

GLAAD. (2016a). *2016 studio responsibility index*. Retrieved September 30, 2016 from http://www.glaad.org/sri/2016.

GLAAD. (2016b). *Where we are on TV '16 –'17*. Retrieved January 7, 2017 from http://www.glaad.org/whereweareontv16.

GLAAD. (2017). *Accelerating acceptance 2017: A Harris Poll survey of Americans' acceptance of LGBTQ people*. Retrieved April 29, 2017 from http://www.glaad.org/files/aa/2017_GLAAD_Accelerating_Acceptance.pdf.

GLSEN. (n.d.(a)). State maps. Retrieved January 7, 2017 from http://glsen.org/article/state-maps.

GLSEN. (n.d.(b)) GSA: Gay–Straight Alliances. Retrieved August 11, 2016 from http://action.glsen.org/page/s/GSAregistration.

GLSEN. (2012). *Playgrounds and prejudice: Elementary school climate in the United States*. Retrieved March 17, 2015 from http://glsen.org/playgroundsandprejudice.

Goldberg, L. (2015, March 19). "Glee" stars on its "groundbreaking" legacy: The show "will live on for generations." *Hollywood Reporter*. Retrieved June 9, 2015 from http://www.hollywoodreporter.com/live-feed/glee-finale-legacy-782952.

Gordon, M. Price, M. S., & Peralta, K. (2016, March 26). Understanding HB2: North Carolina's newest law solidifies state's role in defining discrimination. *Charlotte Observer*. Retrieved June 7, 2016 from http://www.charlotteobserver.com/news/politics-government/article68401147.html.

Gould, D. B. (2009). *Moving politics: Emotion and ACT UP's fight against AIDS*. Chicago, IL: University of Chicago Press.

Graff, E. J. (1996, June 24). Retying the knot. *The Nation*. Reprinted pp. 135–138 in A. Sullivan (ed.), *Same-sex marriage: Pro and con. A reader*. Rev. edn. New York, NY: Vintage Books, 2004.

Graff, E. J. (2004). *What is marriage for?* Boston, MA: Beacon Press.

Grant, J. M., Mottet, L. A., Tanis, J., Harrison, J., Herman, J. L., & Keisling, M. (2011). *Injustice at every turn: A report of the National Transgender Discrimination Survey*. Washington, DC: National Center for Transgender Equality and National Gay and Lesbian Task Force.

Gray, M. L. (2009). *Out in the country: Youth, media, and queer visibility in rural America*. New York, NY: New York University Press.

References

Greenfield, B. (2006, May 26). Intense, unique no-man's lands. *New York Times*. Retrieved October 23, 2015 from http://www.nytimes.com/2006/05/26/travel/26ahead.html?_r=0.

Greenhouse, L. (2003, June 27). The Supreme Court: Homosexual rights; Justices, 6–3, legalize gay sexual conduct in sweeping reversal of Court's '86 ruling. *The New York Times*. Retrieved May 25, 2016 from http://www.nytimes.com/2003/06/27/us/supreme-court-homosexual-rights-justices-6-3-legalize-gay-sexual-conduct.html?pagewanted=all.

Gremore, G. (2016, September 23). Asexuals are tired of your crap, demand greater visibility. *Queerty*. Retrieved April 29, 2017 from https://www.queerty.com/asexuals-tired-crap-demand-greater-visibility-20160923.

Griffin, P., & Ouellett, M. (2003). From silence to safety and beyond: Historical trends in addressing lesbian, gay, bisexual, transgender issues in K-12 schools. *Equity & Excellence in Education*, 36, 106–114.

Griffin, P., Lee, C., Waugh, J., & Beyer, C. (2004). Describing roles that Gay–Straight Alliances play in schools: From individual support to school change. *Journal of Gay & Lesbian Issues in Education*, 1(3), 7–22.

Grinberg, E. (2017, January 31). Boy Scouts open membership to transgender boys. *CNN.com*. Retrieved April 29, 2017 from http://www.cnn.com/2017/01/30/us/boy-scouts-transgender-membership/index.html.

Grindley, L. (2012, January 12). EricJames Borges, 19, leaves behind message of love. *Advocate.com*. Retrieved June 23, 2015 from http://www.advocate.com/news/daily-news/2012/01/13/ericjames-borges-19-leaves-behind-message-love.

Grindley, L., & Ring, T. (2017, May 4). Trump signs religious order but drops "license to discriminate." *Advocate.com*. Retrieved May 7, 2017 from http://www.advocate.com/politics/2017/5/04/trump-signs-order-drops-license-discriminate.

Gross, L. (1993). *Contested closets: The politics and ethics of outing*. Minneapolis, MN: University of Minnesota Press.

Gross, L. (2001). *Up from invisibility: Lesbians, gay men, and the media in America*. New York, NY: Columbia University Press.

Grossman, A. H., & D'Augelli, A. R. (2007, October). Transgender youth and life-threatening behaviors. *Suicide and Life-Threatening Behavior*, 37(5), 527–537.

GSA Network. (n.d.). History and accomplishments. Retrieved May 26, 2015 from https://www.gsanetwork.org/about-us/history.

GSA Network. (2016, April 17). GSA Network unveils new name and tagline. Retrieved September 22, 2016 from https://gsanetwork.org/GSA-Network-Unveils-New-Name-and-Tagline.

Guo, J. (2016, January 8). Sorry, grammar nerds. The singular "they" has been declared Word of the Year. *Washington Post*. Retrieved January 11, 2016 from https://www.washingtonpost.com/news/wonk/wp/2016/01/08/donald-trump-may-win-this-years-word-of-the-year.

References

Haas, A. P., Rodgers, P. L., & Herman, J. L. (2014, January). *Suicide attempts among transgender and gender non-conforming adults*. New York, NY and Los Angeles, CA: American Foundation for Suicide Prevention and the Williams Institute.

Harding, N. (2016, August 10). Nike's first ever ad starring a transgender athlete is actual #lifespo. *Cosmopolitan*. Retrieved October 13, 2016 from http://www.cosmopolitan.com.au/fashion/nike-chris-mosier-transgender-ad-16037.

Harkinson, J. (2015, June 26). Sweet vindication for Gavin Newsom, who staked his career on same-sex marriage. *Mother Jones*. Retrieved May 31, 2016 from http://www.motherjones.com/politics/2015/06/san-francisco-mayor-gavin-newsom-supreme-court-ruling-same-sex-marriage.

Harris, D. (1997). *The rise and fall of gay culture*. New York, NY: Ballantine Books.

Harrison, J., Grant, J., & Herman, J. L. (2011/2012). A gender not listed here: genderqueers, gender rebels, and OtherWise in the National Transgender Discrimination Survey. *LGBTQ Policy Journal at the Harvard Kennedy School*, 2: 13–24.

Heller, K. (2016, June 28). How North Carolina's idyllic hipster haven is being hurt by the "bathroom bill" boycott. *Washington Post*. Retrieved January 5, 2017 from https://www.washingtonpost.com/lifestyle/style/how-north-carolinas-idyllic-hipster-haven-is-being-hurt-by-the-bathroom-bill-boycott/2016/06/28/28fc707a-33d4-11e6-8758-d58e76e11b12_story.html?utm_term=.36008600a9fe.

Hempel, J. (2016, September 12). My brother's pregnancy and the making of a new American family. *Time*. Retrieved October 7, 2016 from http://time.com/4475634/trans-man-pregnancy-evan/.

Herzog, D. (2008). *Sex in crisis: The new sexual revolution and the future of American politics*. New York, NY: Basic Books.

Hetter, K. (2012, January 13). Girl Scouts accepts transgender kid, provokes cookie boycott. *CNN.com*. Retrieved March 12, 2015 from http://www.cnn.com/2012/01/13/living/girl-scout-boycott/.

Heywood, T. A. (2008, April 10). HRC leader stands by non-inclusive ENDA decision. *Pridesource*. Retrieved November 13, 2015 from http://www.pridesource.com/article.html?article=29930.

Highleyman, L. (2002). Radical queers or queer radicals? Queer activism and the global justice movement. Pp. 106–120 in B. Shepard & R. Hayduk (eds.), *From ACT UP to the WTO: Urban protest and community building in the era of globalization*. London, UK: Verso.

Hirshman, L. (2013). *Victory: The triumphant gay revolution*. New York, NY: Harper Perennial.

Hoffman, J. (2016, August 11). Gay and lesbian high school students report "heartbreaking" levels of violence. *New York Times*. Retrieved September 30,

2016 from http://www.nytimes.com/2016/08/12/health/gay-lesbian-teenagers-violence.html.

hooks, b. (1984). *Feminist theory: From margin to center.* Boston, MA: South End Press.

Hooper, J. (2015, June 29). Pat Buchanan doubles down on 1983 column claiming AIDS is nature's punishment. Retrieved August 19, 2016 from http://www.goodasyou.org/good_as_you/2015/06/pat-buchanan-doubles-down-on-1983-column-claiming-aids-is-natures-punishment.html.

HRC. (n.d.). *Answers to questions about marriage equality.* Retrieved July 17, 2017 from http://gaymarriage.procon.org/sourcefiles/HRC-answers-to-questions-about-marriage-equality.pdf.

HRC. (2015). *Beyond marriage equality: A blueprint for federal non-discrimination protections.* Washington, DC: Human Rights Campaign. Retrieved November 19, 2015 from http://www.hrc.org/campaigns/beyond-marriage-equality-a-blueprint-for-federal-non-discrimination-protect.

Hughes. S. A. (2011, September 21). Jamey Rodemeyer, bullied teen who made "It Gets Better" video, commits suicide. *Washington Post.* Retrieved June 23, 2015 from http://www.washingtonpost.com/blogs/blogpost/post/jamey-rodemeyer-bullied-teen-who-made-it-gets-better-video-commits-suicide/2011/09/21/gIQAVVzxkK_blog.html.

Hunt, L. (2013, March 5). Transgender MMA fighter Fallon Fox faces licensing problems. *Sports Illustrated.* Retrieved January 15, 2016 from http://www.si.com/mma/2013/03/05/fallon-fox-transgender-mma.

Hutchins, L., & Ka'ahumanu, L. (eds.) (1991). *Bi any other name: Bisexual people speak out.* Los Angeles, CA: Alyson Books.

Ito, M., et al. (2010). *Hanging out, messing around, and geeking out: Kids living and learning with new media.* Cambridge, MA: MIT Press.

James, S. E., Herman, J. L., Rankin, S., Keisling, M., Mottet, L., & Anafi, M. (2016). *The Report of the 2015 U.S. Transgender Survey.* Washington, DC: National Center for Transgender Equality.

Jarvis, E. (2015, June 10). Meet Ruby Rose, the new *Orange Is the New Black* star who won't be mistaken for Justin Bieber much longer. *Vanity Fair.* Retrieved May 7, 2017 from http://www.vanityfair.com/hollywood/2015/06/ruby-rose-orange-is-the-new-black.

Jennings, K. (2006). *Mama's boy, preacher's son: A memoir of growing up, coming out, and changing America's schools.* Boston, MA: Beacon Press.

Jurney, C. (2016, November 3). North Carolina bathroom bill flushes away $630 million in lost business. *Forbes.* Retrieved January 8, 2017 from http://www.forbes.com/sites/corinnejurney/2016/11/03/north-carolinas-bathroom-bill-flushes-away-750-million-in-lost-business/#325e01e6405c.

Juro, R. (2004, May 7). If not now, when??? Retrieved July 17, 2017 from http://lostkidz.livejournal.com/53329.html.

References

Juro, R. (2013, April 1). Even after all these years, HRC still doesn't get it. *Huffington Post*. Retrieved November 13, 2015 from http://www.huffing tonpost.com/rebecca-juro/even-after-all-these-years-hrc-still-doesnt-get -it_b_2989826.html.

Juro, R. (2014a, July 25). Op-ed: Why Janet Mock's new job gives me hope. *Advocate.com*. Retrieved January 15, 2016 from http://www.advocate.com/ commentary/2014/07/25/op-ed-why-janet-mocks-new-job-gives-me-hope.

Juro, R. (2014b, September 5). Transcript: HRC President Chad Griffin apologizes to trans people at Southern Comfort. *Advocate.com*. Retrieved November 13, 2015 from http://www.advocate.com/politics/transgender/2014/09/05/ transcript-hrc-president-chad-griffin-apologizes-trans-people-speech.

Kahrl, C. (2015, June 2). The meaning of Caitlyn Jenner. Grantland.com. Retrieved July 16, 2015 from http://grantland.com/hollywood-prospectus/ caitlyn-jenner-vanity-fair-cover-announcement/.

Kapadia, S. (2016, August 23). Seahawks Russell Wilson moved wedding due to North Carolina law. *ESPN.com*. Retrieved October 13, 2016 from http:// www.espn.com/nfl/story/_/id/17369825/seattle-seahawks-quarterback-russell-wilson-ciara-marriage-changed-north-carolina-due-state-transgender-bathro om-laws.

Katz, J. N. (1992). *Gay American history: Lesbians and gay men in the USA*. Rev. edn. New York, NY: Meridian.

Katz, J. N. (2007). *The invention of heterosexuality*. Chicago, IL: University of Chicago Press.

Kayal, P. M. (1993). *Bearing witness: Gay Men's Health Crisis and the politics of AIDS*. Boulder, CO: Westview Press.

Keegan, C. (2014, October 22). Op-ed: How *Transparent* tried and failed to represent trans men. *Advocate.com*. Retrieved October 10, 2016 from http:// www.advocate.com/commentary/2014/10/22/op-ed-how-transparent-tried-and-failed-represent-trans-men.

Keisling, M. (2015, July 23). Op-ed: The Equality Act is the LGBT rights bill we want and need. *Advocate.com*. Retrieved November 13, 2015 from http:// www.advocate.com/commentary/2015/07/23/op-ed-equality-act-lgbt-rights-bill-we-want-and-need.

Kellaway, M., & Brydum, S. (2015, July 27). These are the US trans women killed in 2015. *Advocate.com*. Retrieved July 29, 2015 from http://www.advocate. com/transgender/2015/07/27/these-are-trans-women-killed-so-far-us-2015.

Kim, C. (2013, April 10). Ladies, are you ready for Michfest? *Advocate. com*. Retrieved October 30, 2015 from http://www.advocate.com/ women/2013/04/10/ladies-are-you-ready-michfest.

Kimport, K. (2014). *Queering marriage: Challenging family formation in the United States*. New Brunswick, NJ: Rutgers University Press.

Kinsella, J. (1989). *Covering the plague: AIDS and the American media*. New Brunswick, NJ: Rutgers University Press.

References

Kinser, J. (2012, June 19). Chris Colfer tells how Kurt and Blaine helped gay teens. *Advocate.com*. Retrieved June 9, 2015 from http://www.advocate.com/arts-entertainment/television/2012/06/19/watch-chris-colfer-tells-how-kurt-and-blaine-helped-gay.

Kinsman, G., & Gentile, P. (2010). *The Canadian war on queers*. Vancouver, BC: UBC Press.

Klein, R. (2014, October 8). LGBT kids of color are more likely to be disciplined in school, study shows. *Huffington Post*. Retrieved January 7, 2016 from http://www.huffingtonpost.com/2014/10/08/lgbt-kids-of-color-_n_5949008.html.

Kramer, A. E. (2017, April 21). "They starve you. They shock you": Inside the anti-gay pogrom in Chechnya. *New York Times*. Retrieved April 29, 2017 from https://mobile.nytimes.com/2017/04/21/world/europe/chechnya-russia-attacks-gays.html?smid=tw-share&_r=0&referer=https://t.co/4yHkrKUDyE.

Kramer, L. (1983, March 14–27). 1,112 and counting. *New York Native, 59*. Reprinted pp. 33–51 in L. Kramer, *Reports from the holocaust: The story of an AIDS activist*. New York, NY: St. Martin's Press, 1994.

Kramer, L. (1987, March 10). The beginning of ACTing UP. Speech. Reprinted pp. 127–139 in L. Kramer, *Reports from the holocaust: The story of an AIDS activist*. New York, NY: St. Martin's Press, 1994.

Kramer, L. (1994). *Reports from the holocaust: The story of an AIDS activist*. New York, NY: St. Martin's Press.

Kosciw, J. G., Greytak, E. A., Giga, N. M., Villenas, C., & Danischewski, D. J. (2016). *The 2015 national school climate survey: The experiences of lesbian, gay, bisexual, transgender, and queer youth in our nation's schools*. GLSEN. Retrieved January 7, 2017 from http://www.glsen.org/article/2015-national-school-climate-survey.

Lambda Legal. (2015, February 3). Changing birth certificate sex designations: State-by-state guidelines. Retrieved July 12, 2017 from https://www.lambdalegal.org/know-your-rights/article/trans-changing-birth-certificate-sex-designations.

Lesbian Avengers. (n.d.). An incomplete history . . . . Retrieved December 8, 2016 from http://www.lesbianavengers.com/about/history.shtml.

LGBTQ Nation. (2013, May 29). Mass. High school awards Prom Queen title to transgender student. Retrieved June 3, 2015 from http://www.lgbtqnation.com/2013/05/mass-high-school-awards-prom-queen-title-to-transgender-student/.

Long, M. G. (ed.) (2014). *Gay is good: The life and letters of gay rights pioneer Franklin Kameny*. Syracuse, NY: Syracuse University Press.

Lorde, A. (1984). *Sister outsider*. Berkeley, CA: Crossing Press.

Lubold, G. (2017, August 23). White House sets rules for military transgender ban. *Wall Street Journal*. Retrieved August 24, 2017 from https://www.wsj.com/articles/white-house-sets-rules-for-military-transgender-ban-1503534757.

References

Macgillivray, I. K. (2004). *Sexual orientation and school policy: A practical guide for teachers, administrators, and community activists*. Lanham, MD: Rowman & Littlefield Publishers, Inc.

Malloy, P. M. (2014a, March 13). Debunking the "surgery is a top priority for trans people" myth. *Advocate.com*. Retrieved January 14, 2016 from http://www.advocate.com/politics/transgender/2014/03/13/watch-debunking-surgery-top-priority-trans-people-myth.

Malloy, P. M. (2014b, May 16). Michfest urges attendees to rally behind its performers. *Advocate.com*. Retrieved October 23, 2015 from http://www.advocate.com/arts-entertainment/2014/05/16/michfest-urges-attendees-rally-behind-its-performers.

Malloy, P. M. (2014c, July 2). Op-ed: Happy birthday, Sylvia Rivera, LGBT rights pioneer. *Advocate.com*. Retrieved July 15, 2016 from http://www.advocate.com/commentary/2014/07/02/op-ed-remembering-our-queer-history-and-wishing-happy-birthday-sylvia-rivera.

Malloy, P. M. (2014d, July 10). Laverne Cox, Emmy trailblazer. *The Daily Beast*. Retrieved January 15, 2016 from http://www.thedailybeast.com/articles/2014/07/10/laverne-cox-emmy-trailblazer.html.

Malloy, P. M. (2014e, July 26). Trans celebs are great; trans leaders are better. *The Daily Beast*. Retrieved January 15, 2016 from http://www.thedailybeast.com/articles/2014/07/26/trans-celebs-are-great-trans-leaders-are-better.html.

Mandell, S. (2015, March 3). "The Fosters" features same-sex kiss between two 13-year-olds, possibly youngest in US TV history. *Towleroad.com*. Retrieved June 10, 2015 from http://www.towleroad.com/2015/03/the-fosters-features-what-could-be-the-youngest-same-sex-kiss-between-two-13-year-old-boys-video.html.

Marcus, E. (2002). *Making gay history: The half-century fight for lesbian and gay equal rights*. New York, NY: HarperCollins.

Mayberry, M. (2006). The story of a Salt Lake City Gay–Straight Alliance: Identity work and LGBT youth. *Journal of Gay & Lesbian Issues in Education*, 4(1), 13–31.

McCormack, M. (2012). *The declining significance of homophobia: How teenage boys are redefining masculinity and heterosexuality*. New York, NY: Oxford University Press.

McGuire, J. K., Anderson, C. R., Toomey, R. B., & Russell, S. T. (2010). School climate for transgender youth: A mixed method investigation of student experiences and school responses. *Journal of Youth and Adolescence*, 39, 1175–1188.

MentalHelp.net. (2016). Mental health in the LGBT community. *Mentalhelp.net*. Retrieved January 8, 2017 from https://www.mentalhelp.net/mental-health-in-the-lgbt-community/.

Meyerowitz, J. (2002). *How sex changed: A history of transsexuality in the United States*. Cambridge, MA: Harvard University Press.

References

Miceli, M. (2005). *Standing out, standing together: The social and political impact of Gay–Straight Alliances*. New York, NY: Routledge.

Michaelson, J. (2016, November 16). The GOP's anti-LGBT, anti-women "religious freedom" law on steroids. *The Daily Beast*. Retrieved January 6, 2017 from http://www.thedailybeast.com/articles/2016/11/16/the-gops-anti-lgbt-anti-women-religious-freedom-law-on-steroids.html.

Michelson, N. (2016, June 3). What to do if your kid is "frightened" by a trans person in the bathroom. *Huffington Post*. Retrieved June 7, 2016 from http://www.huffingtonpost.com/entry/maya-dillard-smith-transgender_us_575179a7e4b0eb20fa0d9475.

Michfest (n.d.). Welcome to Michfest. Retrieved October 23, 2015 from http://michfest.com/welcome-to-michfest/.

Mize, T. D. (2016). Sexual orientation in the labor market. *American Sociological Review*, 81(6), 1132–1160.

Mock, J. (2014). *Redefining realness: My path to womanhood, identity, love and so much more*. New York, NY: Atria Books.

Mock, J. (2015, February 16). A note on visibility in the wake of 6 trans women's murders in 2015. Retrieved July 29, 2015 from http://janetmock.com/2015/02/16/six-trans-women-killed-this-year/.

Molloy, S. (2015, January 14). Ruby Rose says she doesnt [*sic*] identify as female or male, after releasing a gender-bending short film. *News.com.au*. Retrieved May 7, 2017 from http://www.news.com.au/entertainment/music/ruby-rose-says-she-doesnt-identify-as-female-or-male-after-releasing-a-gender bending-short-film/news-story/c45af1108f39bff4594778e4cc4abe74.

Montgomery, P. (2015, Winter). What to do when "I do" is done. *American Prospect*. Retrieved June 8, 2016 from http://prospect.org/article/what-do-when-i-do-done.

Moodie-Mills, D. (2011, September 8). The kids are not alright: The plight of African American LGBT youth in America's schools. *Center for American Progress*. Retrieved March 20, 2015 from https://www.americanprogress.org/issues/lgbt/news/2011/09/08/10362/the-kids-are-not-alright/.

Moore, D. L. (2014, October 17). Black freedom fighters in Ferguson: Some of us are queer. *The Feminist Wire*. Retrieved May 5, 2017 from http://www.thefeministwire.com/2014/10/some-of-us-are-queer/.

Morland, I. (2014, May). Intersex. Pp. 111–115 in P. Currah & S. Stryker (eds.), Postposttransexual: Key concepts for a twenty-first-century transgender studies. Special Issue of *Transgender Studies Quarterly*, 1(1–2).

Morn, R. (2013, August 29). New Mexico gay marriage legal since … 2004? *AMERICAblog*. Retrieved April 14, 2017 from http://americablog.com/2013/08/new-mexico-gay-marriage-since-2004.html.

Movement Advancement Project, BiNetUSA, and Bisexual Resource Center. (2014). *Understanding issues facing bisexual Americans*. Denver, CO: Movement Advancement Project.

Murphy, T. (2014, July 14–27). Forgetting HIV. *New York Magazine*, 40–47.

NAMES Project Foundation. (n.d.). The AIDS Memorial Quilt. Retrieved January 9, 2017 from http://www.aidsquilt.org/about/the-aids-memorial-quilt.

National LGBTQ Task Force. (n.d.). Historic Victory: US Senate passes Employment Non-Discrimination Act. Retrieved November 13, 2015 from http://www.thetaskforce.org/historic-victory-u-s-senate-passes-employment-non-discrimination-act/.

Navarro, M. (1994, November 12). Life of 22 years ends, but not before many heard message on AIDS. *New York Times*. Retrieved December 15, 2016 from http://www.nytimes.com/1994/11/12/us/life-of-22-years-ends-but-not-before-many-heard-message-on-aids.html.

Northrop, A. (2003, May 28). Interview, conducted by Sarah Schulman. ACT UP Oral History Project. Retrieved August 5, 2016 from http://www.actuporalhistory.org/interviews/images/northrop.pdf.

Obergefell et al. v. Hodges (2015) *The US Supreme Court decision on marriage equality, as delivered by Justice Anthony Kennedy.* Brooklyn, NY: Melville House.

Ochs, R. (2009a). Biphobia. Pp. 248–254 in R. Ochs & S. E. Rowley (eds.), *Getting bi: Voices of bisexuals around the world.* 2nd edn. Boston, MA: Bisexual Resource Center.

Ochs, R. (2009b). Bisexual. Pp. 7–9 in R. Ochs & S. E. Rowley (eds.), *Getting bi: Voices of bisexuals around the world.* 2nd edn. Boston, MA: Bisexual Resource Center.

O'Donnell, N. (2014, October 1). How authentic is "Transparent"? A transgender activist on Jeffrey Tambor and other portrayals. *IndieWire*. Retrieved October 10, 2016 from http://www.indiewire.com/2014/10/how-authentic-is-transparent-a-transgender-activist-on-jeffrey-tambor-and-other-portrayals-69529/.

O'Hara, M. E. (2014, June 11). AMA says transgender people shouldn't require surgery to change their birth certificate. *VICE News*. Retrieved January 14, 2016 from https://news.vice.com/article/ama-says-transgender-people-shouldnt-require-surgery-to-change-their-birth-certificate.

O'Hara, M. E. (2017a, April 8). This law firm is linked to anti-transgender bathroom bills across the country. *NBC News*. Retrieved April 29, 2017 from http://www.nbcnews.com/feature/nbc-out/law-firm-linked-anti-transgender-bathroom-bills-across-country-n741106.

O'Hara, M. E. (2017b, May 2). Over 200 members of Congress file federal LGBTQ-rights bill. *NBC News*. Retrieved May 5, 2017 from http://www.nbcnews.com/feature/nbc-out/over-200-members-congress-file-federal-lgbtq-rights-bill-n754006?cid=sm_npd_nn_fb_np.

Padawer, R. (2014, October 15). When women become men at Wellesley. *New York Times Magazine*. Retrieved October 16, 2015 from http://www.nytimes.com/2014/10/19/magazine/when-women-become-men-at-wellesley-college.html.

References

Padug, R.A., & Oppenheimer, G.M. (1992), Riding the tiger: AIDS and the gay community. Pp. 245–278 in E. Fee & D.M. Fox (eds.), *AIDS: The making of a chronic disease*. Berkeley, CA: University of California Press.

Pascoe, C. J. (2007). *Dude, you're a fag: Masculinity and sexuality in high school*. Berkeley, CA: University of California Press.

Patton, C. (1990). *Inventing AIDS*. New York, NY: Routledge.

Patton, C. (1996). *Fatal advice: How safe-sex education went wrong*. Durham, NC: Duke University Press.

Pepin, J. (2011). *The origins of AIDS*. Cambridge, UK: Cambridge University Press.

Percelay, R. (2015, June 3). 17 school districts debunk right-wing lies about protections for transgender students. Retrieved January 8, 2016 from http://mediamatters.org/research/2015/06/03/17-school-districts-debunk-right-wing-lies-abou/203867.

Peters, J. W., Becker, J., & Davis, J. H. (2017, February 22). Trump rescinds rules on bathrooms for transgender students. *New York Times*. Retrieved May 7, 2017 from https://www.nytimes.com/2017/02/22/us/politics/devos-sessions-transgender-students-rights.html.

Peters, S. (2016, February 22). New HRC report reveals unprecedented onslaught of state legislation targeting transgender Americans. Retrieved April 14, 2017 from http://www.hrc.org/blog/new-hrc-report-reveals-unprecedented-onslaught-of-state-legislation-targeti.

Peterson, C. M., Matthews, A., Copps-Smith, E., & Conard, L. A. (2016, August 19). Suicidality, self-harm, and body dissatisfaction in transgender adolescents and emerging adults with gender dysphoria. *Suicide & Life-Threatening Behavior* [serial online], 1–8.

Pew Research Center. (2015, June 26). Gay marriage around the world. Retrieved January 9, 2017 from http://www.pewforum.org/2015/06/26/gay-marriage-around-the-world-2013/.

Pierceson, J. (2016). *Sexual minorities and politics: An introduction*. Lanham, MD: Rowman & Littlefield.

Polikoff, N. D. (2008). *Beyond (straight and gay) marriage: Valuing all families under the law*. Boston, MA: Beacon Press.

Poteat, V. P., et al. (2015, January/February). Contextualizing Gay–Straight Alliances: Student, advisor, and structural factors related to positive youth development among members. *Child Development*, 86(1), 176-193.

Pride Divide. (1997, documentary). Directed by Paris Poirier.

Quart, A. (2008, March 16). When girls will be boys. *New York Times Magazine*. Retrieved October 16, 2015 from http://www.nytimes.com/2008/03/16/magazine/16students-t.html?pagewanted=all&_r=0.

Queer Nation. (n.d.). Queer Nation NY History. Retrieved December 8, 2016 from http://queernationny.org/history.

Quinlan, C. (2015, October 22). School official said a shirt was "an open invitation to sex." *Think Progress*. Retrieved January 7, 2016 from http://thinkprogress.org/education/2015/10/22/3715051/lesbian-students-t-shirts/.

Ray, A., & Saliers, E. (2013, April 14). A note from Amy & Emily. Retrieved July 18, 2017 from http://indigogirls.com/?p=2079.

Raymond, D., & Highleyman, L. A. (1995). Brief timeline of bisexual activism in the United States. Pp. 333–337 in N. Tucker (ed.), *Bisexual politics: Theories, queries, and visions*. New York, NY: The Haworth Press.

Raymond, J. G. (1994[1979]). *The transsexual empire: The making of the she-male*. New York, NY: Teachers College Press.

Republican National Committee. (2016). *Republican platform 2016*. Retrieved January 6, 2017 from https://www.gop.com/the-2016-republican-party-platform/.

Rhode, D. L. (2016, May 2). Op-ed: Why is adultery still a crime? *Los Angeles Times*. Retrieved May 5, 2017 from http://www.latimes.com/opinion/op-ed/la-oe-rhode-decriminalize-adultery-20160429-story.html.

Rich, F. (1985, April 22). Theater: "The Normal Heart," by Larry Kramer. *New York Times*. Retrieved December 11, 2016 from http://www.nytimes.com/1985/04/22/theater/theater-the-normal-heart-by-larry-kramer.html.

RichardsFink, P. (2013, January 28). For bi guys thinking of coming out. *Huffington Post*. Retrieved October 8, 2015 from http://www.huffingtonpost.com/patrick-richardsfink/for-bi-guys-thinking-of-coming-out_b_2530612.html.

Richman, K. D. (2009). *Courting change: Queer parents, judges, and the transformation of American family law*. New York, NY: New York University Press.

Rimmerman, C. A. (2002). *From identity to politics: The lesbian and gay movements in the United States*. Philadelphia, PA: Temple University Press.

Rimmerman, C. A. (2008). *The lesbian and gay movements; Assimilation or liberation?* Boulder, CO: Westview Press.

Ring, T. (2012, January 9). Marriage equality is a trans issue, too. *Advocate.com*. Retrieved January 9, 2017 from http://www.advocate.com/print-issue/advance/2012/01/09/marriage-equality-trans-issue-too.

Ring, T. (2015, April 21). This year's Michigan Womyn's Music Festival will be the last. *Advocate.com*. Retrieved October 23, 2015 from http://www.advocate.com/michfest/2015/04/21/years-michigan-womyns-music-festival-will-be-last.

Ring, T. (2017, May 2). Trump moves to dump trans-inclusive health care rule. *Advocate.com*. Retrieved May 7, 2017 from http://www.advocate.com/health/2017/5/02/trump-moves-dump-trans-inclusive-health-care-rule.

Rinkunas, S. (2016, January 28). The trans athlete behind the Olympic Committee's new gender policy. *New York Magazine*. Retrieved October 13, 2016 from http://nymag.com/thecut/2016/01/chris-mosier-transgender-athltes-olympics.html.

Rivera, S. (2001 June). History is a weapon: "Our armies are rising and we are getting stronger." Retrieved July 15, 2016 from http://www.historyisaweapon. com/defcon1/riverarisingandstronger.html.

Roberts, M. (2007, October 8). Why the transgender community hates HRC. *TransGriot*. Retrieved July 6, 2017 from http://transgriot.blogspot. com/2007/10/why-transgender-community-hates-hrc.html.

Roberts, M. (2013, April 8). Why the trans community loathes HRC. *TransGriot*. Retrieved November 13, 2015 from http://transgriot.blogspot.com/2013/04/ why-trans-community-loathes-hrc.html.

Robinson, J. P., & Espelage, D. L. (2011). Inequities in educational and psychological outcomes between LGBTQ and straight students in middle and high school. *Educational Researcher*, 40(7), 315–330.

Rodriguez, C. Y., & Santana, M. (2013, November 26). Victoria's Secret petitioned to hire first transgender model. *CNN.com*. Retrieved January 15, 2016 from http://www.cnn.com/2013/11/14/showbiz/transgender-model-victorias-secret/.

Rodriguez, H. (2015, August 21). We can't let increased transgender visibility lead to more vulnerability. *Guardian*. Retrieved January 19, 2016 from http:// www.theguardian.com/commentisfree/2015/aug/21/transgender-visibility-vul nerability.

Rodríguez Rust, P. C. (2000a). The biology, psychology, sociology, and sexuality of bisexuality. Pp. 403–470 in P.C. Rodríguez Rust (ed.), *Bisexuality in the United States: A social science reader*. New York, NY: Columbia University Press.

Rodríguez Rust, P. C. (2000b). Popular images and the growth of bisexual community and visibility. Pp. 537–553 in P.C. Rodríguez Rust (ed.), *Bisexuality in the United States: A social science reader*. New York, NY: Columbia University Press.

Rodríguez Rust, P. C. (2000c). Preface. Pp. xiii–xviii in P.C. Rodríguez Rust (ed.), *Bisexuality in the United States: A social science reader*. New York, NY: Columbia University Press.

Rodríguez Rust, P. C. (2000d). Review of statistical findings about bisexual behavior, feelings, and identities. Pp. 129–184 in P.C. Rodríguez Rust (ed.), *Bisexuality in the United States: A social science reader*. New York, NY: Columbia University Press.

Rofes, E. (1990, Spring). Gay Lib vs. AIDS: Averting civil war in the 1990s. *OUT/LOOK*, 2(4), 8–17.

Rofes, E. (1998). *Dry bones breathe: Gay men creating post-AIDS identities and cultures*. New York, NY: Harrington Park Press.

Rofes, E. (2002). Beyond patient and polite: A call for direct action and civil disobedience on behalf of same-sex marriage. Pp. 150–155 in B. Shepard & R. Hayduk (eds.), *From ACT UP to the WTO: Urban protest and community building in the era of globalization*. London, UK: Verso.

The Rogue Feminist (2013, December 2). Why shouldn't we be using the asterisk? If you don't mind my asking. Retrieved January 19, 2016 from http://

theroguefeminist.tumblr.com/post/68799403787/why-shouldnt-we-be-using-the-asterisk-if-you.

Rolling Stone (2014, January 26). Macklemore, Queen Latifah turn "Same Love" into mass grammy wedding. *Rolling Stone.com*. Retrieved May 26, 2016 from http://www.rollingstone.com/music/news/macklemore-queen-latifah-turn-same-love-into-mass-grammy-wedding-20140126.

Román, D. (1998). *Acts of intervention: Performance, gay culture, and AIDS*. Bloomington, IN: Indiana University Press.

Ross, R. (2015, June 8). *The Fosters* is doing something really important and you should be watching. *TVGuide.com*. Retrieved June 10, 2015 from www.tvguide.com/news/the-fosters-connor-jude-peter-paige-hayden-byerly.

Rotello, G. (1997). *Sexual ecology: AIDS and the destiny of gay men*. New York, NY: Dutton.

Roth, B. (2017). *The life and death of ACT UP/LA: Anti-AIDS activism in Los Angeles from the 1980s to the 2000s*. Cambridge, UK: Cambridge University Press.

Rovzar, C. (2011, June 15). New Paltz mayor Jason West: Even I came late to the marriage-equality game. *New York Magazine*. Retrieved May 25, 2016 from http://nymag.com/daily/intelligencer/2011/06/new_paltz_mayor_jason_west_eve.html.

Rupp, L. J. (1999). *A desired past: A short history of same-sex love in America*. Chicago, IL: University of Chicago Press.

Rupp, L. J. (2009). *Sapphistries: A global history of love between women*. New York, NY: New York University Press.

Rupp, L. J., & Taylor, V. (2003). *Drag queens at the 801 cabaret*. Chicago, IL: University of Chicago Press.

Russo, V. (1987). *The celluloid closet: Homosexuality in the movies*. Rev. edn. New York, NY: Harper & Row.

Rust, P. C. (2000). Neutralizing the political threat of the marginal woman: Lesbians' beliefs about bisexual women. Pp. 471–495 in P.C. Rodríguez Rust (ed.), *Bisexuality in the United States: A social science reader*. New York, NY: Columbia University Press.

Ryan, H. (2014, June 29). We didn't queer the institution of marriage. It straightened us. *Guardian*. Retrieved April 29, 2017 from https://www.theguardian.com/commentisfree/2014/jun/29/same-sex-marriage-straightened?CMP=share_btn_tw.

Sadowski, M. (2016). *Safe is not enough: Better schools for LGBTQ students*. Cambridge, MA: Harvard Education Press.

Same-sex marriage laws. (2015, June 26). National Conference of State Legislatures. Retrieved April 8, 2016 from http://www.ncsl.org/research/human-services/same-sex-marriage-laws.aspx.

San Filippo, M. (2013). *The B word: Bisexuality in contemporary film and television*. Bloomington, IN: Indiana University Press.

References

San Francisco Human Rights Commission LGBT Advisory Committee. (2011). *Bisexual invisibility: Impacts and recommendations.* San Francisco, CA: San Francisco Human Rights Commission.

Savage, D. (2011). Introduction. Pp. 1–8 in D. Savage & T. Miller (eds.), *It gets better: Coming out, overcoming bullying, and creating a life worth living.* New York, NY: Dutton.

Savage, D., & Miller, T. (eds.) (2011). *It gets better: Coming out, overcoming bullying, and creating a life worth living.* New York, NY: Dutton.

Savin-Williams, R. C. (2005). *The new gay teenager.* Cambridge, MA: Harvard University Press.

Schilt, K. (2010). *Just one of the guys? Transgender men and the persistence of gender inequality.* Chicago, IL: University of Chicago Press.

Schulman, M. (2014, January 3). Bisexual: A label with layers. *New York Times.* Retrieved October 8, 2015 from http://www.nytimes.com/2014/01/05/fashion/Tom-Daley-Bisexual-LGBT.html.

Schulman, S. (1998). *Stagestruck: Theater, AIDS, and the marketing of gay America.* Durham, NC: Duke University Press.

Screaming queens: The riot at Compton's Cafeteria. (2005, documentary). Directed by Victor Silverman & Susan Stryker.

Segal, C. (2017, February 20). Same-sex marriage laws linked to fewer youth suicide attempts, new study says. *PBS NewsHour.* Retrieved April 29, 2017 from http://www.pbs.org/newshour/rundown/same-sex-marriage-fewer-youth-suicide/.

Seidman, S. (2002). *Beyond the closet: The transformation of gay and lesbian life.* New York, NY: Routledge.

Serano, J. (2007). *Whipping girl: A transsexual woman on sexism and the scapegoating of femininity.* Berkeley, CA: Seal Press.

Serano, J. (2010, October 9). Bisexuality does not reinforce the gender binary. *The Scavenger.* Retrieved August 4, 2015 from http://www.thescavenger.net/sex-gender-sexual-diversity/glb-diversity/64-sex-gender-sexuality-diversity-archived/glb/467-bisexuality-does-not-reinforce-the-gender-binary-39675.html.

Serano, J. (2013). *Excluded: Making feminist and queer movements more inclusive.* Berkeley, CA: Seal Press.

Shapiro, S. M. (2015, October 25). Chris Mosier: The definition of an athlete. *ESPN.com.* Retrieved October 13, 2016 from http://www.espn.com/olympics/triathlon/story/_/id/13950017/definition-athlete.

Shepard, B. H. (1997). *White nights and ascending shadows: An oral history of the San Francisco AIDS epidemic.* London, UK: Cassell.

Shepard, B. H. (2002). The reproductive rights movement, ACT UP, and the Lesbian Avengers: Benjamin Shepard interviews Sarah Schulman. Pp. 133–140 in B. Shepard & R. Hayduk (eds.), *From ACT UP to the WTO: Urban protest and community building in the era of globalization.* London, UK: Verso.

Shilts, R. (1982). *The mayor of Castro Street: The life and times of Harvey Milk.* New York, NY: St. Martin's Press.

Shilts, R. (2007). *And the band played on: Politics, people, and the AIDS epidemic.* 20th anniversary edn. New York, NY: St. Martin's Press.

Sieczkowski, C. (2013, February 7). Lake County School Board may slash all student clubs to blockade Gay–Straight Alliance. *Huffington Post.* Retrieved May 8, 2015 from http://www.huffingtonpost.com/2013/02/07/florida-school-board-student-clubs-gay-straight-alliance_n_2638124.html.

Signorile, M. (2003). *Queer in America: Sex, the media, and the closets of power.* 3rd edn. Madison, WI: University of Wisconsin Press.

Signorile, M. (2015). *It's not over: Getting beyond tolerance, defeating homophobia, and winning true equality.* New York, NY: Houghton Mifflin Harcourt.

Signorile, M. (2016, April 7). How our complacency led Mississippi to pass an anti-LGBT hate law on steroids. *Huffington Post.* Retrieved June 7, 2016 from http://www.huffingtonpost.com/michelangelo-signorile/how-our-complacency-led-mississippi-to-pass-an-anti-lgbt-hate-law_b_9633150.html.

Singh, S., & Durso, L. E. (2017, May 2). Widespread discrimination continues to shape LGBT people's lives in both subtle and significant ways. *Center for American Progress.* Retrieved May 7, 2017 from https://www.americanprogress.org/issues/lgbt/news/2017/05/02/429529/widespread-discrimination-continues-shape-lgbt-peoples-lives-subtle-significant-ways/.

Skinner-Thompson, S. (2016, May 16). North Carolina's catch-22. *Slate.com.* Retrieved June 7, 2016 from http://www.slate.com/blogs/outward/2016/05/16/north_carolina_s_hb2_puts_transgender_people_in_an_impossible_catch_22.html.

Smith-Rosenberg, C. (1975). The female world of love and ritual: Relations between women in nineteenth-century America. *Signs,* 1(1), 1–29.

Socarides, R. (2013, March 8). Why Bill Clinton signed the Defense of Marriage Act. *New Yorker.* Retrieved April 8, 2016 from http://www.newyorker.com/news/news-desk/why-bill-clinton-signed-the-defense-of-marriage-act.

Solomon, M. (2014). *Winning marriage: The inside story of how same-sex couples took on the politicians and pundits – and won.* Lebanon, NH: ForeEdge.

Somashekhar, S., Brown, E., & Balingit, M. (2017, February 22). Trump administration rolls back protections for transgender students. *Washington Post.* Retrieved May 1, 2017, from https://www.washingtonpost.com/local/education/trump-administration-rolls-back-protections-for-transgender-students/2017/02/22/550a83b4-f913-11e6-bf01-d47f8cf9b643_story.html?utm_term=.8d7d377b7705.

Sontag, S. (1988). *Illness as metaphor and AIDS and its metaphors.* New York, NY: Picador.

Spade, D. (2011). *Normal life: Administrative violence, critical trans politics, and the limits of law.* Brooklyn, NY: South End Press.

References

Stacey, J. (2011). *Unhitched: Love, marriage, and family values from West Hollywood to Western China*. New York, NY: New York University Press.

Stack, L. (2016a, June 23). Chris Mosier is first transgender athlete in ESPN's "Body Issue." *New York Times*. Retrieved October 13, 2016 from http://www.nytimes.com/2016/06/24/sports/transgender-athlete-chris-mosier-pose-espn-magazine-body-issue.html.

Stack, L. (2016b, November 30). Mike Pence and "conversion therapy": A history. *New York Times*. Retrieved January 6, 2017 from http://www.nytimes.com/2016/11/30/us/politics/mike-pence-and-conversion-therapy-a-history.html.

Staggenborg, S. (2016 ed.). *Social movements*. 2nd edn. New York, NY: Oxford University Press.

Steele, L. (2016, August 2). Chris Mosier on making history as first trans member of Team USA. *Rolling Stone*. Retrieved October 13, 2016 from http://www.rollingstone.com/sports/features/chris-mosier-first-trans-team-usa-member-w432272?utm_content=inf_10_2720_1&utm_source=facebook&utm_medium=cpc&utm_campaign=tseaug2016&tse_id=INF_b2ad47005d8611e6b7dc69ca5c618d1.

Stein, A. (1997). *Sex and sensibility: Stories of a lesbian generation*. Berkeley, CA: University of California Press.

Stein, A. (2001). *The stranger next door: The story of a small community's battle over sex, faith, and civil rights*. Boston, MA: Beacon Press.

Stein, A. (2013). What's the matter with Newark? Race, class, marriage politics, and the limits of queer liberalism. Pp. 39–65 in M. Bernstein & V. Taylor (eds.), *The marrying kind? Debating same-sex marriage within the lesbian and gay movement*. Minneapolis, MN: University of Minnesota Press.

Stein, J. A. (2015, June 26). Celebrating marriage; mourning the queer revolution. *Slate.com*. Retrieved June 8, 2016 from http://www.slate.com/blogs/outward/2015/06/26/does_the_success_of_gay_marriage_mean_the_queer_revolution_has_failed.html.

Stein, L. (2017, March 15). In conservative America, small cities stand up for LGBTQ rights. *NBC News*. Retrieved May 5, 2017 from http://www.nbcnews.com/feature/nbc-out/conservative-america-small-cities-stand-lgbtq-rights-n733821.

Stein, M. (2012). *Rethinking the gay and lesbian movement*. New York, NY: Routledge.

Steinmetz, K. (2014, June 9). The transgender tipping point. *Time Magazine*, 38–46.

Stern, M. J. (2014, July 21). Obama signs historic LGBT non-discrimination order. *Outward*. Retrieved November 13, 2015 from http://www.slate.com/blogs/outward/2014/07/21/obama_signs_history_executive_enda_forbidding_lgbt_discrimination.html.

Stewart-Winter, T. (2015, June 26). The price of gay marriage. *New York Times*.

References

Retrieved June 8, 2016 from http://www.nytimes.com/2015/06/28/opinion/ sunday/the-price-of-gay-marriage.html?_r=0.

Stewart-Winter, T. (2016). *Queer clout: Chicago and the rise of gay politics*. Philadelphia, PA: University of Pennsylvania Press.

Stoddard, T. (1989). Why gay people should seek the right to marry. *OUT/ LOOK*. Reprinted pp. 398–401 in William B. Rubenstein (ed.), *Lesbians, gay men, and the law*. New York, NY: The New Press, 1993.

Stone, A. L. (2009). Like sexual orientation? Like gender? Transgender inclusion in nondiscrimination ordinances. Pp. 142–157 in S. Barclay, M. Bernstein, & A. Marshall (eds.), *Queer mobilizations: LGBT activists confront the law*. New York, NY: New York University Press.

Stone, A. L. (2012). *Gay rights at the ballot box*. Minneapolis, MN: University of Minnesota Press.

Streitmatter, R. (2009). *From "perverts" to "fab five": The media's changing depiction of gay men and lesbians*. New York, NY: Routledge.

Stryker, S. (2008). *Transgender history*. Berkeley, CA: Seal Press.

Stryker, S., & Currah, P. (2014, May). Introduction. Pp. 1–18 in P. Currah, & S. Stryker (eds.), Postposttransexual: Key concepts for a twenty-first-century transgender studies. Special Issue of *Transgender Studies Quarterly*, 1(1–2).

Stryker, S., Currah, P., & Moore, L. J. (2008, Fall/Winter). Introduction: Trans-, trans, or transgender? *Women's Studies Quarterly*, 36(3/4), 11–22.

Sullivan, A. (1995). *Virtually normal: An argument about homosexuality*. New York, NY: Alfred A. Knopf.

Sullivan, A. (2003, June 22). The conservative case for gay marriage. *Time Magazine*. Retrieved March 24, 2016 from http://content.time.com/time/mag azine/article/0,9171,460232,00.html.

Sullivan, A. (2004a). *Same-sex marriage: Pro and con. A reader*. Rev. edn. New York, NY: Vintage Books.

Sullivan, A. (2004b, February 8). Why the m word matters to me. *Time Magazine*. Retrieved March 24, 2016 from http://content.time.com/time/magazine/ article/0,9171,588877,00.html.

Sullivan, A. (2014, May 27). Hey, wait a minute, Mr. Kramer. *The Dish*. Retrieved December 17, 2016 from http://dish.andrewsullivan.com/2014/05/27/hey-wait-a-minute-mr-kramer/.

Sullivan, A. (2015, June 26). It is accomplished. *The Dish*. Retrieved June 7, 2016 from http://dish.andrewsullivan.com/.

Talusan, M. (2015, April 25). From a symbol of athletic power to a symbol of gender transition. *BuzzFeed*. Retrieved July 16, 2015 from http://www.buzz feed.com/1demerith/from-athletic-power-to-gender#.wgA5rQJKmN.

Tanne, J. H. (1987, January 12). Fighting AIDS: On the front lines against the plague. *New York Magazine*. Retrieved January 3, 2017 from http://nymag. com/health/features/49240/.

Taylor, V., Kimport, K, Van Dyke, N., & Anderson, E. A. (2009, December).

References

Culture and mobilization: Tactical repertoires, same-sex weddings, and the impact on gay activism. *American Sociological Review*, 74: 865–890.

Taylor, V., & Rupp, L. J. (1993, Autumn). Women's culture and lesbian feminist activism: a reconsideration of cultural feminism. *Signs: Journal of Women in Culture and Society*, 19(1), 32-61.

Terkel, A. (2015, March 26). Indiana governor signs anti-gay "Religious Freedom" bill at private ceremony. *Huffington Post*. Retrieved June 7, 2016 from http://www.huffingtonpost.com/2015/03/26/indiana-governor-mike-pen ce-anti-gay-bill_n_6947472.html.

"This week's cover: How 'Glee' is leading TV's gay-teen revolution." (2011, January 20). *Entertainment Weekly*. Retrieved June 9, 2015 from http://www. ew.com/article/2011/01/20/glee-gay-teens-ew-cover.

Tompkins, A. (2014, May). Asterisk. Pp. 26–27 in P. Currah & S. Stryker (eds.), Postposttransexual: Key concepts for a twenty-first-century transgender studies. Special Issue of *Transgender Studies Quarterly*, 1(1–2).

Toomey, R. B., Ryan, C., Diaz, R. M., & Russell, S. T. (2011). High school Gay–Straight Alliances (GSAs) and young adult well-being: An examination of GSA presence, participation, and perceived effectiveness. *Applied Development Science*, 15(4), 175–185.

Tourjee, D. (2015a, December 16). "He's not done killing her": Why so many trans women were murdered in 2015. *Broadly*. Retrieved January 8, 2016 from https://broadly.vice.com/en_us/article/hes-not-done-killing-her-why-so-many-trans-women-were-murdered-in-2015.

Tourjee, D. (2015b, December 16). Why do men kill trans women? Gender theorist Judith Butler explains. *Broadly*. Retrieved January 8, 2016 from https://broadly.vice.com/en_us/article/why-do-men-kill-trans-women-gender-theorist-judith-butler-explains.

Travers A. (2006). Queering sport: Lesbian softball leagues and the transgender challenge. *International Review for the Sociology of Sport*, 41(3/4), 431–446.

Trevor Project. (n.d.). Facts about suicide. Retrieved July 7, 2015 from http://www.thetrevorproject.org/pages/facts-about-suicide.

Trnka, S., with Tucker, N. (1995). Overview. Pp. 9–13 in N. Tucker (ed.), *Bisexual politics: Theories, queries, and visions*. New York, NY: Haworth Press.

TrueBlueMajority (2008, December 3). Proposition 8 – the musical! (now with full transcript). *Daily Kos*. Retrieved May 31, 2016 from http://www.dailykos.com/story/2008/12/3/668922/-.

Tucker, N. (1995). Bay Area bisexual history: An interview with David Lourea. Pp. 47–61 in N. Tucker (ed.), *Bisexual politics: Theories, queries, and visions*. New York, NY: Haworth Press.

Udis-Kessler, A. (1995). Identity/politics: A history of the bisexual movement. Pp. 17–30 in N. Tucker (ed.), *Bisexual politics: Theories, queries, and visions*. New York, NY: The Haworth Press.

References

UNAIDS. (2016a). *AIDS by the numbers: AIDS is not over, but it can be.* Retrieved December 17, 2016 from http://www.unaids.org/en/resources/documents/2016/AIDS-by-the-numbers.

UNAIDS. (2016b, November). Fact sheet November 2016. Retrieved December 17, 2016 from http://www.unaids.org/en/resources/fact-sheet.

UNESCO. (2012). *Education sector responses to homophobic bullying.* Good Policy and Practice in HIV and Health Education, booklet 8. Paris, France: United Nations Educational, Scientific and Cultural Organization.

US Department of Justice. (2016, May 13). Dear colleague. Retrieved October 13, 2016 from https://www.justice.gov/opa/pr/us-departments-justice-and-education-release-joint-guidance-help-schools-ensure-civil-rights.

Vaid, U. (1995). *Virtual equality.* New York, NY: Anchor Books.

Valentine, D. (2007). *Imagining transgender: An ethnography of a category.* Durham, NC: Duke University Press.

Van Deburg, W. L. (1992). *New day in Babylon: The Black Power movement and American culture, 1965–1975.* Chicago, IL: University of Chicago Press.

Vogel, L. (2014, May 9). Letter to the community – May 9, 2014. Retrieved October 23, 2015 from http://michfest.com/letter-to-the-community-5_9_14/.

Vogel, L. (2015, April 21). Letter to the Michfest community. Retrieved October 30, 2015 from http://michfest.com/community-statements/.

Walls, N. E., Kane, S. B., & Wisneski, H. (2010, March). Gay–Straight Alliances and school experiences of sexual minority youth. *Youth & Society*, 41(3), 307-332.

Walters, M. L., Chen, J., & Breiding, M. J. (2013). *The National Intimate Partner and Sexual Violence Survey (NISVS): 2010 findings on victimization by sexual orientation.* Atlanta, GA: National Center for Injury Prevention and Control, Center for Disease Control and Prevention.

Walters, S. D. (2001). *All the rage: The story of gay visibility in America.* Chicago, IL: University of Chicago Press.

Walters, S. D. (2014). *The tolerance trap: How God, genes, and good intentions are sabotaging gay equality.* New York, NY: New York University Press.

Warner, M. (1999). *The trouble with normal: Sex, politics, and the ethics of queer life.* Cambridge, MA: Harvard University Press.

Westbrook, L., & Schilt, K. (2014, February). Doing gender, determining gender: Transgender people, gender panics, and the maintenance of the sex/gender/sexuality system. *Gender & Society*, 28(1), 32–57.

White, C. T. (2009). *Pre-gay LA: A social history of the movement for homosexual rights.* Urbana, IL: University of Illinois Press.

Whiteside, A. (2008). *HIV/AIDS: A very short introduction.* New York, NY: Oxford University Press.

Williams, C. (2013, April 9). Michigan Womyn's Music Festival. *The Transadvocate.* Retrieved October 30, 2015 from http://www.transadvocate.com/michigan-womyns-music-festival_n_8943.htm.

References

Williams, C. (2014a, May). Transgender. Pp. 232–234 in P. Currah & S. Stryker (eds.), Postposttransexual: Key concepts for a twenty-first-century transgender studies. Special Issue of *Transgender Studies Quarterly*, 1(1–2).

Williams, C. (2014b, August 17). How TERF violence inspired Camp Trans. *Transadvocate*. Retrieved October 30, 2015 from http://www.transadvocate. com/how-terf-violence-inspired-camp-trans_n_14413.htm.

Williams Institute. (2017, January 17). New estimates show that 150,000 youth ages 13 to 17 identify as transgender in the US. Los Angeles, CA: The Williams Institute, UCLA School of Law. Retrieved April 29, 2017 from https:// williamsinstitute.law.ucla.edu/research/transgender-issues/new-estimates-show-that-150000-youth-ages-13-to-17-identify-as-transgender-in-the-us/.

Wilson, C. (2011, May 8). The reluctant transgender role model. *New York Times*, p. S-1.

Wilson, S. (2016, January 24). IOC relaxes guidelines on transgender athletes. *AP: The Big Story*. Retrieved October 13, 2016 from http://bigstory.ap.org/art icle/1ba0be1a281e4fd388eab155f8fec15e/ioc-relaxes-guidelines-transgender-athletes.

Winning marriage: What we need to do. (2005, June 21). Retrieved May 26, 2016 from https://s3.amazonaws.com/s3.documentcloud.org/.../final-marri age-concept-paper.pdf.

Witosky, T., & Hansen, M. (2015). *Equal before the law: How Iowa led Americans to marriage equality*. Iowa City, IA: University of Iowa Press.

Wolf, R. (2017, April 4). Federal appeals court: Civil rights law covers LGBT workplace bias. *USA Today*. Retrieved April 29, 2017 from https://www.usa today.com/story/news/politics/2017/04/04/federal-court-civil-rights-act-protec ts-lgbt-workplace-bias/100046514/.

Wolfson, E. (2004). *Why marriage matters: America, equality, and gay people's right to marry*. New York, NY: Simon & Schuster.

Wong, C. (2017, April 10). Emmys tell non-binary star they can choose their award category. *Huffington Post*. Retrieved May 7, 2017 from http://www. huffingtonpost.com/entry/asia-kate-dillon-emmy-awards_us_58e66f55e4b07 da813248728.

Yoshino, K. (2000, January 1). The epistemic contract of bisexual erasure. *Stanford Law Review*, 52(2), 353-461.

Yoshino, K. (2015). *Speak now: Marriage equality on trial. The story of Hollingsworth v. Perry*. New York, NY: Crown Publishers.

Zarrella, K. (2014, July 24). Exclusive: Andreja Pejic is in her own skin for the very first time. *Vogue*. Retrieved January 15, 2016 from http://www.vogue. com/13268577/model-andreja-pejic-sex-reassignment-surgery/.

Zeigler, C. (2013, March 5). Fallon Fox comes out as trans pro MMA fighter. *Outsports*. Retrieved January 15, 2016 from http://www.outsports. com/2013/3/5/4068840/fallon-fox-trans-pro-mma-fighter.

Zeigler, C. (2014, February 27). Should Jared Leto's *Dallas Buyer's Club* performance be lauded or loathed? *Playboy.* Retrieved October 10, 2016 from http://playboysfw.kinja.com/should-jared-letos-dallas-buyers-club-perfor-mance-be-1530239316.

Zirin, D. (2015, June 2). The Olympic bravery of Caitlyn Jenner. *The Nation.* Retrieved July 16, 2015 from http://www.realclearpolitics.com/2015/06/06/the_olympic_bravery_of_caitlyn_jenner_358515.html.

Index

Index

Index

Index

Index

Index

Index

Index

Index

CPSIA information can be obtained
at www.ICGtesting.com
Printed in the USA
BVHW040124181219
566953BV00020B/222/P